COMANDANTE

'[A] deeply informative, sprightly chronicle of Venezuela's
dizzying journey under its Comandante . . .
Here is a lively portrait of a new Latin American genus:
the democratically elected caudillo'

Washington Post

'The best things in Rory Carroll's fine, timely book are
the small details . . . These snippets, collected by Mr Carroll
while he was reporting for the *Guardian*, are woven
into a compelling story that comes close to answering
the riddle of Mr Chávez'

The Economist

'In cool, lucid prose, Rory Carroll unpicks the threads
that weave together to form a modern-day dictatorship,
no less sinister for its relative absence of bloodshed.
The portrait of Venezuela that emerges is as nuanced
as it is ultimately chilling'

Michela Wrong, author of *In the Footsteps of Mr Kurtz*

'To some, "El Comandante"
is a tin-pot dictator; part clown, part geopolitical agitator.
To others, he's a breath of fresh air in a world sold out to safe,
centrist governments and corporate interests . . .
Rory Carroll is well positioned to provide a verdict'

Independent

'Carroll uses interviews and anecdotes effectively to describe Chávez's bizarre court'

Mail on Sunday

'Carroll's book should serve as a useful reminder of what el Comandante did and didn't achieve'

New York Times

'In this incisive portrait of a histrionic ruler who brooks little criticism, Carroll, the *Guardian's* Latin American bureau chief, captures the tragic absurdity of life in a country flush with petrodollars but where many go without adequate health care'

Publishers Weekly

'Carroll deftly retells the familiar narrative and then adds something new'

The New Republic

COMANDANTE

THE LIFE AND LEGACY OF
Hugo Chávez

RORY CARROLL

CANONGATE
Edinburgh · London

This paperback edition published by Canongate Books Ltd in 2013
First published in Great Britain in 2013 by
Canongate Books Ltd,
14 High Street,
Edinburgh EH1 1TE

www.canongate.tv

1

First published in the USA in 2013 by The Penguin Press,
a member of Penguin Group (USA) Inc, 375 Hudson Street,
New York, New York 10014, USA

Photograph credits
Insert page 1, 2 (both), 8 (middle): Luis Cobelo/Latin Focus; 3 (both): Jose Francisco
Sanchez Torres; 4 (all three): Guaicaipuro Lameda; 5 (top): Photo by Geraldine Ahuni; 5
(bottom): Vladimir Marcano; 6 (both): Raul Baduel; 7 (all four): Sean Smith/ *Guardian*; 8
(top and bottom): Reuters/Miraflores Palace/handout

British Library Cataloguing-in-Publication Data
A catalogue record for this book is available on
request from the British Library

ISBN 978 0 85786 153 5

Designed by Amanda Dewey

Printed and bound in Great Britain by
Clays Ltd, St Ives plc

For Ligi, for my parents, Kathy and Joe,
and in memory of Heidi Holland

CONTENTS

★

Acknowledgments   ix

PROLOGUE   1

THRONE

1. HELLO, PRESIDENT!   9
2. INSIDE MIRAFLORES   32
3. DEFECTORS   53
4. THE YOUNG LIEUTENANT   84

PALACE

5. SURVIVAL OF THE FITTEST   107
6. THE ART OF WAR   139
7. THE DEVIL'S EXCREMENT   156
8. THE STORYTELLER   180

KINGDOM

9. Decay *203*

10. The Great Illuminating Journey *225*

11. Protest *251*

12. The Illusionist *270*

Bibliography 293

Index 295

Acknowledgments

I didn't know it at the time, but this book began upon my arrival in Venezuela in September 2006. I was a correspondent for the *Guardian* and found an apartment in Caracas, my new home after a decade covering Africa, Iraq, and the Mediterranean. Caracas was to be a base for covering Latin America, but the best story was on my doorstep. On trips to Colombia, Cuba, Mexico, Haiti and elsewhere, my mind would wander back to Venezuela and its unfolding revolution. When I returned, I would catch up with interviews and reporting trips, talking to street vendors, taxi drivers, security guards, housewives, farmers, prisoners, pensioners, professors, palace functionaries, ministers. All told different stories, but all, one way or another, lived in the shadow of the president, Hugo Rafael Chávez Frías. He bestrode society like a colossus, commanding attention, everywhere his voice, his face, his name. It did not matter whether you despised or adored him; you looked. Covering Venezuela was like wandering through a vast, boisterous audience that simultaneously booed and cheered the titan who turned the presidential palace, Miraflores, into a stage.

ACKNOWLEDGMENTS

My notebooks filled and I filed copy to London, but there was never enough scope to capture this experiment by the Caribbean that supporters called *el proceso,* the process. A laboratory of power and charisma that veered between hope, dread and farce. There was no capturing that in five-hundred-word news stories. Thus Chávez retained a mystique abroad, depending on partisanship, as a tyrant or a messiah. Cartoonish images. The reality was more complex, strange and fascinating. Thus was born the idea for this book. By 2012, I had four boxes bulging with notebooks, but they were not enough. I needed to see how Chávez constructed his stage. I needed to get inside the walls of Miraflores. I took six months' leave from the *Guardian* to seek and interview those who had, at one time or another, access to the throne. Aides, ministers, courtiers, body-guards, supplicants, all played a role in the court of Hugo Chávez. All, in different ways, bore witness. Some spoke eagerly to criticise and settle scores with a ruler they no longer believed in. Others spoke to laud, to eulogise a one-off, a man of unique, unforgettable talents. Others had to be cajoled, or offered anonymity, for fear their testimony would create ructions in what was left of the revolution. Most sources are named. A few are not. To all who spoke, named or not, I am grateful. Private letters from Chávez published in Cristina Marcano and Alberto Barrera Tyszka's excellent 2004 biography helped plug gaps.

I owe a debt to many others: Marianella García, my assistant, for her contacts, generosity and friendship; Virginia López for her ideas, solidarity and humour. Heidi Holland, Francisco Toro, Brian Ells-worth, Phil Gunson, Andrés Domínguez and Dan Cancel, fonts of expertise, for reading the draft and intercepting blunders; Lolybel Negrin for the transcriptions; Will Lippincott, my agent, for shep-herding each step with agility and wisdom; Ginny Smith, Laura

Stickney, Ann Godoff and Scott Moyers at the Penguin Press, Nick Davies, Anya Serota, Jamie Byng and the team at Canongate, for flair and dedication in turning a manuscript into a book; my colleagues at the *Guardian* for indulgence and support; my family in Caracas and Dublin for encouragement; and, above all, my wife, Ligi, for her patience, passion and belief in helping me to write about her country. To all, thank you.

Los Angeles, July 2012

COMANDANTE

VENEZUELA

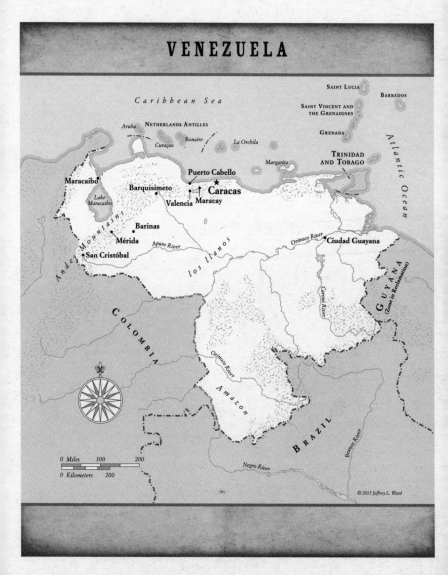

Caribbean Sea

SAINT LUCIA

BARBADOS

SAINT VINCENT AND
THE GRENADINES

Aruba

NETHERLANDS ANTILLES

GRENADA

Curaçao

Bonaire

La Orchila

Atlantic Ocean

Margarita

TRINIDAD
AND TOBAGO

Puerto Cabello

Maracaibo

★ Caracas

Barquisimeto

Valencia Maracay

Lake
Maracaibo

Barinas

Andes Mountains

Mérida

Apure River

Los Llanos

Orinoco River

Ciudad Guayana

San Cristóbal

GUYANA
(Zone in Reclamation)

Caroni River

COLOMBIA

Orinoco River

Amazon

BRAZIL

Branco River

Negro River

0 Miles   100   200

0 Kilometers   200

© 2013 Jeffrey L. Ward

PROLOGUE

It was approaching midnight when the Venezuelan air force plane climbed over Havana and wheeled south, skimming over a moon-lit Caribbean, bound for Caracas. Gabriel García Márquez sat with a pen and notebook next to Hugo Chávez. There was little physical resemblance between the two men. The writer was small, with a white mustache, dark eyebrows and grey, retreating curls over a lined, alert face. Chávez was not especially tall but was powerfully built, still athletic, with cropped black hair, a hatchet nose and a smooth, dark complexion. Standing next to him, García Márquez resembled a gnome. Seated and buckled, however, they shrank to more equal dimensions.

Both men had been guests of Fidel Castro. Cuba's old fox had taken close interest in the Venezuelan, and now it was the turn of the Nobel laureate. It was January 1999, and Chávez was returning to his homeland to be sworn in as president. He had won an election a few weeks earlier and was now set, at forty-four, to become the republic's youngest leader. A Colombian magazine had commissioned García Márquez to write a profile. Before finding fame as a novelist, Gabo, as friends called him, had been a newspaper reporter and still had a newsman's instinct to interview and probe. 'We had met three days earlier in Havana,' he subsequently wrote. 'The first thing that impressed me was his body of reinforced concrete. He had an immediate friendliness and a homegrown charm that were unmistakably Venezuelan. We both tried to meet up again, but it was not possible for either of us, so we decided to fly together to Caracas so we could chat about his life and other miracles.'

Chávez had yet to take office, and already his rise seemed extraordinary. Venezuela had once been considered South America's most successful and therefore boring country, a realm of oil wealth and beauty queens that sat out the region's cold-war–era dictatorships and revolutions in a haze of petrodollar complacency and bloodless elections. That changed one explosive night in February 1992 when an unknown lieutenant colonel named Hugo Chávez attempted a coup and sent tanks and soldiers with camouflage-painted faces to assault the presidential palace, Miraflores. President Carlos Andrés Pérez escaped, the coup failed, and Chávez went to jail, but six years later he stormed back as an election candidate, swept aside rivals, and here he was, president-to-be, flying beneath the stars to an unwritten fate. Who was this man?

García Márquez had special reason to accept this assignment. In novels such as *The Autumn of the Patriarch* and *The General in His Labyrinth,* he had explored the psychologies of Caribbean leaders. Many dictators had thrived on these humid coasts over two centuries and woven themselves into the culture as mythic personages. The master of magical realism studied and did not necessarily condemn them. Fidel, in fact, was a personal friend. Having just won a clean, landslide election, Chávez was no dictator but came with a whiff of cordite. Supporters called him comandante.

García Márquez's pen skimmed across the notepad as his interviewee related his childhood and political rise. The article observed: 'The February coup seems to be the only thing that did not turn out well for Hugo Chávez Frías. He views it positively, however, as a providential reverse. It is his way of understanding good luck, or intelligence, or intuition, or astuteness, or whatever one can call the magic touch that has favoured him since he entered the world in Sabaneta, in the state of Barinas, on 28 July 1954, born under Leo, the sign of power. Chávez, a fervent Catholic, attributes his charmed existence to the hundred-year-old scapular that he has worn since childhood, inherited from a maternal great-grandfather, Colonel Pedro Pérez Delgado, one of his tutelary heroes.'

The son of poor primary-school teachers, as a boy he found among his mother's books an encyclopedia whose first chapter seemed heaven-sent: 'How to Succeed in Life'. Young Hugo did not last long as an altar boy ('he rang the bells with such delight that everyone recognised his ring') but excelled at painting, singing and baseball. His dream was to pitch in the major leagues, and for that the best route was the military academy. The cadet gradually abandoned his fantasy of a roaring stadium because in the academy he fell in love with military theory, political science and the history of Simón Bolívar, the Liberator who expelled the Spanish from much of the continent in the nineteenth century. Lieutenant Chávez received his graduation saber from Carlos Andrés Pérez, the president he would try to overthrow two decades later, an irony he acknowledged. García Márquez prodded at this. 'What's more, I told him, "You were about to kill him." "Not at all," Chávez protested. "The idea was to set up a constituent assembly and return to barracks."'

Here the author of *One Hundred Years of Solitude* noted that in fact he did share one striking similarity with his concrete-built interlocutor. 'From the first moment I realised that he was a natural storyteller, a product of Venezuela's creative, exhilarating popular culture. He has a great sense of timing and a memory that has a touch of the supernatural, allowing him to recite poems by Pablo Neruda or Walt Whitman, or entire passages of Rómulo Gallegos.' The profile continued recounting Chávez's narrative: his fascination with family history; his indignation at Venezuela's social inequalities; his reluctant counterinsurgency hunt for Venezuela's dwindling guerrilla bands in the 1970s; his gathering of fellow officers into a conspiracy in the 1980s to overthrow a corrupt state and usher in a real democracy to make Bolívar proud. Chávez gave García Márquez a small scoop, revealing a previously unknown coup co-conspirator, 'a fourth man', who happened to be on the plane. 'He pointed a finger at a man in a seat by himself and said: "Colonel Baduel!"'

All this the article related in an affectionate tone that was not surprising. In addition to storytelling, the famous chronicler shared Chávez's leftward political tilt, friendship with Fidel and anger at Latin America's extreme wealth inequalities. When the plane landed, it was 3:00 a.m., and Caracas glowed in the distance, a swamp of lights. Chávez embraced García Márquez farewell and invited him to attend his inauguration. The old man stood on the asphalt and watched his subject disappear into the night, bound for power. Chávez had promised his followers utopia and seemed in a hurry.

We do not need to wonder what thought went through García Márquez's mind, a mind revered the world over as that of some kind of oracle. At the end of his article, a few short lines shook loose like a kaleidoscope everything that preceded them. 'While he sauntered off with his bodyguards of decorated officers and close friends, I was overwhelmed by the feeling that I had just been travelling and chatting pleasantly with two opposing men. One to whom the caprices of fate had given an opportunity to save his country. The other, an illusionist, who could pass into the history books as just another despot.'

THRONE

★

To understand revolutions and their
participants, we must observe them at close
range and judge them at great distance.

— SIMÓN BOLÍVAR

1

HELLO, PRESIDENT!

A quiet Sunday morning in February 2010, the eleventh year of the revolution, and the comandante took a stroll outside the palace's peach-coloured walls. The sun was shining, the mood light. From a distance he was recognisable by the familiar walk, arms and legs in unison, one two, one two, a soldier still. Time had registered its passage in the face, fleshier than before, jowlier, and in a thickening of the torso, but old age remained at bay. Not a grey hair on his head, and the extra bulk, distributed evenly, carried well. A bear of a man. He wore black trousers and a red T-shirt beneath a tailored olive-green military jacket. It was plain, without medals or stripes or insignia, and fit perfectly. A favourite outfit. His daughter María, a gold chain glinting around her neck, held his hand and matched his pace. Aides and ministers in red T-shirts swarmed a few feet behind. When the entourage entered the plaza, a church bell pealed and pigeons fluttered.

'What's that song?' asked the comandante, slowing his stride.

'Do you remember that song, María?' The young woman shook her head. He paused, concentrating, and the lyrics floated out. 'Walking through Caracas, Caracas/the people passing and greeting me/I would raise my fraternal hand/and Caracas would embrace me.' He had a nice tenor voice and sang well. In fits of modesty he sometimes fibbed that it was a bad voice, prompting protests. '¡No, mi comandante!' He turned to his daughter. 'María, do you remember when you were little? You would run around here chasing pigeons and then cry because you couldn't catch any.' She blushed and smiled. 'María, look, there's one coming, grab it!' Everybody laughed.

The comandante slowly circled the plaza, lined with evergreen *jabillo* trees and colonial-era buildings, scrutinising the facades, then walked to the center of the plaza toward a giant equestrian statue on a marble pedestal. The bronze black stallion reared on its hind legs, veins and muscles bulging in its shiny flanks. It had a short mane, a broad, thick neck and the head angled to the side, as if looking where to crash the mighty hooves. The rider astride this thrusting energy wore breeches, boots and a magnificent tunic with epaulettes and braid. A cape flowed over his shoulder. He was composed in the saddle and held the reins with one hand. For over a century he had gazed down at the plaza, serene and commanding, holding out his hat as if in salutation to a cheering crowd and glory eternal.

'Look at Bolívar,' said the comandante. 'Bolívar, Bolívar,' he repeated, savouring each syllable. Everyone looked. A small, darting movement caught his eye. 'Look, a squirrel! Over there, look, look, look, there goes a squirrel.' Everyone looked. His attention returned to the statue. 'Bolívar. Simón Bolívar, liberator of Venezuela, New Granada, Ecuador, and Peru, founder of Bolivia. Since when has that statue been there?' Before anyone could answer, he addressed one of the officials standing nearby. 'What age are you, compadre?'

Fifty-two, Comandante, came the reply. 'Almost my age.' Turning to a woman. 'And you?' Before she could reply, he answered: 'You're thirty.' She gasped. 'Yes, absolutely.' The comandante nodded. 'And how are you?' Before she could answer, he turned to his daughter. 'You're younger, you're twenty-five, right, María?' She nodded. 'I remember I used to love coming here with Rosita, María, Huguito – they were very small – and we'd visit the house across the old plaza there where Bolívar was born.'

The comandante paused at the statue and adopted a pedagogical tone, a cue for the entourage to cluster and form an audience. 'The year they brought Bolívar's remains here, they named it Plaza Bolívar, 1842. The oligarchy brought his remains here after expelling him in life. There was a lot of popular pressure to bring him back, and his remains stayed in the cathedral for a while. Then General Guzmán Blanco came and ordered them to put up the statue. Ah, there's the date, look, 1874! That was after the federal war, another betrayal. They killed Zamora, and the oligarchy continued owning power. Then they started to use Bolívar, his myth, make him almost a saint, but for their own interests, to exploit the people using Bolívar himself. I started to understand all this when I was a cadet and we used to come here in dress uniform, white gloves, blue cap, there at the Pantheon and at the house he was born.' The audience nodded. Guzmán Blanco had been a dictator, Ezequiel Zamora a famous rebel.

The comandante continued. 'I wasn't born here. You know that. I was born far away, in the south, but I love Caracas now. I was afraid of it when I came here as a kid, but I love it now. Bolívar. How does the song go, María?' He sang another ballad, this one comparing the Liberator's voice to a candle showing the true way. Applause when he finished. The president turned to the statue. 'Advancing again with

Simón. We have arrived, we have come, and he leading the battle from the front.' More applause. The comandante squinted in concentration to remember a poem about the Liberator. Squinting turned his eyes into impenetrable slits, the more so now he had put on weight, and masked the object of his gaze. He always sought eye contact and would continue scrutinising his audience left to right, right to left, a minesweeper of faces, appraising expressions. Mural artists tried to render that look by furrowing the brow and narrowing the eyes. The toy dolls of him had a little lever at the back of the neck to swivel them. When the real comandante's brown eyes flashed back open, whoever was in his sight line at that moment would jolt.

He turned to his daughter and asked her to find him the poem 'The Toothless Ones' by Venezuela's great writer Andrés Eloy Blanco from her smart phone. 'María has a little machine that finds everything. She presses a button like this, *raaaa!,* and everything appears.' She laughed. He returned to the theme of oligarchs exploiting Bolívar's legacy. 'They made him into something he wasn't, the way some Catholics have made Jesus into something he wasn't. Christ was a great rebel, and for that he died crucified. He was an anti-imperialist. He was born and died among the poor and for the poor and with the poor. And that's what happened with Bolívar, the bourgeoisie transformed him.' This was a not-so-veiled criticism of the Catholic Church hierarchy, which the comandante regularly accused of elitism and siding with his enemies.

A silence descended on the entourage. Rooted to the spot, a statue himself, the comandante lowered his voice to paint another graphic scene. At this very spot, he said, patriots from a 1797 rebellion were brought to execution scaffolds, some to be hanged, others beheaded. Among the transfixed spectators was a group of teenage boys, sons of criollo landowners, who sat on horses and watched from a corner of the square, flinching as nooses and axes did their work. The youngest of them was Bolívar, and he vowed vengeance against the Spanish Empire. 'Right here!' The comandante's audience seemed to shiver, oblivious to the baking sun, for they were on hallowed ground. 'You realise,' he continued, 'where we come from, what flesh and clay we are made of. You see? That is why we are here today saying more than ever: Fatherland, socialism, or death! We will prevail!'

The entourage roared back: 'We will prevail!'

The comandante: '¡Viva Bolívar!'

Entourage: '¡Vivaaa!'

The comandante beckoned the municipal mayor, Jorge Rodríguez. A psychiatrist by profession, Rodríguez had been the comandante's favourite egghead in the early years, appointed head of the National Electoral Council, a key position, then promoted to vice president despite having crashed his Audi into a friend's Audi in a posh part of the city one night, a minor scandal that provoked scorn from the revolution's poorer sectors. Rodríguez later lost the comandante's patronage – he was blamed for his one electoral defeat, a referendum in 2007 – and was cast out of the palace's golden circle. Demoted to mayor, desperate to win back favour, Rodríguez ruled over a shrivelled fiefdom that included Plaza Bolívar, and now the boss summoned him to his side, a glint in his eye.

'The plaza has improved, changed, but it's still missing something, no? Missing a special touch. That building over there, an old theatre, right, but now in government hands?'

Rodríguez: 'Yes, at this moment it's in government hands.'

He pointed to a handsome ten-storey block partly obscured by red banners suspended from lampposts: 'And that building?'

An expectant pause, a little intake of breath, because everyone knew, the comandante knew, that this was La Francia, a famous landmark filled with the country's best jewellery shops. High-ranking government officials shopped there. Tourists did too until cruise ships stopped coming. Rodríguez himself recently bought an expensive emerald ring.

He replied: 'That is a building of private jewellery shops.'

The comandante, arm outstretched, finger pointing, unleashed his bolt: 'Expropriate it! Expropriate it!'

Rodríguez simultaneously stiffened and bowed: 'Okay.' The entourage gazed at the building as if expecting flames to shoot out. Some began to clap.

The comandante wheeled and pointed at the other side of the square. 'And that building over there, on the corner?'

'That is also filled with shops,' said Rodríguez.

The comandante looked affronted. 'Bolívar lived there when he was newly married, right there in that house with two balconies. And now it has shops! Expropriate it!'

The applause swelled, and Rodríguez caught the rhythm. 'Yes! Why not, President!'

The comandante pointed at another building. 'This building here, what is it?'

Rodríguez: 'That's also a center of private shops.'

Comandante: 'Expropriate it! Mr. Mayor, expropriate it!'

Rodríguez, face shining: 'Why not!' Now cheers as well as applause.

Comandante: 'Yes, expropriate. We have to make this into a great historic center. Well, it already is, but we have to make more of it, make . . . architectural projects, historic projects. We are in the heart of Caracas.'

Rodríguez: 'That's right.'

The comandante patted him on the shoulder. 'Caracas, Caracas, the city of rebels. How are you, Jorge?'

What just happened? On one level it was obvious. Our own eyes and ears told us. Hugo Chávez had seized some buildings in the name of the state. We knew this because it was live on television. This was episode 351 of *Hello, President,* a weekly live show. The host and star, indignant at commercial desecration of the Liberator's memorial, had taken swift, resolute action, earning acclaim and gratitude. How could there be doubt? We saw and heard it. Over the course of the show's next five hours – some lasted eight – we would see the mayor prepare the expropriation paperwork and submit it to the president for inspection. The process could not be more transparent. It had been like this since Hugo Chávez was inaugurated in February 1999 and made live television a central part of his rule, inviting cameras to transmit official meetings, family events and public engagements to twenty-eight million Venezuelans. In Plaza Bolívar we were able to see the buildings, the context of the president's decision and the reaction of those around him. Government literally in sunlight. Media mastery had helped the comandante win successive elections and turn his administration into what he called the Bolivarian revolution, a self-styled radical effort to transform state and society into a vision worthy of Bolívar, a beacon of democracy, socialism and enlightenment. All on television.

Except the cameras avoided panoramic sweeps, pointed only in certain directions, were selective about close-ups. Plaza Bolívar was pretty, but the rest of downtown Caracas in 2010 was decaying. Once it had seemed blessed, a verdant valley on Venezuela's northern tip close to the Caribbean and protected from humid, coastal torpor (and eighteenth-century pirates) by the Ávila mountain range, which kept the air fresh. In the 1950s it seemed a modernist wonder of daring architecture and gleaming towers but half a century later reeked of dysfunction. Buildings peeled and crumbled, graffiti from old referenda stained walls ('Vote no' signalled 2004; 'Now yes' meant 2007), potholes cleaved the asphalt, motorbikes roared through belching, paralysed traffic, pavements were clogged with stalls selling knickers, bras, socks, jeans, pirated DVDs, batteries, mangoes, onions, fried chicken. The blackened shell of Parque Central, a fifty-six-storey octagonal tower wrecked in a fire six years earlier (a sister tower was undamaged) and still unrepaired, scarred the skyline. Once South America's mightiest skyscraper, now a hulking, charred reproach.

None of that decay appeared in the February 2010 broadcast, which confined itself to the city's vestige of colonial-era charm. The cameras were just as careful about timing because to film the expropriated buildings too soon or too late – that is, before or after Chávez gave the word on their fate – would have confused the narrative. Here, for example, were scenes not televised. Weeks before the broadcast, government officials sniffed around La Francia's ninety-five little jewellery shops, asking questions, taking photographs. The owners, some of whom had been there since the 1950s, huddled in conference. Pessimists feared revenge for the shop owners' having once joined a nationwide antigovernment strike. Optimists noted the mayor and other high-rolling Chavistas were regular visitors to their gleaming display cases and that the shops employed two thousand people – surely that would count for something? The day before the comandante's show a rumour gathered force: expropriation. With trepidation, owners and employees switched on *Hello, President* the following morning. The programme shifted location each week, the palace, a factory, a farm, you never knew where Chávez would show up. Seated at home, they watched the opening credits, a cascade of trumpets, drums and whizzing graphics, then they saw the coman-dante leading his entourage into Plaza Bolívar.

Later that night under cover of darkness, after the show had packed up and the plaza was deserted, the shop owners crept into their shops – the national guard had yet to move in – and poured all their gold, silver, pearls, rubies and diamonds into cardboard boxes. By dawn they had loaded up and driven away. Fast-forward a year, to February 2011, and if you visited the expropriated shops, everything was boarded up, dusty, dilapidated, the architectural and historic projects yet to begin, possibly forgotten. A lone sentry, a teenager in khakis with a rifle over his shoulder, leaned against a doorway. He was bored and fiddled with his phone. 'Nobody here but me,' he said, smiling.

Chávez dominated screens day after day, year after year, nation-alising an industry here, hosting a summit there, hiring ministers, firing ministers, explaining, denouncing, reminiscing, campaigning. By the time of the Plaza Bolívar broadcast, state television had been airing increasingly polished, professional images for eleven years. The revolution was thriving. A new 'geometry of power' had replaced old, corrupt ways with direct democracy. State enterprises espousing solidarity and dignity were replacing capitalist greed and individual-ism. Venezuela was leading Latin America to an era of unity and sov-ereignty free from Yankee imperialism, an example to the world. The comandante was more popular than ever and on track to win a third term in 2012.

But turn off the television, wander the streets (taking care to avoid potholes), and the picture looked murkier. The comandante's name and face were everywhere: billboards, murals, T-shirts. He presided over an authoritarian democracy, a hybrid system of personality cult and one-man rule that permitted opposition parties, free speech, and free, not entirely fair elections. A third of the population adored Chávez, a third detested him, and the rest were *ni-nis,* neither one nor the other, floaters adrift in the middle. Years of record oil revenues – Venezuela had the world's biggest reserves – had flooded the country with cash and eased poverty. The state offered free education, medical care, loans, grants, scholarships, courses, jobs. But distortions were buckling the economy. Inflation burned through wallets, shortages left supermarket shelves sporadically bare of staple goods, and red tape choked businesses and ordinary people. Cuba and a few other allies bowed to Chávez (while eyeing his checkbook), but most of Latin America politely shunned his model. The rest of the world looked at this Caribbean drama from afar, intrigued but not really understanding, and according to taste cast the comandante as hero, demon or clown. Venezuela's opposition, a fractious coalition drawn from the middle class and traditional elites, had disgraced itself in Chávez's early years by trying to oust him in a coup and a strike. By 2010 it remained weak but was staging a tentative comeback through the ballot box, clawing back city halls and governors' mansions and hoping the presidential palace was next.

A muddy mound by the Orinoco resembled a log until it came to life, swished a tail, and blinked a yellow crocodile eye. On the plains of Apure a ship's mast appeared to shimmer on the horizon, but there was no ocean, no ship, just immense, motionless grassland with a single palm trunk. Every night lightning flashed over Lake Maracaibo, sometimes twenty thousand bolts, but the clouds were so high no thunder sounded.

This realm of impossible waterfalls and gigantic plants had long bewitched interlopers. Columbus called it the Land of Grace and declared the Orinoco waters so sweet that they must come from the fabled Terrestrial Paradise. He never found it, nor treasure, and ended up manacled by a disappointed Spanish monarch. More white men crossed the ocean. They saw humble thatched huts on stilts and coined the sarcastic name Venezuela. Little Venice. A country named in scorn. It played a joke of its own. While the Aztec and Inca empires enriched conquistadores in what is now Mexico and Peru, Venezuela offered only nomadic tribes, swamps, mosquitoes and jaguar teeth necklaces. But its glinting light continued to hypnotise invaders. Diego de Ordaz saw a link between gold and the sun and led six hundred men into the Orinoco delta, following the celestial yellow orb. Insects stung, burrowed into skin, and rotted flesh, turning feet into blackened claws and driving the treasure hunters into murderous rages against the Indians. Their quest disintegrated, but others took their place. Indian prisoners told of a kingdom in the interior where pyramids rose over the jungle canopy and every day a monarch was dusted with gold: El Dorado. The invaders grew excited. Where, where? The answer always the same: a brown finger pointing to the horizon, there, over there. Expeditions clanked into the jungle, hacking vines, and perished as starved, diseased cannibals. Lope de Aguirre went insane, declared a kingdom of wilderness, and butchered his own men, murdering even his own daughter. After he was finally cornered, shot and dismembered, Aguirre's head was displayed in a cage in El Tocuyo to reassure all that the monster was dead.

The quests abandoned, Venezuela slumbered for two centuries, a coffee- and cacao-exporting backwater of Spain's American empire. By the late eighteenth century, with revolution shaking France and North America, Venezuela grew restive. Criollo elites, the landowning descendants of Spanish settlers, wanted to be rid of Madrid's regulations and taxes; mulatto artisans and merchants yearned for better land and jobs; at the bottom of the pyramid black slaves demanded freedom, and Indians wished just to be left alone. Bolívar's wars ousted the Spanish and delivered independence, but his dream of a South America united into a single, enlightened country evaporated. Republics seceded, and caudillos, regional strongmen, carved personal fiefdoms that perpetuated colonial inequalities. Bolívar died in 1830, broken and disillusioned. 'America is ungovernable. Those who serve the revolution plow the sea.'

Venezuela returned to slumber, an impoverished tropical outpost, until 1914, when it discovered a new illusion. An optical trick so spectacular it spent the next hundred years applauding. The black ooze that Indians had used for millennia to caulk canoes on Lake Maracaibo began to be pumped in commercial oil wells. The land of El Dorado, it turned out, floated on black gold that would fuel the automobile age and a fantasy of everyone becoming rich. The petrodollars turned a scrawny state muscular, built roads, railways, barracks, schools, then, after oil prices quadrupled in the 1970s, skyscrapers, shopping malls, the Caracas metro. The wealthy flew to Miami for shopping weekends and became famous for their delighted squeal: 'So cheap, give me two!' Peasants migrated to bleak hills overlooking cities and became labourers, taxi drivers, maids and security guards, meagre wages supplemented by government subsidies, crumbs from the banquet. When oil prices collapsed in the 1980s, the cash-strapped government raised the price of crumbs, so in February 1989 the slums revolted, a wave of rage called the Caracazo that looted city centers and shattered the mirage. The state panicked, and troops mowed down hundreds, maybe thousands.

The stage was set for Chávez's 1992 coup, a military fiasco but propaganda victory for the previously unknown lieutenant colonel. The unpopular, despised government gave him two minutes on television to make a statement of surrender, a fateful mistake. Wearing a red beret and crisp uniform, eloquent and confident, even dashing, he introduced himself to a stunned nation and said his movement's objectives had not been met 'por ahora', for now. Two words gleaming with defiance, promising return. He deserved thirty years in jail, went the joke: one for the coup, twenty-nine for failing. Pardoned after only two years, he stormed the 1998 election, an insurgent candidate, telling Venezuelans their old model of oil dependence and corrupt politics, their mirage of development, was dead. It was time, he said, for reality.

A decade in power later, what was one to make of Chávez? Part of my job as a foreign correspondent based in Caracas from 2006 to 2012 was to answer that question. An exotic assignment, and I thought I had come prepared. Born and raised in Dublin, I had started my career at a newspaper in Northern Ireland disentangling propaganda and verity from IRA violence and sectarian conflict. After joining the *Guardian,* I was posted to Rome, around the time Chávez was inaugurated, and covered the intrigues of the Vatican, the Mafia, and Silvio Berlusconi. I caught the end of the Balkan wars and, after 9/11, the fall of the Taliban in Afghanistan and the rise of the anti-U.S. insurgency in Iraq. Between stints in Baghdad, where I was kidnapped, I lived in Africa for four years, seeing democracy take root in South Africa and wither in Zimbabwe, a cautionary tale of a 'big man' hijacking power. The ruins of Angola, Congo and Liberia showed me what happened when countries fall apart.

When the *Guardian* asked me to open a Latin America bureau, the obvious location was Caracas. Perched on the Caribbean between Central and South America, it straddled the region and hosted its most exciting story: Hugo Chávez. My arrival at the Caracas airport was not propitious. It was dark, raining and chaotic. A viaduct connecting the airport road to the capital had collapsed some months earlier, forcing travellers onto narrow, winding mountain roads while a new viaduct was built. Taxis and trucks navigated mud and potholes and hillside slums to reach Caracas. From there I took an overnight bus to Mérida, a pretty university town in the Andes, to study Spanish and Latin American history.

I returned to Caracas with a suitcase of books and notepads and moved into an apartment overlooking the Ávila in time for Chávez's triumphant reelection in December 2006. The economy was roaring, support was electric and opposition was feeble. It was, in hindsight, his apogee. The tank commander he once was had smashed through domestic and international obstacles, consolidating power and popularity. His votes were not so much counted as weighed.

As a newcomer to Spanish, I appreciated Chávez's communication skills. For all his idiosyncratic, colloquial Venezuelan expressions, he spoke clearly, enunciating each word and repeating key phrases until his meaning gleamed. The catch was he never shut up. Turn on the TV or radio at any time and there, invariably, he was. Talking about anything. The price of milk, aluminium production, George Bush, baseball, his granddaughter. In bars, offices and hotels but mainly at home, I would plant myself in front of the screen. It felt counterintuitive, shameful, to be so sedentary. Revolution in a strange land, and me with my feet up. Elsewhere the rule had been to get out and hunt stories. Here too, but only after watching Chávez. After trips overseas or to the Amazon, I would return to Caracas and anxiously phone colleagues. 'What did I miss?' It was worse for agency reporters compelled to stay in their offices every day and watch every minute, a cumulatively cloying, claustrophobic ordeal that drove many to quit. A young English colleague fled, vowing to move to Iran's Zagros Mountains to write a novel.

It was easy taking the political temperature. Chávez was everywhere. Over a breakfast of mango, arepa (a type of corn-bread sandwich), and coffee, I would read the local papers – polarised partisans that either demonised or praised the comandante – and throughout the day hear opinions about him on the metro, at street stalls, in offices. Perched on the back of a motorbike taxi weaving along motorways at breakneck speed, I would listen to its owner defend or attack the president, yelling his opinion over the roar of traffic. '¡Así es, mi amigo!' That's how it is, my friend!

Every government leader uses the media to justify and persuade, project and burnish, but none like Chávez. He was on television almost every day for hours at a time, invariably live, with no script or teleprompter, mulling, musing, deciding, ordering. His word was de facto law, and he specialised in unpredictable announcements: nationalisations, referenda, troop mobilisations, cabinet shuffles. You watched not just for news value. The man was a consummate performer. He would sing, dance, rap; ride a horse, a tank, a bicycle; aim a rifle, cradle a child, scowl, blow kisses; act the fool, the statesman, the patriarch. There was a freewheeling, improvised air to it all. Suspense came from not knowing what would happen.

State television, which under Chávez multiplied from one to eight channels, showed him continuously. On occasion it was just his voice when he phoned chat shows other than his own to chime in on whatever debate was under way. Under exceptional circumstances the executive was allowed to interrupt programming of all channels, state and private, to make live presidential broadcasts. Such broadcasts were called *cadenas,* chains. Predecessors had used this sparingly, for emergencies or major events, but Chávez used it every few days. There would be no warning. Soap operas, films and baseball games would dissolve and be replaced by the familiar face seated behind a desk or maybe the wheel of a tractor. If you were listening to radio, the music would suddenly stop. 'Good afternoon, compatriots. There is something important I want to share . . .' It could last minutes or hours. Sometimes Chávez wouldn't be talking, merely attending a ceremony. If you missed the beginning of such a *cadena* and tuned in to the radio, you would hear maybe a brass band, or marching feet, or applause, and be left wondering what the event was. One time Chávez decided to personally operate a machine on the Caracas-to-Charallave rail tunnel. A television and radio announcer improvised commentary for the first few minutes but gradually ran out of things to say as the president continued drilling, drilling, drilling. Radio listeners, blind to Chávez pounding away, were baffled and then alarmed by the mechanical roar monopolising the airwaves. Some thought it signalled a coup.

Rhonny Zamora, a producer of the marathon Sunday show, said Chávez directed himself and chose locations, themes, camera angles, guests. 'It's wild, untamable, very complex. We tried to give it a fixed time, keep it down to two or three hours, but that was impossible. The president decides everything; it's his show. It was called *Hello, President* because people would call in, but it became like the lottery, everyone looking to get a job, a house, something. That's no way to run a country. Now it's pretty much just him talking. The team runs on adrenaline and anxiety. The president can ask for anything at any moment. Ministers come prepped on the day's themes, but the president is magnificent at knocking them off balance, throwing out something they're not ready for. Does it reflect reality? The question, my friend, is what is reality? You can present reality whatever way you want, beautiful, ugly, happy, sad.'

Hello, President had a fixed starting time, but since most of Chávez's television appearances came without warning, it was best to leave the television perpetually on and on channel 8, the main state network, Venezolana de Televisión. From morning to night it would flicker in the corner, mute, half ignored, until the comandante surfaced. Then grab the control, click volume, tune in. 'Good morning, citizens, I greet you from Miraflores Palace on this beautiful day.' There was no knowing when it would end. On days off you could leave your apartment, take the metro across town, pay utility bills, meet a friend for coffee, buy groceries, pick up laundry, come home and find him still talking. Watching required patience and a sixth sense. You would pay close attention at the beginning to note the location and apparent theme – agriculture, a new social programme, the armed forces, U.S. relations – and then gradually undertake another task, reading, writing, ironing, while keeping an ear and an eye on the president. Over the years an internal antenna developed that detected subtle changes in tone and expression, a dropping of the voice, a twitch, which signalled something important requiring full attention.

Television was just one dimension, a controlled, electronic stage that concealed as well as revealed. What was happening in the wings, behind the cameras? Here there was darkness because when the comandante was not performing, the lights went out, the show stopped, draping a great virtual curtain across government. Chávez abolished individual ministry press offices and centralised all news through the Ministry of Communication and Information, known as

MinCI, a few blocks from the palace. Its young employees, friendly, charming, casually dressed in jeans and T-shirts, would issue press credentials and ply visitors with state publications (*Thoughts of President Chávez,* volumes 1 to 4) but could never arrange interviews, because officials and ministers were not authorised to speak. Not even the succession of information ministers. They dodged interviews and phone calls and appeared in public only as silent, nodding assistants to the president. Venezuelans were by nature garrulous and effusive, but it was as if a cord had been pulled, silencing officialdom.

This reserve applied only to ministers and courtiers. Those outside the golden circle, the revolution's lower ranks and the opposition, compensated for irrelevance by shouting. They started soon after Chávez took office and were still at it a decade later, a relentless cacophony in print and on airwaves. One side – political parties, private media, business owners, the middle class – shrieking apocalypse, ruin, tyranny. The other – ruling party members, militias, the slums – ululating for the president and hailing progress, development, modernity. It was as if they inhabited different planets. They couldn't both be right, and maybe both were wrong. If one wanted to understand the revolution and make sense of García Márquez's prophecy, the trick was to skirt the shouters and do three things: follow the president on television, seek out the courtiers and functionaries who hovered behind him and tramp through farms, factories, villages and cities to see firsthand what the revolution had wrought.

Sublime, unexpected moments lit up the screen and showed why the comandante remained popular even after a decade in power. Having dispatched the mayor to draft expropriation documents –

'no time to lose, Jorge' – Chávez sat at a large desk in the center of the square, facing rows of cameras and seated officials. As usual, he talked torrents, one idea following another in a twisting, looping narrative: lauding newly established communal councils as instruments of direct democracy; a theological discourse on the revolution's holy trinity of Christ, Bolívar and Karl Marx; a folk song; a family anecdote; a solution to Venezuela's electricity crisis; denunciation of U.S. perfidy; a joke about a Spanish barber; a greeting to his mentor Fidel Castro. 'Hey, Fidel! How are you?' This said in English with a thick accent. Most Venezuelans could not speak English, and the comandante always exaggerated and revelled in his bad pronunciation – khellow! khow are yoo? – signalling that the gringo tongue, the language of superpower, was nothing to be feared.

By now it was 2:00 p.m., and he had been talking without pause for three hours, a seamless narrative flow punctuated with little, gleeful prods to the mayor, who was occasionally summoned to the desk for updates on the expropriation.

'Is the expropriation decree signed yet?'

Rodríguez, looking anxious: 'We are preparing it, President.'

Chávez, with a hint of impatience: 'You are preparing it.'

As a posh, unpopular figure with the revolution's more humble sectors, the mayor made a good fall guy.

Then, polished as a network anchor, the comandante switched gears. 'Let's now go to the satellite.' The monitor cut to a gathering of about two hundred people in red baseball caps amid ploughed fields just outside Caracas. The camera panned over a tractor, tools, seeds, baskets of vegetables and newly built houses. A spokesman explained that these 3,400 acres originally belonged to Bolívar and had been neglected by subsequent owners. Now thirty-two communal councils comprising fifty-nine hundred families were making them fertile.

Chávez: 'Long live the communes! This is creation, heroic creation.'

All this was standard fare for *Hello, President*. Last week happy factory workers, this week happy peasants. But Chávez almost always found a way to cut through the staging and show something real, which in this case turned out to be an elderly woman lurking behind the spokesman. A weathered grandmother, decades of poverty and manual labour etched on her face, who was clearly nervous with the attention.

'Good afternoon, my comandante.' The voice quavered, and she looked anxiously at the microphone. Back in Plaza Bolívar, his face beamed on a monitor, Chávez smiled and nodded encouragingly. She continued. 'My name is Laura Thais Rojas, and I belong to the Brisas del Paraíso commune. Excuse me, I'm suffering stage fright.' The voice quavered again. From her accent and age, she had probably left school very young and barely literate. Chávez nodded, signalling, willing her to go on. She gathered confidence. 'But I'm going to speak with you.'

And she did, leading the camera to a little house and vegetable patch. 'This is where I've grown lettuce, tomato, radish, what else . . . cucumber, carrot, beetroot. The harvest has been good.'

Chávez grinned: 'Let's give applause to Laura.' Everybody clapped. 'She said she had stage fright but explained everything perfectly well. Laura, you spoke very well, do you know that?' She smiled shyly. 'Yes, you told us about the lettuce, tomato, radish, cucumber, carrot, beetroot. So, Laura, you have that garden. How many metres is it? Tell me.'

'Well, my comandante, it's four flower beds, each six metres long, one metre wide. I also cultivate earthworms and spread them around the soil. I don't have many, but they do the trick. Go ahead, Comandante.'

'I bet the worms do do the trick, Laura. What a thing, natural fertiliser, nothing chemical or polluting. We have to make use of all these resources, all this technology in the hands of the people. How many people work in that garden with you?'

Laura, the voice now firm: 'My son, my grandson, my daughter, my husband. We work together. Before we were living on waste ground. Here I feel happy because I have a vegetable garden and I'm proud of it.'

'Proud of your garden and we are proud of you, Laura. Tell me something, what type of support have you received? Tell me a little about that.'

'Well, Comandante, apart from the land, we received a spade, a weeding hoe, a water tank, a hose, seeds. Technical advisors have been with us constantly, the Cuban teachers Sonia and Arbello.'

Chávez grinned and clapped his hands: 'Look how you explained everything so well. And you who said you had stage fright!' The audience applauded long and loud, and the camera zoomed in on the old woman's face. Laura seemed fit to explode with happiness. This was the moment. There was nothing staged about the shine in her eyes, the joy creasing her cheeks. A long, humble life of scratching subsistence from baked earth, a life anonymous like those of her ancestors, had just been sprinkled with magic. A president asked her name, about her family, about her garden. A camera recorded her words, and a satellite in space delivered them to the nation.

Most Venezuelans lived in towns and cities but had nostalgia for rural relatives and land abandoned in migrations to hillside slums. Laura could have been anyone's grandmother, and her surge of pride and dignity melted hearts.

The broadcast continued. An eclectic monologue about Native Americans being naturally socialist, a lament about Chávez's baseball team, Magallanes, losing to Caracas, a warning about profiteering capitalists, a recommendation to read Lenin. Soon after church bells tolled 3:00 p.m., the mayor, face shining with relief, returned to the comandante's side. 'Mr. President, I have just signed the Request for a Declaration of Public Utility for the four buildings on the four corners of Plaza Bolívar. Tomorrow they will be officially declared public utilities, President.'

Chávez examined the document. 'Correct!'

Another satellite linkup, this time to the state of Barinas, where the comandante's brother Adán, the governor, toured a plantain processing factory. The comandante, following from his desk, asked a worker to peel a plantain. 'Look at that, tremendous. Let's cook some *tostones*!' His home state, he said, would be transformed by motorways, railways, quarries, dredged rivers. A little boy appeared by his desk. 'Hey, hey, the *gallito* is here! Gallitooo!' A nickname for his grandson. They cuddled. 'Are you well? Look at Bolívar. See Bolívar. Say hello to everyone. How do you greet soldiers?' The boy saluted. 'That's it. This is a soldier.' The audience applauded. 'You sing about Bolívar. How does it go?' Together comandante and grandson sang ballads, then the national anthem. A final satellite linkup to Haiti, where Venezuelan and Cuban doctors ran a camp for earthquake survivors.

Two final announcements: a canal to link the Orinoco to the Caribbean, an ancient dream, would become reality thanks to a deal with Argentina. And China and Russia had just pledged billions to modernise the creaking electric grid. Every home would have power. Music wrapped up the show. Hip-hop artists performed a rap about resistance. The comandante jived, waving a red handkerchief. 'Bravo, bravo, bravo!' Then a folk group with a harp rhapsodised about Venezuela's plains. The comandante sang the last verse. The closing image, as credits rolled, was joyful. Morning heat had turned to evening cool, shadows stretching, everybody singing, dancing, laughing. A few blocks away the Ministry of Communication and Information's young, diligent officials stayed till midnight typing up the show's transcript. It ran to eighty-nine pages, about average. Some shows filled more than a hundred.

2

INSIDE MIRAFLORES

It was the comandante's custom to rise late. The well-known fact he worked late, until three or four in the morning, gave rise to the legend he slept just two or three hours a night. In fact he tended to surface between eight and nine in the morning. Though impatient to start work, he took care over personal hygiene and grooming, important rituals. A vigorous shower – he timed himself to keep it under three minutes – followed by fastidious shaving, nail clipping and combing of his cropped, frizzy hair. Body odour repelled him, so he used lotions and deodorant to combat the tropical heat, prompting aides to privately wonder how the comandante spent so many happy years soldiering amid sweat, dirt, and grease.

Soon after the February 1999 inauguration he acquired the habit of spending nights in Miraflores Palace rather than cross the city to La Casona, the presidential residence, where his wife, Marisabel, and children lived behind high white walls. It was practical since he had no desire to wake up his family, nor half the city, with a predawn convoy of armour-plated vehicles. Also, he had spent most of his adult life in barracks and liked the order of having work and private life in the same place. And of course the palace, the same palace his soldiers had stormed during the coup attempt seven years earlier, symbolised the power he had so long strived for.

His quarters were austere, almost monastic in their denial of adornment, with a small, well-ordered bookcase with tracts on history, politics, philosophy and literature. Some, such as Bolívar's writings, would inhabit these shelves for many years. Others were fleeting guests, lodging just a few days or weeks before making way for new arrivals. Upon Chávez's emerging from this chamber, a waiter in a white jacket immediately served sweet black coffee in a small porcelain cup. The comandante would carry this down to the *sala situacional,* the situation room, an underground den accessed with infrared swipe cards. Inside about two dozen civilians and military officers huddled over computers, reports and newspapers, muttered into phones, wrote on boards, and pinned notes to walls covered with maps and charts. This was the nerve center of the palace, the president's eyes and ears. The first briefing began with a media digest, including the regional papers outside Caracas and who said what on the early morning talk shows. Then a sketch of international events and the day's agenda of government and party business. In contrast to his bombastic public persona, the president would be reserved and listen attentively.

If there were no emergencies, he took breakfast – arepas – on a terrace with a thatched roof, potted plants, a hammock and a large wooden table that served as a desk and dining table. While eating, he would review letters thrust into his hand by supplicants during public events the day before.

*mr. president I direct myself to you to make a request for a house
in the name of our lord jesus christ I am a mother of two children
and unemployed I don't have anywhere to live for twelve years I
live cursed 0416-3627075 and 0426-7238700 24 of july barrio 170
N street 49E-89 it's my mothers.*

Nouvy Pirela

*A cordial bolivarian greeting, I would like to please ask your help
with a job and a pension for my mother. I give you my telephone
number 02123228014 and 4129376741. Awaiting your prompt
answer this comrade bids you farewell. MAY GOD BLESS YOU
MY PRESIDENT.*

Gloria Camejo Mujica

*Mr. President I need your help I am disabled I want to work in
the government like a true revolutionary . . . you are the true son
of Simon Bolibar may God bless you.*

Hernán Cortés

*Mr. president my greetings, I write to you because in reality I
need your help my name is jorge camacho of pensionable age I
ask your intervention I have been married for 18 years and now
want a divorse and have not been able to get it because of an
error in the marriage certificate the number does not match my
identity document and I have exhausted all my resources and
have not been able to achieve anything I am an evangelical
Christian and I want to marry the woman who has been my
partner for 10 years . . .*

Jorge Camacho

On and on, some just a few lines, others stretching over pages, stories of thwarted ambition, bad luck, ruined health, insurmountable problems, callous bureaucracy, all requesting something: a hip replacement, money to start a business, Christmas gifts for children, a car, a tractor. When he plunged into crowds, the president was mobbed by so many petitions an official wish taker accompanied him. 'The palace gave me a waistcoat and backpack and I would follow the president through the crowds taking all the letters people thrust at him,' said a retired wish taker, whom I shall call Carmen. 'My God, the whole city would turn up. We were asphyxiated by the quantity of people and the love they had for him. Everybody wanted to embrace him and ask him something.' The letters became so numerous the palace created a special department of clerks to summarise them overnight in typed digests. This was what the president read over breakfast. When he put down his fork to circle a petition with a pen, it would receive attention from the special department, which archived every letter. It was called the Sala de la Esperanza, the Office of Hope.

The comandante liked the terrace in the morning for the breeze, the rustic feel and the fact it overlooked Caracas. A century earlier Miraflores stood apart, a secluded mansion amid fields, but now the city tumbled in from all sides, a riot of concrete and honking horns. To the south rose a steep hill of grubby tower blocks with laundry hanging from the windows, the January 23 slum, named for the date in 1958 when this and other neighborhoods chased the dictator Marcos Pérez Jiménez into exile. Now it was a bastion of loyalty to the comandante. Beyond it, looking east, shimmered the green slopes and cream condominiums of Valle Arriba, home to bankers and diplomats. Turn north and downtown's jumble of office buildings and shops started just a block from the main palace entrance. You could hear but not quite see the roaring motorbikes and hissing buses. This urban maze stopped abruptly in the middle distance at the foot of a great wall of green, the Ávila mountains, which marked the city's northern limit. On the other side, invisible, were fishing villages, resorts, and the Caribbean Sea.

After breakfast, more coffee and perhaps a cigarette – he smoked on occasion, never in public – the comandante went back inside and followed a shiny corridor leading to honour guards who flanked the yellow door of his office, the *despacho del presidente*. A hymn to cream and gold, its furniture largely unchanged since the night President Carlos Andrés Pérez, pajamas beneath his rumpled suit, grabbed an Uzi from a black briefcase to repel Chávez's storm troops. There were Shah Abbasi Persian rugs, damask curtains, French Restoration armchairs whose legs tapered into bronze claws, an oval table of green alpine marble and a rectangular writing desk of dark rosewood. Facing the desk, with its back to the window, was a wide leather chair with the nation's coat of arms on a headrest and a gold-plated sphinx under each arm. The seat of power. There was a lever to adjust the height.

Normally this would command attention, but the eye was drawn to thick, heavy pillars of solid iron welded from floor to ceiling. Samson himself could not tear them down. They were designed to withstand the earthquakes that periodically jolted Caracas. Venezuelan presidents were haunted by the fear of falling masonry. When Joaquín Crespo built Miraflores, he requested an 'anti-seismic room' but died in battle in 1898 before moving in. His successor, Cipriano Castro, immediately occupied it to avoid repeating the experience of having once jumped from a second-storey balcony during a tremor. The president, according to a ditty of the era, unfurled an umbrella to slow the fall but still broke an ankle and shat himself in fright. Chávez too was said to fear earthquakes.

A door connected the president's office to the cabinet meeting room, the *consejo de ministros,* a rectangular room with panelled walls, a large portrait of Bolívar and a long oval table. The president's chair was slightly taller than the others. In his first year he held weekly meetings here, quizzing each of his fourteen ministers in turn. In later years, after his interest in such meetings dwindled, the connecting door would remain shut, and the vice president would host the ministers (their numbers doubling as new ministries were created), leaving them all to peek at the door and wonder if the comandante was on the other side in his office, or perhaps in another part of the palace, and wonder what he was up to.

Some afternoons he would visit his family at La Casona. It was in the east of the city surrounded by leafy, middle-class villas but still had the feel of the coffee plantation it once was, with hacienda architecture, mango trees, rustic gardens, a murky swimming pool, a bowling alley and an outdoor cinema. In the election campaign he had blasted it as a symbol of oligarchy, saying his family could live in an apartment, and in truth he did not like it much. But still his family lived there. In late afternoon, if there were no public events to attend, the president returned to the palace and the *sala situacional* for another briefing: intelligence reports; a media update; political flash points; economic indicators. If something grabbed his attention, he would use one of his mobile phones to give instructions on the spot, or take the elevator to his office upstairs and get his secretary to make the calls. Visitors waiting in the annex would learn if they were to receive an audience or should return another day. If there was no official event that evening, the president would play softball with his guards or entertain guests in the Japanese suite. Whispers of romantic assignations swirled around this part of the comandante's day.

Whatever their truth, the comandante's real passion blossomed later at night when he returned to the thatched-roof terrace and, fuelled by fresh coffee shots, ploughed through piles of documents, his pen circling, stabbing, underlining. At 11:00 p.m., he would turn up the volume of the television on a corner shelf to watch *The Razorblade,* a nightly chat show on the main state channel. The host, Mario Silva, a heavy, bearded man with a keen intelligence and lupine grin, wore red baseball caps and leather jackets. Seated at a desk surrounded by images of Che Guevara, Karl Marx, Bolívar and Chávez, he interviewed occasional guests but mostly assailed the comandante's foes in monologues of lip-smacking relish. He was famous for showing photographs that embarrassed the opposition. Silva also played excerpts of intercepted phone calls revealing, or purportedly revealing, opponents' sleaze and hypocrisy. Some were edited to the accompaniment of farm animal noises. The host said the material came from anonymous sources, which everyone assumed to be the Directorate for Intelligence and Prevention Services, DISIP, the main intelligence agency. It was the comandante's favourite show, and he urged followers to watch it. Some nights he phoned in for on-air banter with Silva, or to make policy announcements.

After *The Razorblade*'s credits rolled around 1:00 a.m., he would phone ministers with questions and instructions. Has your department finished that report? Have you seen these statistics? Speed up this, change that, talk to so-and-so. Other times he would phone just to chat and tell stories. Finally, with the city asleep and no ministers left to call, he would pluck a book from the stacks on his desk, or from the little bookcase in his chamber, and tumble into its pages.

The best-thumbed volume contained Bolívar's speeches and letters, which the president had memorised. For a time he was much taken with *Path of the Warrior* by the Argentine writer Lucas Estrella Schultz. 'Warrior, when you win a battle, don't lose time sheathing your sword, because tomorrow will only bring more battles,' it counselled. For months the president publicly praised the book, extolling its wisdom and erudition, but after jokes spread that the text was a gay metaphor, he never mentioned it again. Before being elected, Chávez denied he was a socialist, saying he had never read Marx, and in 1999 that was still true. Instead, he reached for García Márquez, Nietzsche and, above all, Plekhanov. Several times he told the nation of the moment he discovered the Russian revolutionary's philosophical tome *The Role of the Individual in History* while hunting guerrillas in the mountains as a young officer in the 1970s. 'I remember that it was a wonderful starry night and I read it in my tent by flashlight.' (The Mexican writer Enrique Krauze was one of the first to recognise Chávez's Plekhanov fixation.) The president kept his copy through the decades. 'The same little book with the same little underlinings a person makes, and the same little arrows and the same cover I used as camouflage so that my superiors wouldn't say "what are you doing reading that?" ' Now that Chávez was in power, this book, published a century earlier, seemed to speak to him with more urgency than ever. 'A great man is a beginner precisely because he sees further than others, and desires things more strongly than others.'

The comandante would lie in his monastic chamber turning pages, making fresh notes and underlinings, embryos of future plans, and drift toward somnolence. By sunrise, when the first rays glinted off palace windows, he would be asleep.

The president had won the December 1998 election with 56 per cent of the vote, crushing the two establishment parties, the social democratic Democratic Action and the Christian democratic COPEI. They had alternated power since Pérez Jiménez's fall in 1958, a cosy system called the Punto Fijo Pact, which peacefully rotated presidents constitutionally barred from serving consecutive terms. From afar it looked an enviably stable, democratic arrangement, and Venezuela was called a model for the region. But the 1970s oil-boom sugar rush turned bitter when prices collapsed in the 1980s, bankrupting the economy. The two parties, by now ossified vehicles of patronage, flailed in vain at the crisis. The 1989 Caracazo riots, followed by Chávez's 1992 coup attempt and a second, separate coup attempt by other military officers later the same year, exposed the system's hollowness. Chávez, released from jail after only two years, swept to power as the charismatic figurehead of the Movement for a Fifth Republic, MVR, a coalition of trade union activists, environmentalists, students, former military officers and small left-wing parties.

By the time he was inaugurated in February 1999, the excitement of starting anew, turning the page, infected even those who had voted against him. When he took the dais of Congress to be sworn in, polls showed 90 per cent of the country supported him. The priority, he declared, was a new constitution. The right hand aloft, the left resting on the constitution he had just vowed to expunge, he quoted a line from the Chilean poet Pablo Neruda: 'It is Bolívar coming back to life every hundred years. He awakes every hundred years when the people awake.' The face was taut and the eyes gleamed. Years later people returned to this moment, paused the video frame by frame, and froze the expression. Look at the eyes, they cried. You can see it! See what? See what is to come!

When he strode out of Congress, a cheering human magma carried him to Miraflores. Having tried and failed with the gun, Chávez now took Miraflores without blood, the guards standing aside, grinning, as the crowd surged through open gates.

New ministers fizzed with ideas to boost this, tweak that, fingers twitching over levers, but the comandante called them to order. The priority, he repeated, was a new constitution. The old elite was wounded but still dangerous, still held a majority of seats in Congress. Power flowed through not just institutions but time, surging and ebbing to the pendulum's rhythm. Now, with momentum on his side, he quickly held and won an April referendum to approve a constituent assembly, then the July vote to elect it. Dominated by his supporters, the assembly raced to produce a charter that proposed additional human rights guarantees, state benefits, protection for the environment and indigenous communities and a more powerful presidency. The term was extended from five to six years with the right to immediate reelection. The executive would also gain control over promotions within the armed forces and be rid of the bothersome Senate with the merging of Congress's two houses into one National Assembly. The draft constitution fluttered with progressive, enlightened language while offering a hammer to the palace.

The Ávila is part of Venezuela's coastal mountain range and runs east to west along the Caribbean shore. Really it is an extension of the Andes, a fact best appreciated from the sea, where you gaze up at sheer cliffs that rise and rise and disappear into cloud. The Ávila National Park is fifty miles long and ten miles wide and jags along the valleys of Caracas, Guatire, Guarenas and Barlovento. Its highest point, Pico Naiguatá, at 9,071 feet, is cold, sometimes close to freezing, but the rest of the range is lush and tropical.

Human settlements climb up the slopes. They started arriving in the 1950s, migrants forsaking scrabbly little farms in the interior in the hope of jobs in the booming capital. They could not afford homes in the valley, so they built shacks called ranchos on the Ávila's foothills. As more migrants arrived over ensuing decades, these little homes, of wood and tarpaulin at first, then cinder block and corrugated tin, crept higher up and spread across the slopes. They sprouted winding paths and crooked steps and turned into barrios, a word that according to tone can denote neighborhood or slum. Families lived here for generations, poaching electricity from power lines, hauling water up in buckets, neglected by successive governments. On one flank of the mountain they overlooked the Caracas of privilege, which nestled on the valley floor. On the other, which was in the state of Vargas, they overlooked fishing villages, the port of La Guaira and beach resorts where the wealthy had weekend homes. When Hugo Chávez was born in 1954, Venezuela's population was five million. By 1999 it was an estimated twenty-one million, with 80 per cent crammed into crowded towns and hillside slums.

Close to the equator and warm year-round, Venezuela traditionally had two seasons. The dry baked the earth from November to April, and the wet drenched it in short, thunderous bursts for the rest of the year. The Indians called this the rhythm of sun and rain. During heavy downpours gorges directed rocks and mud onto the Ávila interlopers, smattering their tin roofs. Two weeks before the constitutional referendum, Venezuela's sun and rain lost their rhythm. Thunderstorms continued into December, saturating Caracas and much of the country day after day. On the fourteenth, the eve of the vote, the rain strengthened into fierce, hammering sheets. The comandante urged supporters to go out and vote regardless. 'If nature opposes us, we will fight against her and force her to obey us.' It was a famous, defiant quotation from Bolívar after an earthquake destroyed Caracas in 1812, a catastrophe the pro-Spanish Catholic Church interpreted as divine retribution for Bolívar's rebellion.

Chávez's invocation proved fateful. The weather turned even worse, a wild, savage tempest that dumped months' worth of rain within hours. As polls closed on the evening of the fifteenth – less than half the electorate voted – the peaks of the Ávila, sealed in cloud and night, began to move. Sodden soil liquefied, as if melting, and slithered down the slopes. Rocks, boulders and trees, unmoored from the earth, tumbled and crashed in pursuit, one landslide begetting another, multiplying and fusing and accelerating into an avalanche of unimaginable dimension and force, hurtling through the blackness toward the sea in a great roar. Those in the way stood no chance. The cataclysm engulfed barrios on the upper slopes, sucking homes and lives into the whirling mash and throwing them onto neighbours below, and the ones below that, devouring all in nature's maw. The mountain rushed down and down until there was nothing left to seize and it crashed into the foaming sea.

It was Venezuela's worst natural disaster. Hundreds of communities disappeared, washed out to sea or entombed in an alien, unrecognisable landscape. Around a thousand bodies were recovered, but estimates of the dead ranged from ten thousand to thirty thousand. The only people who knew their names were family and neighbours killed alongside them, so victims died as they lived, anonymous, their existence effaced. Vargas state was in ruins, its houses, bridges, roads, and port destroyed. Hundreds of thousands needed shelter.

Sooner than he or anybody had expected here was an urgent test of Chávez's leadership. At first he flunked it. While the nation clamoured for news and reassurance, he disappeared from view, apparently paralysed by the tragedy's dimensions. On the second day he recovered and took personal command, surveying devastation from a helicopter, ordering evacuations, turning sports stadiums and even the presidential residence, La Casona, into temporary shelters, coordinating military, civilian and international recovery efforts, driving himself over muddy trails, appearing on television, emotional but composed, to update, comfort and articulate the nation's grief. The emergency played to his personal strengths and military training.

And then, as weeks passed and the initial shock faded, it played to something else. The crisis became tangled in palace politics. Initially, the comandante had welcomed help from everyone, including the United States, which sent helicopters and dozens of soldiers within two days. The defence minister, Raúl Salazar, accepted a further U.S. offer to rebuild the coastal motorway with 450 marines and navy engineers. Then, after the USS *Tortuga* set sail from Norfolk, Virginia, laden with bulldozers and tractors, Chávez phoned Salazar at four in the morning to say the gringos could not come. It was a matter of sovereignty, he said. The general was furious and suspected Fidel had whispered concerns about imperialist troops rehearsing beach landings. Chávez's relations with the U.S. president, Bill Clinton, were cordial, and clearly there was need for the aid, but not at the cost of inviting in the meddling Yankee superpower. Projecting a revolutionary image counted for more. Salazar obeyed and told the Americans they were no longer wanted. The USS *Tortuga* turned around.

With the rain clouds finally dissolved in early 2000, the Ávila, with its new topography, was once again visible from the palace terrace. But the comandante's attention drifted the other way, into the hallways of Miraflores and a political battle unfolding within. His longtime comrade and fellow coup conspirator General Jesús Urdaneta was unhappy. Chávez had appointed his friend, typically blunt and outspoken like people from the western state of Zulia, to head DISIP, the intelligence service. Urdaneta received reports that two of the president's most important civilian allies, Luis Miquilena, head of the National Assembly, and José Vicente Rangel, the foreign minister, were lining their pockets. Both were veteran political operators who had guided the comandante, a political neophyte, after his release from jail on the hidden strings between state, media and business interests in the so-called Fourth Republic. Urdaneta complained to Chávez that they were bringing the old, corrupt habits into the fledgling Fifth Republic. According to the general, the president acknowledged the duo's corruption but said he needed their dark arts to consolidate power. The feud spilled into the Vargas aftermath when security forces were accused of executing looters. Of eight thousand men in the field, only sixty were from DISIP, but Urdaneta found his agency singled out and pilloried – allegedly due to Miquilena and Vicente Rangel pulling their invisible strings. (Years later Miquilena fell out with Chávez and was charged but acquitted of corruption. Vicente Rangel was never charged with any crime.) Chávez barred Urdaneta from speaking to the press. His old friend claimed he had been set up and resigned in protest, the revolution's first major defection.

There were rumblings that others would follow, that some of those closest to the throne were plotting, sharpening daggers. The comandante spent less time gazing at the Ávila or touring the ruins of Vargas. So although the government released emergency funds, disbursed tens of millions of dollars in international aid, hired foreign consultants, announced ambitious reconstruction plans and said survivors should be called not *damnificados,* which means those rendered homeless by a natural disaster, but *dignificados,* the dignified ones, it all came to little.

With the palace distracted, the recovery effort crawled, then stopped. Lethargy infected Vargas. Bulldozers came late or not at all, engineers made blueprints but did not come back, cement went missing. Aid seemed to evaporate in the haze. As months passed, survivors left their refuges and returned to the shells of collapsed homes to eke out existence amid the debris, boulders and dried mud. More than a decade later they were still there, still waiting for help, and climbing the bare, slippery slopes above them was not scrub but the cinder blocks and tarpaulin of new ranchos. The cycle repeating itself. But that is to skip ahead of the story, to miss important stages in the evolution of the palace.

B y 2000, Hugo Chávez cut a colourful, curious figure on the international stage. Foreign governments did not know what to make of a coup leader turned democrat who lauded Fidel Castro and proclaimed himself a revolutionary but said he was neither capitalist nor socialist but seeker of a third way. On his frequent travels, punishing marathons, he included Venezuelan businessmen in his entourage, courted investors, rang the New York Stock Exchange bell, pitched a ball at the Mets' Shea Stadium, met Bill Clinton at the White House, shook the hand of a Texas governor called George Bush in Houston, expressed third-world solidarity with African leaders, lauded Asia's economic success. Chávez fizzed with energy, ambition and irreverence, overturning protocol with glee. He broke into a sprint on China's Great Wall, hugged Japan's emperor, who was not supposed to be touched, greeted the Russian president Vladimir

Putin with a judo pose, visited Saddam Hussein in Baghdad and crooned to Colombia's young female foreign minister. Hosts were perplexed and charmed. Who was this man?

The U.S. ambassador in Caracas, John Maisto, urged his wary masters in Washington to relax. 'Watch what Chávez does, not what he says.' Fidel adoration aside, the young president retained a conservative finance minister from the previous government, improved tax collection, punctually paid Venezuela's debts and pursued conventional economic policies. His most radical move was convening a meeting in Caracas of OPEC, the oil producers' cartel to which Venezuela belonged, and herding its squabbling members to production cuts. Partly because of this the price of a barrel, just $8 when Chávez was elected, began to rise sharply, boosting the government's meagre treasury. On swings through Venezuela's Andean towns, Amazon jungle, Caribbean ports and pampa-type plains, a varied landscape nearly twice the size of Spain, he always honoured local saints, folklore figures and independence war heroes. His entourage would return to Miraflores exhausted, but Chávez with his superhuman energy would immediately go on television with maps and photographs to explain in detail where he had been, whom he had met and what he had done.

But the internal discontent rumbled and erupted in mid-2000. Two veteran comrades, Francisco Arias Cárdenas and Yoel Acosta, army officers who collaborated in the 1992 rebellion and swept into government with Chávez, announced that they were breaking with him. They accused him of authoritarianism, of ruling as if on a throne and allowing civilian allies to stuff their bank accounts while flattering his ego. In the army they were roommates and held equal rank. Was it too much to see their comrade now on an elevated perch giving orders? Arias Cárdenas was a year older, which under military custom made him senior, yet in government he struggled to have his voice heard. In the July 2000 presidential election – the new constitution required fresh elections – he ran against Chávez with the support of other disaffected groups. In a bitter campaign he accused Chávez of cowardice during the 1992 coup, of cooping himself up in his headquarters while other conspirators fought and died. He placed a chicken on a desk and called it Hugo, and on a stage in Caracas he pointed toward the palace and bellowed to the crowd: 'Let's turn that chicken into soup!' It stung the comandante, now thoroughly diverted from the ruins of Vargas. He mobilised a hyperkinetic campaign that crisscrossed the country and dominated the airwaves, rousing supporters and depicting Arias Cárdenas as a traitor and tool of the oligarchy. 'Burn the Judas!' he cried, and voters did, giving Chávez 59.7 per cent and Arias Cárdenas 37.5 per cent, an even bigger landslide than his 1998 victory. Crushed, the traitor limped into the wilderness.

Through all these early dramas and triumphs, a glamorous figure with perfect teeth and an uncertain smile hovered by the comandante's side. Marisabel Rodríguez, wife, mother, first lady, trophy. Her physical contrast with the comandante was striking. Pale skin, blue eyes, blond hair, delicate features. *Una muñeca*. A doll. She seemed incongruous, cast in the wrong movie, but she had chased this role, chased it and grasped it, and now blinked in the spotlight, co-star of elections, referenda, trips and palace intrigues.

Rodríguez started her career as a radio journalist in Barquisimeto, a western city known as Venezuela's music capital for the number of groups that rehearsed and performed in its plazas. In 1995 she was in her thirties, a small-time broadcast success and single mother with a young child, when Chávez came to town. He had just been released from prison and was touring the country as a renegade politician. Crowds who turned up to hear him speak tended to be small, sometimes fewer than a dozen people, but on this day there were several hundred, among them Rodríguez, infant son in her arms. Chávez's charisma captivated her, and she scribbled an improvised note. 'Comandante, our homeland deserves everything, without reservations, and I am with you heart and soul. When you need me for your struggle, please call me.' In those days Chávez did not have an official wish taker, or Office of Hope archivists, and the message went astray.

A year later, when he passed back through Barquisimeto, a mutual friend introduced them. After notes and phone calls they became a couple on 14 January 1997. Their first date recalled with precision because it was the day of the Divine Shepherdess, the region's patron saint, and they were part of a huge religious procession in the cattle town of Carora. It was also the day they conceived a daughter, Rosinés, in Chávez's Volkswagen. A detail revealed with nudges and winks in a joint interview a year later, by which time they were married and Rodríguez was campaigning hard to get her husband elected.

The timing was fortuitous. Chávez had been married before, to Nancy Colmenares, a reserved, unassuming woman from his home state of Barinas. They had three children, Rosa Virginia, María Gabriela and Hugo Rafael. They divorced soon after the 1992 coup attempt when Chávez became a celebrity and full-time politician. Around that time he also ended a decade-long affair with a Caracas-based historian, Herma Marksman, who had helped his clandestine plotting. Once released from jail, the dashing, articulate rebel enjoyed liaisons with swooning female admirers. Rodríguez, however, became pregnant and then his wife. Eloquent and pretty, she proved a huge asset in the 1998 election by soothing voters worried by Chávez's rough, military edge. The following year Rodríguez was herself elected, to the Constituent Assembly, and became the country's most popular politician after the president.

They appeared on the balcony of Miraflores – now dubbed the People's Balcony – and elicited roars from the crowd below by kissing. They rode past a military procession in an open-top car, evoking comparisons with Eva and Juan Perón. During a Valentine's Day broadcast in 2000, Chávez leered at the camera and said, 'Marisabel, you're going to get yours tonight.' Some thought it vulgar; plenty others chortled. It underlined not only his virility – in Venezuela to sleep with someone is to 'conquer' the person – but also his leaping over race and class barriers. In this multi-toned society many parents encouraged daughters to find pale-skinned partners to produce white babies and thus 'improve the race'. And yet here was this porcelain Desdemona sharing a bed with a *zambo,* the name for those of mixed race, with copper-toned skin.

Rodríguez hosted *dignificados* in La Casona, enjoyed brief sway in the Constituent Assembly and had her aerobics instructor appointed deputy sports minister. Her political influence faded along with her marriage. Chávez was a moody workaholic; Rodríguez clashed with the president's mother, his teenage children and his entourage. They whispered that she was crazy, that the *primera dama* was a prima donna who ordered a military helicopter to bring her milk and cereal on the beach and took the presidential jet to Disney World. Their arguments, as well as his distaste for La Casona, prompted the comandante to spend more nights at Miraflores. By 2001 he had moved her out of the spotlight, and by 2002 she had moved out of La Casona and returned to Barquisimeto. They soon divorced.

This could have dented the comandante's image, especially after the couple got into a tawdry, public dispute over their daughter and Rodríguez married her tennis instructor. Instead, a curious thing happened. Chávez vowed to remain a bachelor at least until 2021, the two hundredth anniversary of Bolívar's final, definitive victory over the Spanish, and shunned public romances. There would be no more raunchy declarations to the camera or balcony smooches. The only women to hold his hand in public henceforth would be his daughters and mother. The comandante's romantic life officially ceased to exist. In the public eye he became married to the revolution.

Rumours rippled through and beyond the palace of relationships with actresses, journalists, ministers and ministers' daughters. The bull, officials said with a twinkle, was not retired. But it was all handled with circumspection, even decorum. The media, even hostile, privately owned newspapers and television channels, drew a veil, breathed not a word, as if modern tabloid journalism and electronic gossip belonged to another era. Venezuela recalled Bolívar's serial fornication – he merrily bedded peasant women, merchants' wives and duchesses during the independence wars – with an indulgent smile. Many Venezuelan husbands had girlfriends on the side. If Chávez was emulating the libidinous Liberator, went the smirking consensus, good for him.

Miraflores was filled with passed-on whispers, but few really knew firsthand. Those functionaries who did tended to be ciphers afforded knowledge not through seniority but through palace quirk, a cubbyhole in a strategic spot, a desk adjacent to sensitive conversations.

Carla had worked in the protocol office. She was retired and did not wish to endanger her pension, so her name is changed. She said: 'Even before he divorced Marisabel, the president had very beautiful lovers. One of the early ones was one of my bosses, a department head. Green eyes, red hair, pale skin, a great body. I wondered how someone so beautiful could be with someone so ugly even if he was the president. I joked with her one day that he must be a bad lover because she wasn't looking her best. She just laughed. When a Venezuelan woman has a bad lover she becomes dowdy, you see. The hair loses its shine.' Carla was in her sixties but had a flirty, husky manner and notably shiny hair. 'Most days my boss looked well. She was passionate about the cause and enjoyed a good life. Whenever she had her car stolen, the next day she'd be given a new one. Colleagues counted thirty-nine lovers and said there were offspring here, there and everywhere, children who looked like the president, but I don't know about that. I knew only about La Loca [the Crazy One] who visited him in prison, La Hermosa [the Beautiful One], an Argentine, really stunning, and a minister's daughter. They all seemed content, so maybe the president was skilful. But they also say a bad dancer is a bad lover. And that man doesn't know how to dance.'

3

DEFECTORS

For Carlos García no single moment, no epiphany, signalled the revolution's change. Denim jeans, boots, bushy mustache, powerful hands with chipped nails, sun-crinkled face, he did not care much for politics or Caracas, hundreds of miles and a world away. He cared for his family, workers and cattle on his 1,400-acre farm, a patchwork of fields and dirt roads on the plains, the llanos, of Barinas state.

García had voted for Chávez to shake things up. These fertile prairies could be the breadbasket of South America, but migration had drained the life out of them. For decades peasants had sold their little plots and moved to coastal cities to the north, chasing the mirage of oil wealth, leaving land in the hands of a few wealthy farmers who only half worked their vast estates. You could drive for hours over bumpy tracks with no sign of man or livestock or crops. At harvesttime, farmers hired what labourers were left to haul sugar, corn, sorghum and plantains, then the labourers returned to their shacks and poverty.

The rancher supported Chávez because he excoriated the waste, the old excuses, and he was a local son, born and bred in Sabaneta, a gritty, sun-bleached town not far from García's farm. 'At last,' he told his children in his hushed, raspy voice, 'a guy with guts. Someone to get things moving.' Some of García's neighbors, conservative old ranchers, did not vote for Chávez, but by his inauguration they too had been swept up in the excitement at having a young, charismatic rebel in Miraflores. In those heady weeks Chávez's popularity nation-wide touched 90 per cent.

García's labourers, of course, had all voted for the comandante. Their ancestors had fought in militias during the civil wars following independence from Spain, and a flinty rebelliousness endured. García had known these thin, leathery men with tattered jeans and machetes since childhood. Some lived on his land in houses of brick, wood and tin, others on a no-man's scrubland where they inhabited small adobe houses with tiny windows, as in Bolívar's day. When there was work, he gave them work; when there wasn't, they made do. García had a good relationship with them, but other land-owners could be ruthless. During disputes over pay or conditions, they would summon police, or private armed guards, and if necessary crack skulls.

García usually paid little heed to politics. His days started in the cool just before dawn when he started touring his land, the moon still glimmering overhead, continued through the sun's blinding midday glare, and wound down after dusk when he dined with his family in a big, air-conditioned living room. García got his news in snatches from the radio when his mud-splattered Ford pickup passed through areas with reception. He caught fragments of

Chávez's speeches, which were often 'chained', meaning every radio and television station was obliged to carry them.

Every day there seemed to be a speech, sometimes several. The president, García said with a chuckle, liked to talk. And he was obviously thinking big. Just a few months after being sworn in, he declared: 'We have to rescue the nation, rebuild it, make it beautiful. Venezuela is emerging from a terrible nightmare ... Venezuela will again be dignified; it is marching toward dignity. Venezuela will again be great; it is marching toward greatness. Venezuela will again be glorious; it is raising the banner of its glory, the people's glory, the people's hope.'

To García the comandante's first year justified such optimism. There was a new constitution, higher oil prices, talk of investment in agriculture and inclusive vocabulary. Chávez spoke of the nation being reborn 'para nosotros', for us, and the revolution being 'para todos', for everybody. But as the autumn rains of 2000 gave way to the humid spring and baking summer of 2001, something nagged at García. There was a shift in the president's tone, a creeping defensive bellicosity. He started referring to himself in the third person and harped on criticism, no matter how obscure the source or outlandish the content. When a visiting academic compared him to Mussolini, Chávez could have ignored it but instead, referring to himself in the third person, made it a central part of a speech in June 2001. 'He is not disrespecting Chávez, don't think I complain for myself, I do it for all of you because this people, our people, deserve respect. Here we have a democracy. And when someone comes to say that Chávez is a tyrant, a dictator, well, he's abusing the people who elected me.'

By now there was something about the way he said 'nosotros' and 'todos', the way he railed at the 'oligarquía', that bothered García. As a candidate, Chávez had said the same things, but now he was on the throne, not the stump, and supposed to be ruling, not campaigning. The president's resentment seemed to fill the airwaves. He announced 'frontal attacks' and 'offensives' against political obstacles as if still a tank commander. Denunciations of the 'oligarquía' unspooled into tirades against 'ellos', them, and 'esa gente', those people.

What García found troubling in the president's discourse, his labourers found stirring. 'Free land and free men! Free elections, and horror to the oligarchy!' The famous rallying cry, barely heard since the nineteenth-century civil wars, resounded again. Grubby and weary after a day in the fields, García, changing gears as he barrelled down a dirt track, would sit back and shake his head at the radio. The labourers squeezed in beside him, just as grubby and weary, would lean forward to catch every word. For the rancher it was a cumulative realisation. When the president spoke of 'nosotros' and 'el pueblo', he, César García, was not included.

Neighboring ranchers had the same feeling, and soon the cattlemen's association in Caracas lodged a formal protest. But this made the president only more hostile. 'We're not going to keep accepting that there are big landowners who have abandoned their property while most live without a hectare, without a square metre to sow a stalk of sugarcane or bananas,' he railed. Then, in October 2001, the axe fell. 'Let us say you have five hectares and the guy next to you has four hundred,' the president told a rally. He paused to let the unfairness sink in. 'No, that cannot be . . . we have to finish off the *latifundios*!' He raised his voice to a shout. 'The *latifundio* is the enemy of the country.' García looked with alarm at his labourers, his childhood playmates who never had his privileges and now craned their necks toward the radio to better hear the president. Did they see him that way? An exploiter? An agent of prejudice and iniquity? How dare Chávez do this! The hell with him! César García became what Chávez said he was: an enemy of the revolution.

In November 2007, he was still on his ranch, still driving his pickup. Six years had passed since Chávez declared war on *latifundios*. The government had seized almost five million acres of farmland deemed idle or illegally purchased. Thanks to his relatively small holdings, García was still in business, just, but peasants had occupied neighbouring farms with support from police, soldiers and Agriculture Ministry officials. The government called this liberation; ranchers called it invasion. Crops had been burned and equipment and livestock seized. Criminal gangs were kidnapping farmers for ransom. García had hired two guards to patrol the perimetre on horseback but knew they would be powerless if truckloads of red shirts arrived. 'It's very, very bad,' he said in the soft, raspy voice. 'We keep hearing rumours of an invasion. There's not much we can do except keep watch and try to get an idea of how many. And when.' After a day touring what was left of his herds – he was selling off animals – García squinted at the setting sun. 'It's late. Time to head home.' He revved the engine, and we trundled down a deserted track. It had rained, and the earth was mushy. Birds circled overhead, a portent of more rain. There was nothing around except fields and shadows and emptiness, but García checked his mirror and peered side to side as if on a busy motorway. 'With these abductions we vary our routes. And we don't travel at night. We stay indoors and live like prisoners.' The radio stayed off. García no longer tolerated Chávez's voice in his cab.

But this is skipping ahead of the story, overtaking the pace of events. In late 2001 the expropriations, seizures, and 'liberations' were still in the future. No one knew for sure what was to come. But the rancher who had voted for the president with such hope three years earlier now loathed and feared him. García was not alone. Millions underwent a similar transformation, detaching from the collective exhilaration of Chávez's inauguration by growing puzzled, then anxious, then enraged. Millions of others, however, stayed loyal. Their ardour for Chávez burned with greater intensity.

Division was etched into the geography of Caracas. The capital was built along the contours of a narrow valley tucked inside coastal mountains. Its elevation from the sea gave a breezy, tropical savanna climate to the valley floor, and this was where money lived. The wealthiest inhabited spectacular mansions with mango orchards, swimming pools and high walls. The less wealthy lived in sleek apartments with security guards and views of the Ávila. The almost wealthy rented smaller apartments facing the city. The hills that surrounded the valley were for the poor, descendants of peasant migrants who improvised ramshackle homes on vacant slopes. The higher you went, the narrower the tracks and flimsier the structures. Every morning the hill dwellers took little buses down winding paths to the valley floor's realm of glass towers and electronic gates. Here they donned smocks to work as maids, sweeping, cooking, ironing, or clipped on name badges to work as private security guards, observing, registering, saluting. At dusk, when the valley was fed and had ice in its scotch, the buses took the visitors back up the slopes to home and a supper of beans and rice. The hills knew the valley intimately, how it liked its towels folded, its juice squeezed, its steak seasoned. The valley knew the hills not at all. The shacks were ugly, alien, a foreign land 'up there'. In the darkness of night, from a distance, all you could see of the hills were thousands of lights twinkling like the Milky Way. Even this spectacle the valley disdained and so drew its curtains.

Before Chávez this inequality stewed but did not boil. Left-wing radicals, supported by Cuba, attempted a guerrilla insurgency in the 1960s, but the campaign flopped for lack of popular support. Venezuela's young, oil-fuelled democracy bought the population's acquiescence with elections and largesse in the form of subsidies, jobs and housing. The poor did not get much, but it was enough to keep them passive. The one exception was the Caracazo in February 1989, when low oil prices and austerity measures triggered riots and a brutal state crackdown. A decade of stagnation later, the middle class and the wealthy were just as fed up as the poor, and so the two worlds, valley and hill, united behind Chávez, the insurgent candidate.

The traditional elites were so sure of entitlement and power they expected to control the comandante. As a candidate he let them think that, and in these early years of power he left their wealth untouched. His economic policies were moderate – he courted foreign investment and even moved to privatise telecommunications – to the point frustrated radicals accused him of neoliberalism. But he methodically attacked the elite's sources of political influence, dissolving the old Congress, firing judges, purging state institutions. For good measure he insulted them, branding them, among other things, 'rancid oligarchs' and 'squealing pigs'. No president had ever spoken this way, least of all to those who felt they owned the country. Their cry of dismay resounded through the valley. We should have known! He is so vulgar, so uncouth. The elites were nervous. This was the language of class war. Their criollo ancestors had feared slave uprisings, and now it was their turn to scan the hills, fearful the drumming from Miraflores would awaken the barrios.

The puzzle was not Chávez's attacks on the plutocrats – when he accused them of looting the nation's oil wealth, he was essentially correct – but his alienation of the middle class. The comandante proved to have a talent for aggravating not just middling ranchers like César García but other groups who, in his view, obstructed progress. When parents and teachers protested a proposed education regulation – it would rewrite history textbooks and expand military instruction – he called them selfish. 'They live quite well, quite comfortably,' he told a boisterous rally in early 2001, a moment recalled in the Chávez biography by the Venezuelan journalists Cristina Marcano and Alberto Barrera Tyszka. 'Fancy house, fancy apartment, they have no problems; their children attend good schools and travel abroad. Nobody criticises them, but some of them don't realise that in December 1998 a change took place . . . They look down their noses at everyone else, as if the rest of us were mere rabble. Yes, we are the same rabble that followed Bolívar . . . The decree will be enforced and I will be supervisor number one.' The crowd roared, and he threw down a challenge to the middle class. 'Come out to the street and look at me! The more dirt you throw at me, the more I'll throw at you. That is who I am.'

A constituency that initially supported the comandante would challenge him over some issue, leading to tirades and insults. Business leaders were 'vampires'. Catholic bishops were 'ignorant, perverse, or perverts . . . What they need is an exorcism so that the devil that got into them will come out from under their robes.' Critics were worms, bandits, hypocrites, spoiled brats, bags of excrement. On and on, an assault of abuse and taunts rat-a-tat-tatting from the palace. It was not so much what Chávez did as what he said. He collectively branded his opponents 'escuálidos', which in Spanish suggested pale, puny creatures. Few realised then that there was a method to it all, that polarisation was a strategy. A trap. Behind the big mouth there was a mind of cunning, foresight and subtlety.

What Chávez said mattered. He was a master of language and

communication. He toyed with words, revived old ones, coined new ones, made them sing and sting. Words can provoke reactions and create their own reality. In Venezuela words spawned hatred and polarisation. Chávez's spurned allies found their voice and hurled back their own insults. They marched through Caracas with megaphones and banners calling him a tyrant, a dictator, a lunatic. They made racist jokes that 'mi comandante' really meant 'mico mandante', monkey ruler. They banged kitchen pots and casserole dishes, a type of protest known as *cacerolazo* that filled the city with clang, clang, clang. Privately owned newspapers and television stations – at that time a Goliath compared with the state's puny media presence – spewed a venomous mix of factual reports, exaggeration and lies. This hatred generated an equal and opposite reaction in the poor, the vast army of labourers, maids and security guards, who loved Chávez all the more and hated those who hated him. Each side glowered at the other, seething and uncomprehending. A fuse had been lit.

In the revolution's folklore Guaicaipuro, an indigenous name, was shared by two very different men. One a hero, the other a traitor. The hero was a warrior who united the tribes of Caracas valley against the first Spanish interlopers. He was not just a cacique, a chief, but a *guapotori,* a chief of chiefs. Guaicaipuro killed and chased away the bearded gold seekers and successfully protected his ancestral lands for years, inspiring other tribes to resist. But in 1568, Spanish troops located his hut in Paracotos, surrounded it and set it ablaze. Guaicaipuro stormed out amid the smoke and flames and with a captured sword threw himself at the invaders. They cut him to pieces. Chávez hailed the chief as a martyr and commissioned a bronze statue depicting him as a towering, muscular figure leaping into combat. He also renamed 12 October, Columbus Day, the Day of Indigenous Resistance.

The other Guaicaipuro lived in Bello Monte, a quiet neighborhood of pleasant houses and apartments behind high walls in the municipality of Baruta, named after the original Guaicaipuro's son. A tiled hallway with stiff, ornamental chairs led to a compact, well-ordered study. A large, gloomy portrait of Bolívar gazed from one wall. The others were filled with maps and books. A boxer padded in, followed by a Chihuahua, then their master. Guaicaipuro Lameda was in his mid-fifties, of medium height, with a bushy mustache and brown eyes. An ironed short-sleeved shirt was tucked into belted dark blue jeans, which also appeared ironed. He made a slight click with his heels while offering a strong, squeezing handshake. What made his appearance striking was a bald, pointed head in the shape of an egg.

It was March 2011. A decade earlier Lameda had been a key piece on Chávez's palace chessboard, a knight who was supposed to leap over the battle lines and checkmate the opposition. He did as commanded, for a while, but then something happened, and at a climactic moment he changed sides. Lameda had had a privileged seat next to the throne for Chávez's first three years. His defection signalled the moment hatred infected both sides with a recklessness bordering on madness.

Half the country seemed to think he belonged in jail; the other half considered him a hero. His voice was inflected with the authority of the general he once was. At times he would jump up to consult a file – all duplicated, immaculately ordered – to keep his memories in sequential order. His father named him, he said, after the indigenous warrior who once roamed the valley. His father, an army officer and oil industry executive, also bequeathed a passion for the military and for numbers. The army recognised Lameda's administrative bent after he entered the academy in 1971 and trained him in logistics and finance. Lameda briefly crossed paths with a cadet one year behind him, an affable, skinny *llanero* with the plainsman's love of talking and joking. 'We weren't close. We had different interests. Chávez was into sports and theatre. He was forever staging plays and performances. Once we were on a war game in the field, and he was put in charge. It felt more like a work of theatre than a military exercise. I didn't like that.' In the 1980s and early 1990s they fleetingly saw each other at Fuerte Tiuna, the military's sprawling garrison headquarters in Caracas, but Chávez wisely did not try to enlist his stickler-for-the-rules colleague into the coup conspiracy.

Chávez obviously respected his ability because shortly after the 1998 election he asked Lameda, now a brigadier general and the Defence Ministry's budget director, to be the national budget controller. The president-elect said he wanted to replace the corrupt, bureaucratic practices of the 'Fourth Republic' – the inherited, creaking democratic system – with a 'Fifth Republic' of lean, efficient government. Meaning no more presidential slush funds, no more fiscal deficits, financial crises or devaluations. 'We had a long talk. He told me his time in prison had given him a chance to reflect and prepare a plan for government.' Lameda's mission would be to march budget numbers into order and keep them in formation. He clicked his heels and accepted the job.

'Oil was around $10 a barrel, and the treasury was empty. The previous government left us with no money, no budget. It was very hard, but we pulled it off. We made a fiscal adjustment and balanced the budget. Then, in 2000, oil prices started to rise, and we had a surplus.' Lameda helped manage a special fund to store the windfall. The idea was to save for the future and release portions, if necessary, to the executive, state governors and mayors. 'A responsible policy. That lasted until 31 March 2000. That's when the president announced the government would spend more than it received.' The date barely figured in articles and textbooks about the revolution, but for Lameda it was a Rubicon. A crossover to 'irresponsabilidad', from which, he would discover in hindsight, there would be no return. 'At a meeting about it with ministers, Chávez told me I was there to listen and execute, not opine. At the end I told him he had just decreed a devaluation because we were going to spend too much. He bristled and said he didn't want my opinion.' Lameda imitated Chávez's voice and gesticulated: 'My government will not be irresponsible like our predecessors. For me "devaluation" is a dirty word.' The general sighed and shook his head. 'Chávez doesn't care about the economy. That was our big difference. What he cares about is politics. Money is an accessory.'

After that clash in March 2000, Lameda felt as if the clouds that blanketed the Ávila had slid into the valley and formed a mist around El Silencio, the hub of ministries, agencies, banks and offices that ringed the presidential palace. Objectives and strategy turned nebulous, targets drifted into haze. His authority as budget director seemed to dissipate. Ministers did not return calls, mislaid his reports, sent data late or not at all. One morning in September 2000 he discovered that the planning minister, Jorge Giordani, and the finance minister, José Rojas, were holding a crucial meeting over the upcoming national budget. Lameda had not been informed or invited. He raced to the Finance Ministry and notified the ministers, via a secretary, that he was at reception and available to participate. Their door stayed closed. One hour passed. Two hours. Three. Four. The budget director did not budge. What did he do during this time? 'Flicked through magazines.' When the meeting ended, the ministers slipped out by a back door to avoid him. The meeting's conclusions would be submitted to Chávez for his approval, then presented to the National Assembly. Lameda immediately wrote a memo to Chávez denouncing the proposed budget, but how could he be sure aides would deliver it? Power, he realised, hinged entirely on access to the throne.

Lameda's outspokenness had irked Chávez and infuriated ministers, who found their breezy fiscal assessments challenged, but instead of firing the general, Chávez promoted him. He valued the tactical advantage of surprising not only enemies but allies. As a tank commander, he had studied Clausewitz and Sun Tzu on the art of ambush. As a coup conspirator, he learned secrecy and intrigue. Now, in power, he used unpredictability to bolster his authority. Ambitious ministers would devise a policy, or plot against a rival, try to tilt the comandante a certain way, and when least expected, Chávez would yank the carpet so everyone – everyone but him – fell down in a tangle.

Lameda's rivals found their campaign backfired. The annoying general was vaulted in October 2000 to a position of immense power and patronage: president of Petróleos de Venezuela SA (PDVSA), the state-owned petroleum company. Guardian of the golden goose. Venezuela's oil had been drilled by big Western corporations until 1976, when Carlos Andrés Pérez, in his first presidential term, nationalised the industry and turned PDVSA into a corporate behemoth. It employed thirty thousand people, pumped three million barrels daily, making it the world's fifth-largest exporter, and fed the state more than half its revenues. It was hailed as proof that a state enterprise could compete with the likes of BP, ExxonMobil and Chevron.

The problem, from Chávez's viewpoint, was that PDVSA operated as a state within a state. Its Harvard-educated executives considered themselves a technocratic elite. Swaggering, superior beings who flew in private jets over the mess fumbling politicians made of the rest of Venezuela. They fed the state revenue, yes, but retained much for the company to reinvest – too much said some critics – and regulated payments to the state with a wagging finger. Miraflores would plead in vain for more. Sorry, Mr. President, that's it for this year, good luck. This was how Venezuela had long worked, except Chávez had no patience for begging from golf-playing, chinowearing yuppies. He wanted control. Lameda's mission was to tame the executives and increase the petrodollar flow to the state. He had no background in oil but knew numbers and could decipher the accounting tricks and legal ruses PDVSA used to fob off previous governments. Just as important, Lameda was a soldier and therefore had sworn loyalty to his commander in chief.

Lameda patted the boxer nuzzling beside his desk and smiled. 'There had been problems between me and Chávez, but I always told him the truth. There were ministers who tried to hide bad news. I didn't. I told him, and it would bother him. You know the easiest thing in the world is to fool a president.' Lameda took thick brown folders from a drawer and piled them up. 'Each minister puts one of these on his desk. Twenty-eight ministers, it rises and rises. You think the president can read them all? No. So each minister briefs him. Everything's going great, sir, marvellous, humming.' Lameda snorted. 'Well, at that time the deficit was growing way too fast, but nobody dared say it. All the pressure came on PDVSA, every minister clamouring for more money. I arranged a private meeting with the president in the palace. He was having his hair cut. It was the same barber who used to cut our hair when we were cadets, Don Corleone we called him.' Lameda had brought graphs and charts and talked quickly as scissors clipped around the comandante's ears. The republic owed PDVSA $2 billion in unpaid debt, he said, and to fill the gap, the company would have to seek funding abroad. Lameda concluded with typical bluntness. 'Mr. President, they are lying to you.'

The next day his phone rang. Chávez. 'Lameda, I'm here with the ministers, and I'm showing them your graphs. I'll put you on speakerphone so they can hear you explain.' His briefing ended with the ministers' cold anger – even over the phone that was obvious – but no decision from Chávez. The fiscal dilemma was left dangling. 'What the president did was trigger a war. Me versus the ministers. They all started conspiring to get me out of the government.'

In this game of cat and mouse around the throne, the general found himself cornered time and again by Giordani, the planning minister who had locked him out of the budget meeting. 'When the history of this government is written, there should be a chapter just for him. He is a master at pulling the strings of power.' In mid-2001, Lameda found himself bypassed until the last minute in drafting a law to squeeze foreign oil companies for more royalties. A committee of Giordani's allies rejected Lameda's request for more time, then leaked to the press that certain officials were delaying the law, and those that delayed were enemies of the revolution.

It was courtiers' bad luck to serve a micromanaging sovereign in the mobile-phone era. 'About thirty of us, mostly ministers, were given a special phone and told to always answer. Chávez was number one. I don't think I ever received a pleasant call on that phone. He rang me several times at 3:00 a.m. to ask about this and that, but really it was to show he could. A demonstration of power.' Lameda's wife, who entered the room at this part of the interview, shuddered at mention of the phone. 'It was a decade ago, and I can still remember the ring tone.' It had pricked the general's pride to submit so totally to a former lieutenant colonel, and he took refuge in impudence. Chávez once called him when he was in Chile negotiating an $850 million loan to say he had left the country without permission and should return immediately. Lameda refused. The president took this as an affront to his authority and quoted Bolívar: 'To call yourself a leader and not act like one is the height of wretchedness.' Lameda replied that, for his part, 'I am the president of PDVSA, and I am not wretched.' A friend engraved the exchange on a plaque that sat on his desk.

Relations between the two men deteriorated. 'He noticed I didn't use words like "compatriot" and didn't laugh at things that were supposed to be funny but weren't. I'm very transparent; I can't hide my feelings. He said: "Lameda, you don't absorb the revolution." I said I was a technocrat and didn't want to give political statements.' Vacations offered no respite from the growing tension. In the fall of 2001, Lameda received a call from number one. His heart sank. 'Chávez asked where I was. I said, "My president, I will be precise. I am on holiday, sitting on a bench at the Dolphin Mall in Miami opposite Victoria's Secret, where my wife is buying underwear."' The comandante hung up, then rang the next day to order Lameda's immediate return for an urgent meeting. 'It was the eleventh of September. Fifteen minutes later I was watching a plane hit the Twin Towers. Getting back was a nightmare, but I caught the last flight before the airport shut. I reported straight to the palace. I was left waiting, then an aide told me the president no longer needed to see me, that I could go home.'

The comandante honoured Guaicaipuro with pomp and ceremony that December by moving the warrior chief's symbolic remains to join Simón Bolívar's in the National Pantheon. He moved the other Guaicaipuro, slowly and without glory, to irrelevance. Allies in the oil company were pressured to leave. The government bought ailing energy companies against his advice. The comandante ordered Lameda to fire a colleague on suspicion of plotting his assassination. The comandante ordered him to donate $1 million of oil profits to Bolivia's opposition and glowered when Lameda refused, citing regulations. Nicknames mocking his appearance began to surface in state media: Conehead; Bullethead; Egghead. Giordani, the planning minister, returned to the attack, ambushing the general in meetings, withholding reports, contradicting PDVSA estimates. Lameda flailed back. Giordani, by all accounts a man of personal honesty, could not be accused of corruption. Instead, Lameda gave Chávez a private dossier making different allegations about his tormentor: Giordani had been born in the Dominican Republic; Giordani was a Cuban spy; Giordani led a shadowy socialist cabal called the Garibaldi group. Chávez laughed and told Lameda he was imagining things.

In February 2002, Chávez fired him. The president wanted a more cooperative keeper of Aladdin's cave. It was announced on the Saturday of carnival, when Venezuelans were at the beach drinking, drumming and dancing. No one read newspapers that week. The president, Lameda said, told him he could remain in government and pick a lesser job. The general pondered the offer awhile, then declined, and also requested immediate retirement from the armed forces. He wanted to cut all ties.

It was a turning point. Lameda was a symbol of old-fashioned norms, the earnest numbers man who kept the oil flowing and the nation's accounts in order amid Chávez's rhetorical thunder. And now he was leaving. The comandante had given Lameda, and the country, a choice. With him or against him. It was not about ideology or great policy differences. It really boiled down to him. Lameda had been catapulted into PDVSA to bend its Ivy League barons to the comandante's will but, little by little, lost faith in his master. Chávez's personality and style made him wince, while the barons made him feel like one of them. And so he changed sides.

By late 2001 three protagonists were impelling events in Venezuela. One, of course, was Chávez. After obtaining special powers from the National Assembly, he unveiled forty-nine decrees affecting agriculture, industry and state institutions. Few were truly radical, but the lack of consultation and the secret drafting infuriated farmers, business leaders and trade unions. Luis Miquilena, the president's veteran political mentor, and string puller, quit in despair. 'That fake revolutionary language . . . I would say to him, "But you haven't touched a single hair on the ass of anyone in the economic sector! You have created the most neoliberal economy Venezuela has ever known. And yet you go on deceiving the people by saying that you are starting the blah, blah, blah revolution. Which means you deceive the crazy revolutionaries we have here, plus you scare the people, the businessmen who could help you build the country." ' This he said years later to the biographers Marcano and Barrera Tyszka. In late 2001 the shrewd, old fox was still a minister but preparing to jump. He had lost faith in his protégé. And maybe sensed what was coming.

A second protagonist was the privately owned media, especially the television networks Globovisión, RCTV, Venevisión and Televen. They launched a relentless barrage against Chávez, criticising, condemning, exaggerating and distorting everything he said and did. News anchors, reporters and interviewees fused into a shrill, sustained diatribe depicting the president as an ogre, an out-of-control menace to society. It fuelled a protest movement, comprising mostly middle-class professionals. Some adopted his insult 'escuálido' as a badge of honour. They organised strikes and jeered the comandante at baseball games, so he gave up going to stadiums and watched his beloved Magallanes on television. They interrupted outdoor presidential broadcasts with increasingly loud *cacerolazos,* leaning from balconies and occupying street corners to clang pots with ladles. 'Let's record them and make a CD,' Chávez joked to aides, but he hated the *cacerolazos* with passion.

And then there was a third force. *Los amos del valle.* The masters of the valley. Tycoons, executives, generals and bishops, allies of the media lords, who agreed the monkey in the palace was going too far. The cardinal of Caracas, Monsignor Ignacio Velasco, acted as a bridge between the military and civilians. They met in mansions and talked late into the night, consulted the calendar, made plans, clinked tumblers of scotch. They did not emerge into the sunlight, not yet, but rumours swirled. The air turned heavy, expectant.

Watching all this were the Americans. Bill Clinton was gone, and his successor had no intention of inviting Chávez back to the White House. George Bush viewed Venezuela's president through the eyes of Elliott Abrams, John Negroponte and Otto Reich, cold warriors who had served the Reagan administration's counterinsurgency campaigns in Central America in the 1980s. Another way of putting it was they had facilitated right-wing dictators' war crimes. Two decades later the cold war was history, but they returned to the White House just as suspicious of anything left-wing in Latin America. To these agents of U.S. power Fidel Castro was an abomination. And now he seemed to be nurturing an heir. An heir with oil. They spent 2001 sniffing the wind from Caracas and worrying it would gust across the region. After the Twin Towers fell, the stakes rose. In the immediate aftermath of the al-Qaeda atrocity, almost everyone – including Chávez – expressed solidarity with the United States. The unity was

fleeting. A month later Chávez condemned U.S. bombing in Afghanistan as a 'slaughter of innocents', provoking fury in Washington.

The screen shook as if the cameraman was nervous, or maybe just excited. It zoomed on a pair of feet, then panned low and wide across Baralt Avenue. A million feet, maybe more, marching on the palace. By some counts the biggest march in Venezuela's history. They had tramped the city from east to west, stamping and singing – 'he's going to fall, he's going to fall' – and were now just a few blocks from Miraflores. All of a sudden, as if on command, they stopped, hesitated. Something was blocking them. A grey vapour filled a corner of the screen, clouding the picture. Tear gas. A rock hit the asphalt, then another, and another, a meteor shower. The screen shook again, as if the cameraman was running. It was 11 April 2002, and the throne was under siege.

The images from outside Miraflores that mesmerised the country – whoever was not at the march seemed to be watching it – were replaced by a government logo and the sound of trumpets. 'This is a special announcement from the Ministry of Communication and Information.' The president appeared, looking solemn. He was wear-ing a suit and sat at a desk framed by a Venezuelan flag and a portrait of Simón Bolívar. 'Good afternoon, my dear fellow countrymen and countrywomen of Venezuela. Here we are, as ever, facing our respon-sibilities.' The president was in Salón Ayacucho, named after the battlefield that sealed South America's independence, a handsome room of caoba-panelled walls used for televised ceremonies. It was beneath the palace, beside a chapel and a dungeon reinforced to withstand bullets and bombs. He continued. 'I have taken this decision – according to my watch, it is fifteen minutes to four in the afternoon – to call this special radio and television broadcast to send a message to all Venezuelans . . . especially that minority who appear to not want to hear, who appear to not want to see, who appear to not want to accept reality.' All channels had been chained to carry the broadcast. The president wished to show he was in command. But he was not.

While he was talking and monopolising the nation's screens, mayhem erupted outside the palace walls. Molotov cocktails shattered and flamed. Bullets hissed. A voice cried: 'They're shooting!' Who was shooting? The marchers looked around in panic. Gunfire seemed to be coming from all directions. They stampeded, feet tangling and twisting. People collapsed onto the asphalt and lay motionless, blood pooling around them. A massacre was unfolding.

The crisis had started a week earlier when the president made a very different broadcast on his television show. Ebullient and combative, he had fired and humiliated PDVSA executives, reading out names one by one. 'Eddy Ramírez, general director, until today, of the Palmaven division. You're out! You had been given the responsibility of leading a very important business . . . This Palmaven belongs to all Venezuelans. Señor Eddy Ramírez, thank you very much. You, sir, are dismissed.' He blew a whistle, as if he were a football referee. The audience cheered, and the comandante continued working his way through a list. 'In seventh place is an analyst, a lady . . . Carmen Elisa Hernández. Thank you very, very much, Señora Hernández, for your work and service.' The voice dripped sarcasm, and he blew the whistle again. 'Offside!' The broadcast delighted supporters and enraged opponents. They said enough.

Within days the opposition called a general strike, then this march. Ostensibly, it was to demand the executives' reinstatement, but really it was to channel the boiling resentments of those – half the country, according to polls – who hated Chávez. The media lords and the masters of the valley pulled strings behind the scenes. If they were going to attempt a coup, this was the moment. A human river filled streets and avenues, overran plazas, burst onto highways, singing, chanting, drumming, banging pots. Hundreds of thousands of people, some said more than a million. At the front, leading them all, holding a giant Venezuelan flag, three men: Pedro Carmona, Carlos Ortega and Guaicaipuro Lameda. Carmona, patrician and grandfatherly, headed Fedecamaras, the business federation. Ortega, a chunky, gravel-voiced firebrand, headed CTV, the country's biggest union federation. Lameda, just two months out of government, symbolised the fired PDVSA workers and those who had believed in, then broken with, Chávez.

The march was supposed to end at the oil company's headquarters in Chuao, but the speeches demanding the president back down, reverse course, change tune – or else! – didn't satisfy the turbulent sea of banners and faces. It had heard this before and now, intoxicated by its size and energy, demanded more. Demanded that Chávez go. It appeared spontaneous, but opposition leaders, it was later revealed, had planned it. 'Let's go to Miraflores!' yelled Ortega. 'Let's go to Miraflores!' And with a great roar the sea again became a river and surged through the valley, west, toward the palace. Marching on Miraflores was forbidden, but the crowd was heedless and rushed on, rushed to sweep Chávez away.

Halfway up Baralt Avenue, with Miraflores just a few blocks away, national guard troops and pro-Chávez grassroots groups called Bolivarian Circles occupied side streets. They were vastly outnumbered but armed and resolved to protect the president.

Lameda, his suit rumpled and tie askew because he had been carried on shoulders to stay ahead of the crowd, had planned with other leaders to demand to meet Chávez, but the path to Miraflores was blocked. The human river met the improvised Chavista defence. Insults flew, then stones. The marchers sang the national anthem. Each side eyed the other, the atmosphere electric. Lameda hopped on the back of a motorbike and roared toward Venevisión, the country's largest, privately owned television network, 'to explain', he said later, 'what was happening'. There he was met by Carmona, the business leader, and Gustavo Cisneros, the channel's billionaire owner.

While Lameda and other interviewees – all anti-Chávez – explained why the president should resign, the standoff around Baralt Avenue exploded into violence. Stones, rocks, Molotov cocktails, tear gas, gunfire. The president cut in with his broadcast, obliging Venevisión and all other channels to show his soothing message from Salón Ayacucho. Television was driving events, and for as long as he spoke, no channel, in theory, could show the violence unfolding outside. Chávez's tone was calm. He asked those who had marched on the palace to reflect and repent. He told the nation to focus on happy topics, like a new scheme to subsidise vehicles. After ninety minutes he concluded with reassurance. 'The situation isn't serious. The situation is under control.'

It was not under control. His generals refused his order to mobilise army troops around the palace, saying it would cause a massacre, and kept soldiers and tanks inside Fuerte Tiuna. The palace was guarded by only a few hundred national guard troops and civilian supporters. And despite the *cadena* the nation had seen the drama on the streets while he talked because four private stations broke the chain by splitting the screen. On one side the president, on the other live images of smoke, bodies, blood. The juxtaposition made the president look a liar.

After the broadcast the president left Salón Ayacucho using

palace tunnels for fear of snipers and in his office – the same office his fellow coup conspirators had tried to storm a decade earlier – swapped his suit for combat fatigues. He strapped a pistol to his leg and grabbed a rifle. But the most powerful weapon in this battle for power was not the gun but television. That evening while the president hunkered in the palace, private television channels showed more footage, recorded earlier, of pro-Chávez supporters shooting into Baralt Avenue. Then it showed wounded and dead. There were nineteen dead and hundreds wounded. Some of the dead were Chávez supporters, and it remained unclear who had done the killing. Unidentified snipers seemed to have fired down on the crowd from hidden positions. Private television stations simply pointed the finger at Chávez and led the valley in a howl of fury. Butcher! Murderer!

By now it was dark, and Lameda was touring one studio after another denouncing the president and urging his friends and comrades in the military high command to intervene. 'Take advantage of this message, think. And make the right decision.' The meaning was clear: Chávez had innocent blood on his hands and must be removed. Other opposition leaders echoed the call. Within hours the top brass, gathered in Fuerte Tiuna, issued an ultimatum saying it would bomb Miraflores unless the president resigned.

Inside his office, Chávez felt trapped and desperate. Tear gas and bullets had dispersed the march, leaving streets eerily deserted amid debris and blood, but he was being blamed for the massacre. Many generals had abandoned him. Ministers and officials were in hiding, fearing retribution, others roamed Miraflores, frightened and uncertain. Chávez appeared so desolate aides eyed his pistol, which he had placed on his desk, and feared suicide. At this moment, a fateful phone call. Fidel Castro. 'Chávez, do not sacrifice yourself, do not be a martyr like Allende, you must survive.' As midnight approached, he took the advice. Word spread that he agreed to resign on condition he and his family would be exiled in Cuba. He walked through corridors of weeping aides and was driven to Fuerte Tiuna, where he handed himself over to the generals. A prisoner.

The next day, 12 April, a helicopter took Chávez to Turiamo, a Caribbean naval base, then to an island, La Orchila. Chávez could be shot, put on trial, or allowed to go to exile in Cuba. In Washington the White House press secretary, Ari Fleischer, implied Chávez got what he deserved. 'The details are still unclear. We know that the actions encouraged by the Chávez government provoked this crisis. According to the best information available, the Chávez government suppressed peaceful demonstrations. Government supporters, on orders from the Chávez government, fired on unarmed, peaceful demonstrators. . . . The government also tried to prevent independent news media from reporting on these events.' The *New York Times* said Venezuela had been saved from a would-be dictator.

Back in Caracas mobs surrounded the Cuban embassy and elsewhere hunted fugitive officials, ripping their shirts, scratching their faces. Across the valley, relief and cheers. The generals celebrated. We did it! Bishops and businessmen celebrated. We did it! On television, commentators and journalists celebrated. We did it! Some grinned and said it was a conspiracy that had been planned for months. Somewhere during the march the anti-Chávez plotters and protesters had intersected.

Later that day, 12 April, the generals invited Carmona, the business federation leader, to form a provisional government at Miraflores. Small, bald, mild, a former diplomat who spoke French, he was called a conciliator, levelheaded, a safe pair of hands. How, then, to explain what happened next? Was Carmona enchanted by Miraflores? Rafael Castellanos, a historian and palace archivist, warned of its sensual feel of power. 'It seeps from the masonry. You feel it in the air, like an intuition, a spirit, almost supernatural.' The palace walls and ceilings danced with gods and demigods, centaurs and nymphs, products of the 1880s portrait fashion for fables, mythology and cornucopia. Aurora's throne of roses glided into the heavens. Cherubs and fruits tumbled from a huge golden goblet. Page boys heaved platters of food and flowers. A giant bottle of champagne exploded with angels and foam. A bronze Meleager hunted the golden fleece. A sculpted chariot raced toward victory. Independence heroes sat astride muscular stallions, holding swords, seizing destiny.

His whole life Carmona had served power. Economist, advisor, ambassador, board member, token of others' authority, others' money. Now he felt he was man of the hour, saviour of the republic. Bishops, generals, tycoons, politicians and editors rushed to Miraflores, coiled around him, patted his back, whispered in his ear. Carmona flitted as if in a dream from the crystal chandeliers of the Peruvian Sun Room, past the bust of Napoleon in the Vargas Swamp Room, past the lunar rock donated by Richard Nixon and the immense mural of battle and floating heads in Salón Boyacá, past the Mirror Room, his image multiplied, and down into the vault of Salón Ayacucho, from where Chávez had spoken just the previous day, to take the throne.

The assembled elites applauded as Carmona swore himself in as president in a televised ceremony. He took the *silla presidencial,* the presidential chair, and he nodded to the newly appointed solicitor general, who started reading out decrees. The National Assembly was to be dissolved. The audience cheered. All state governors were to be replaced. Louder cheers. The following were to be abolished: the Supreme Court; the Office of the People's Defender; the National Electoral Council. As the list went on, the audience exploded in whoops. When the constitution was revoked, they hugged and wept with joy. There was to be a presidential election the following year. It was the liquidation of Chávez and everything he had created, with no pretence of inclusion or promise of immediate elections. The previous day's protest march had become a coup d'état.

Years later a university professor who had marched against Chávez confessed the moment's sweet guilt. 'In our souls we knew it was wrong. We were taking a shortcut, playing rough. But you must understand. We hated Chávez so much we couldn't help it; we couldn't stand it anymore. It was like a scab you're not supposed to scratch. We scratched and scratched until it bled. We won, or thought we had won. But then we made a terrible mistake. We picked that fucking dwarf.'

In fact Carmona was not really in charge. The generals picked him to give a civilian veneer to their overthrow of Chávez. He was the suit behind which uniforms jockeyed for position, a swirling, turbid contest between rival factions. But Carmona seemed drunk on the paintings of bacchanal that surrounded him and acted as if power truly were his. He offered posts to friends – Lameda was to resume running PDVSA – but nothing to the head of the army, nothing to the trade unions, nothing to anyone from the previous government, nothing to the millions who supported Chávez. His biggest mistake was freezing out Carlos Ortega, the union federation head, who withdrew his movement's support. Blind to his blunders, Carmona settled into Chávez's office and took the seat with the gold-plated sphynx under each arm, adjusting the lever so his legs didn't dangle. The new president was so busy giving orders he was oblivious to the draft that rustled his papers, the cold gazes of guards, the icy tone of switchboard operators, the dropping temperature. The palace, like the country, was rejecting him like a transplanted organ.

Within hours a revolt began in the military city of Maracay, where the commander of the Forty-second Paratrooper Brigade was Raúl Baduel, the clandestine 1992 conspirator Chávez had revealed to García Márquez. He rallied not just his brigade but the entire Fourth Division against Carmona. Word spread and events moved quickly. Other divisions denounced Carmona and demanded Chávez's restitution. By the morning of 13 April the hill dwellers around Caracas had recovered from their shock and began to stream down into the valley, demanding the president's return. Their numbers swelled, and they began to march on the palace. Television stations mentioned nothing of the army mutiny nor the Chávez supporters filling the streets. In fact they carried no news at all besides saying President Carmona was forming a new government and all was well. They filled the hours with cartoons and Hollywood movies. Relax, citizen, put your feet up and watch Julia Roberts in *Pretty Woman*.

Lameda, dressed in pressed jeans and tucked-in shirt, the retired general's civilian uniform, shifted behind his desk. He gazed out at his sun-dappled garden, casting his mind back to those mad days a decade earlier. The boxer's stubby tail wagged, yearning to leave the study's air-conditioned gloom for an afternoon walk. His master may have felt the same way. The coup was the opposition's original sin. A transgression against democratic, legal and moral norms that branded it for years to come. Its leaders were exposed as hypocrites who preached democracy only to usurp it, and to be so inept they made Chávez stronger, a victim and a hero. Lameda, the man whom Chávez had brought into government and trusted, had been in the thick of it. That such a stickler for old-fashioned rules and principles was implicated showed how polarisation spun the country's moral compass, subsuming right and wrong into the greater issue: for or against Chávez. It was, to use a loaded word, squalid.

A decade later, Lameda cleared his throat and defended himself the best he could. No, he had not been part of any pre-11 April conspiracy. Rerouting the march to Miraflores had been a spontaneous decision. No, the opposition had not planted snipers to provoke bloodshed and justify Chávez's removal. No, he had made no deal with Carmona to be named head of PDVSA. And in fact had disapproved of the interim president's inauguration ceremony. Nevertheless, Lameda accepted Carmona's job offer and on the morning of 13 April went to Miraflores to be formally reinstated as head of the oil company. 'I was putting together the list of names for the new board, talking to the new energy minister, getting ready for our swearing in and then' – Lameda paused, shook his head, still struck by the memory – 'a waiter came in. Came in and told us a crowd of Chavistas was approaching Miraflores and that we should go.' The would-be oil lords strode through the corridors, alarmed to find them nearly deserted, and spotted Carmona with a navy admiral scurrying for a car. The crowd had surrounded the palace, but Lameda escaped through an emergency exit and made his way to the military base. He realised the armed forces had turned against the regime but found Carmona and generals squabbling over ministerial appointments, as if they were still in control. 'It was a farce.' Then the penny dropped. 'At a certain moment everyone realised the game was up, and all the uniforms left the room. Carmona was alone. It was a lonely, frightening moment for him.' Doubtless for Lameda too. The two men parted as pro-Chávez troops took control of the base. Carmona was arrested; Lameda was allowed to scuttle home. At the same time commandos dispatched by Baduel rescued Chávez from La Orchila and flew him back to Caracas. Later that night, on television, Lameda watched the denouement: spotlights in Miraflores picked out a helicopter that slowly descended amid a rapturous, jubilant throng. Chávez, resurrected, walked among them, hugging and smiling, bathed in the flash of a hundred cameras. The crowd chanted and sang. 'He's back, he's back, he's back . . .'

The truth about 11 April remained shrouded. Each side accused the other of massacring innocents and manipulating video footage. Witnesses contradicted each other, changed their stories, fled the country. A truth inquiry was suspended, and criminal investigations stalled. Carmona, baptised Pedro the Brief by Chávez, bribed his way to freedom and exile. Lameda was never charged but became a hate figure for the government and even a decade later could, in theory, have been put on trial. The only people jailed were three metropolitan police commanders and eight junior officers accused of siding with the opposition and orchestrating violence. The media oligarchs were disgraced, as were opposition leaders. The CIA, its own documents later showed, knew a coup plot had been bubbling. The U.S. ambassador said he warned Chávez a coup was imminent and that the president shrugged it off, saying he knew about the plot. Whatever the truth of that, the opposition felt emboldened by U.S. antipathy to the comandante, and the Bush administration smirked when he fell. But there was little evidence, as Chávez would later insist, that Washington pulled the strings. An Irish documentary,

The Revolution Will Not Be Televised, became an influential advocate overseas for Chávez's version, casting him as a romantic hero. The coup entered folklore, guilt and innocence tangled in vines, details covered by moss.

4

THE YOUNG LIEUTENANT

I n the late 1960s a tall, stoutly built boy used to lead pupils from
the Daniel Florencio O'Leary High School in Barinas into the
street for boisterous demonstrations: the Vietnam War, the Paris student rebellion, liberation theology, the school's blocked sewers, taste-
less lunches. Rafael Simón Jiménez, head of the student union as well
as the local communist youth group, possessed boundless energy, a
booming voice and a desire to change the world, starting with his
school, named after Bolívar's Irish aide-de-camp, and Barinas, a
quiet, rural town amid the plains of southern Venezuela. His classmates did not always understand exactly why they were demonstrating or throwing stones, only that Rafael Simón instructed them to do
so. Among them was a skinny boy with big feet and a toothy smile
with the nickname Tribilin, the Spanish name for Goofy. He was a
year younger than Rafael Simón, and his name was Hugo Rafael
Chávez Frías.

Huguito had been born on 28 July 1954, on the outskirts of

Sabaneta, a dusty, somnolent village out on the plains. His father, Hugo, and mother, Elena, taught at the primary school. She had named her firstborn Adán and planned to name her next Eve. When it turned out to be a boy, he was named after his father. The family home had an earth floor and a palm leaf roof. As more children arrived (six boys in all, no girls), the overstretched parents sent Adán and Hugo to live with their grandmother, Rosa Inés, a widow who had a small adobe home nearby.

They were poor, like their neighbors, and lacked running water and regular electricity. But Hugo adored this industrious, kind woman who made him rope sandals, cooked dinner over an open fire and told him folktales – 'The Headless Horseman' was a favourite – by candlelight. She also spoke of his great-grandfather Maisanta, an outlaw, who would gallop through the village on his way to join the great rebel leader Ezequiel Zamora. Huguito tidied the yard, picked mangoes, avocados and papayas, and helped Mama Rosa, as he called her, caramelise papayas into spider-shaped sweets that he sold around the village and at school.

'I want you to know that I have always felt proud to have been raised by you and to be able to call you Mama,' he would write to her years later. 'And I ask you to bless me, your loving son.' Poems he wrote long after she died in 1982 stressed the importance of this childhood figure.

Nurtured by this tender, loving bond, the future comandante was an active, happy child. When not at school or helping his grandmother at home, he watched the village men gather to play *bolas criollas,* a type of bocce, or bet on cockfights. He would also draw and paint anything – a tree, a cat, the sky, his grandmother. From the age of eight or nine, relatives recalled, Huguito became fascinated by the sound of his own voice. He was learning to sing folk ballads and corridos and stretched his vocal range, becoming successful enough to be invited to sing at other children's birthday parties. He had a gift for memorising ballads and lengthy corridos about the plains, outlaws, romance and broken hearts.

There was no high school in the village, so from the age of around eleven Hugo and Adán moved with their grandmother to the town of Barinas, an hour's drive away. They shared a little house from which the brothers could walk to the O'Leary school. Rafael Simón disliked the aloof bookworm Adán, who was his own age, but befriended Huguito, also a bookworm but cheerful and chatty and a ready recruit for the older boy's demonstrations. 'When Rafael Simón said we had to throw stones, we threw stones,' Chávez said years later. But whereas Rafael Simón threw them in anger, Hugo did so just to fit in.

What made Huguito's blood race was not politics or even girls (he had 'ugly' girlfriends, which was not surprising, since Hugo himself was no looker, Rafael Simón recalled decades later). What animated him was *el juego de pelota*. Baseball. A game introduced to Venezuela in the 1920s by American oil workers and a national obsession by the time Chávez was born. In Sabaneta he improvised with sticks and bottle tops and by the time he moved to Barinas dreamed of emulating his idol, Isaías 'Látigo' Chávez, a famous Venezuelan pitcher who played in the U.S. major leagues and by coincidence shared his surname. One day in March 1969 grief visited the fourteen-year-old Huguito, a shock he recalled decades later in a state TV documentary. 'My grandmother Rosa was preparing my breakfast and turned on the radio to listen to some music . . . We heard a news flash and for a moment I felt as if death had struck me, right then and there. A plane crashed soon after taking off from Maracaibo and there were no survivors. Látigo Chávez was on that plane . . . I fell apart. I even came up with a little prayer I recited every night, vowing to grow up to be like him.'

Hugo continued to join Rafael Simón's student insurrections, but after graduation in 1971 their paths diverged. The ambitious boy with the foghorn voice went on to study law and history at university before launching a political career in a new political party, the Movement for Socialism (MAS). Chávez joined the army. Not because he wanted to be a soldier, but because it had an excellent sports academy and would get him to the capital, where some of the best baseball teams were based. 'I'm going to get to know Caracas and then I'll quit the military academy and stay there' was the plan, he revealed years later. Once in the academy, however, the seventeen-year-old discovered he adored the camaraderie, the ceremonies, the uniforms. 'By the time I dressed in blue for the first time, I already felt like a soldier,' he recalled. 'A uniform, a gun, an area, close-order formation, marches, morning runs, studies in military science . . . I was like a fish in water. It was as if I had discovered the essence or at least part of the essence of life, my true vocation.' In a letter to Mama Rosa he enthused about marches and pitching tents in the rain. 'Grandma, if you had only seen me firing away like a maniac in our manoeuvres. First we worked on instinctive shooting – immediate action, daytime attack, infiltration etc . . . We walked through little villages where the girls stared at us in awe and the little kids cried, they were so scared.'

On a day of leave in late 1971 he put on his ceremonial blue tunic and white gloves and set out through Caracas, to him still a bustling, alien metropolis, to the cemetery where Isaías Chávez was buried. There he asked the dead pitcher forgiveness for abandoning the vow to follow in his footsteps. 'I started talking to the gravestone, with the spirit that penetrated everything there . . . It was as if I was saying to him, "Isaías, I'm not going down that path anymore. I'm a soldier now." And as I left the cemetery, I was free.'

The cadet fell in love not just with the army but with the books it opened. He studied Mao, Clausewitz, Napoleon, Hannibal, Sun Tzu, masters of strategy and conquest, as well as texts on Bolívar, Zamora, and Venezuela's first caudillo presidents. The academy in Caracas had a tradition of absorbing lads from the slums and impoverished villages and turning them conservative as they rose through the ranks. But times were changing. Visiting cadets from Panama told how back home General Omar Torrijos, who had seized power in a coup, was heading a left-wing, nationalist government and reclaiming the canal from the Yankees. In a visit to Lima in 1974, Chávez and other cadets encountered Peru's revolutionary military government shortly before it fell in a right-wing coup. The group met the president, General Juan Velasco Alvarado, Chávez later recounted. 'One night he received us at the palace . . . the revolutionary manifesto, the man's speeches, the Inca Plan – I read all those things for years.' It opened his eyes to the possibility of fusing the military with nationalism and left-wing politics. Meanwhile, the United States, mired in Vietnam, shored up Augusto Pinochet in Chile and any other brute who could squelch socialists in Latin America. Venezuela's oil-flush democracy needed little U.S. help in snuffing out its own guerrillas – Venezuela's army was well equipped – but tolerated legal, left-wing political parties such as MAS and Radical Cause that slowly gathered strength. Through his brother Adán, who studied physics in Mérida, Chávez met left-wing activists.

While the military trained the young officer in armour and communications – commanders recognised his gift of gab – an idea began forming in his mind. Bolívar's unfinished economic and social liberation; his outlaw great-grandfather; Venezuela's poverty and inequality; progressive activism; military honour and power: it all added up, in the young lieutenant's mind, to one conclusion. His destiny was not just to rise up the military ranks but to pursue a calling. A mission. Revolt. In a diary entry dated 25 October 1977, he appealed to Bolívar. 'Come. Return. Here. It is possible.' A few lines later: 'This war is going to take years . . . I have to do it. Even if it costs me my life. It doesn't matter. This is what I was born to do.'

Rafael Simón Jiménez filled the whole entrance. Big face, big hands and a big body, a ton of a man. He wore a billowing yellow linen guayabera, the four-pocketed, loose-fitting Caribbean shirt. He smiled, revealing dainty white teeth. They seemed too small for the booming voice that gusted through them. He padded into a bright office with Arctic air-conditioning. It overlooked Plaza Altamira, a handsome square with an obelisk and a fountain in eastern Caracas, one of the poshest parts of the city. He eased into a chair that disappeared under his frame. It was April 2011, and Jiménez was fifty-eight years old, but it was easy to see how he had dominated classmates at O'Leary High School four decades earlier. It was not just his size but his volume and exclamatory certainty. Even seated in this small office, he spoke as if addressing thousands in the plaza below. But Jiménez no longer had crowds hooked on his every word. A political career that had begun so precociously and went on to scale great heights had slipped and tumbled down the slopes. A rise and fall rooted in Jiménez's relationship with the onetime apprentice he had called Huguito.

He eased back in his chair and talked for a while about Chávez's childhood. 'You know he almost didn't make it into the academy because he flunked chemistry? Ha! How differently things may have turned out!' Jiménez pondered this alternate history for a moment. 'A real friendly kid. Happy-go-lucky, outgoing. Into sports and theatre. I much preferred him to Adán! What a sourpuss, completely charmless. Their grandmother's house was built by the government, you know. Given to them for a nominal sum, a humble but decent lower-middle-class house. But you never hear that! Nooo, Chávez will make you believe they were desperately poor. All part of the legend. The myth. But that's the way with us *llaneros*. Half-truths, storytelling, folktales, we're masters at it, can spin a yarn out of anything.'

That put a question mark over the credibility of Jiménez's own recollections, of course, but he foghorned on. While he had studied law and history and climbed the ranks of MAS, Chávez went to the academy and gradually became politicised. 'One day in 1975, I was walking down the street in Barinas, and he pulled up in his dad's Dodge. He was home on leave and in uniform. We chatted awhile, then he told me that by 2000 he'd be a general and fix the country, that he had a plan. I thought he was joking.' One night three years later, Jiménez recalled, he was with party comrades pasting MAS posters onto walls when Chávez, again home on leave, stopped by. 'Very affectionate, effusive as ever, then he starts helping us put up the posters – and him in uniform! He could've been drummed out of the army, he was reckless like that, but got away with it.' By the late 1980s the army top brass knew Chávez was plotting something but didn't charge him, said Jiménez. 'There were two rival generals vying to be defence minister, and each thought he could use a conspiracy to his advantage.' Jiménez guffawed. 'That's Venezuela right there.'

After the 1992 coup and Chávez's release from jail, MAS, by now a moderate, left-wing party led by Jiménez, was part of the broad coalition that supported his 1998 presidential bid. 'What a candidate! Chávez is very bright. He doesn't go deep into subjects or grasp the intricacies but can read the dust jacket of a book and then talk as if he's read the whole thing.' From Jiménez, an academic and political fixer, that was both compliment and put-down. 'Chávez was well-intentioned. He wanted social reform and to change a rotten system. He genuinely wanted to spread wealth and ease hardship.' Jiménez became vice-minister of justice and interior, then vice president of the National Assembly. Working with the president was fraught. 'He is very complex, very unpredictable. He can be tender and generous one moment, abrasive and aggressive the next. You never know what you're going to get. I've always said you shouldn't get too close, otherwise you get snagged in his personality, or too far, because then you lose him.'

Jiménez said he was alarmed by Chávez's power grabs and rhetoric in 2001 and 2002 and lobbied him, in vain, to cool it. 'He would listen and nod quietly, seem to agree, then out he'd go the next day shouting so that everybody got riled up again.' Jiménez stayed loyal during the coup and was relieved when Chávez returned to Miraflores apparently chastened rather than vengeful. In his first public responses to what had happened, Chávez was gracious and conciliatory, holding a crucifix, asking forgiveness for his role in precipitating the mayhem and promising dialogue and unity. Jiménez, from his perch in the National Assembly, began talks with the opposition.

There are two versions of what happened next. Jiménez, sensing Chávez's weakness, cut clandestine deals with opponents to make himself president of the National Assembly. Chávez got wind of it and banished the traitor from his ranks at a heated meeting in Miraflores in May 2002. Or, in Jiménez's version, he tried to bridge the country's political differences and was punished by Chávez, who swiftly dropped talk of conciliation and resumed assailing foes. The old friends parted ways. Jiménez lost his National Assembly post and joined the opposition. Their relationship had come full circle. The former schoolboy brawler preached moderation. His former sidekick was now the rebel throwing stones, demanding the world be changed.

Chávez's yen for confrontation started soon after he took the throne, and it still flowed a decade later. Some wondered if it stemmed from childhood, from a psychological wound that never healed. Young Hugo was turned away from his first day at primary school for wearing rope sandals rather than shoes, making his grandmother cry in shame, but poverty did not seem to have scarred him. His relationship with his mother, Elena, a stern, matriarchal figure, was distant and lacked the warmth and adoration he had for Mama Rosa. Elena had openly disapproved of both his wives, and there were rumours they had once stopped talking for two years. But if Chávez felt abandoned or resentful, he never said so. In public and private he seemed to maintain a cordial, affectionate relationship with his parents.

Another explanation was that he was an emotional man who lashed back at vitriolic enemies who believed themselves superior. Before he took office, some branded him a communist ogre, a charlatan and a would-be despot. By 2001 this invective was amplified, day after day, by privately owned newspapers and television stations, and Chávez countered with his own verbal barrage. However, after 2006 opponents started toning down their aggressive rhetoric, while the president not only continued but escalated his, raining abuse year after year upon increasingly mute targets.

Some of those closest to him suspected a manic-depressive disorder. Before his death in 2010, Alberto Müller Rojas, a socialist army general, advisor and vice president of Chávez's party, told an interviewer: 'People have to feign, at the very least, absolute submission to him, which reveals a total lack of self-confidence . . . He goes from one position to another very easily. He is an individual who has a tendency toward cyclothymia – mood swings that range from moments of extreme euphoria to moments of despondence.' Salvador Navarrete, a doctor and family friend who treated Chávez during his first years in office, publicly opined, years later, that the president was bipolar.

There was an alternative – or additional – explanation for Chávez's aggression that had nothing to do with his mental state. Throwing stones worked. The insults against opponents appeared spontaneous outbursts but were in fact calculated, measured provocations. Time and again opponents took the bait. They lunged, veins throbbing, faces contorted with loathing and rage, to choke their tormentor. It was a trap that exposed their arrogance, economic power and sense of entitlement. Forced to choose between the comandante and tomato-faced aristocrats, most Venezuelans – meaning the poor – chose the comandante. The genius of the strategy was its durability. The perpetually indignant elites inhabited a self-contained echo chamber of boardrooms, golf clubs, dinner parties and private media. They thought they were Venezuela. They could not see how their hysterics repelled and radicalised less-privileged compatriots. Thus they kept lunging and, in election after election, would keep losing.

January 17, 2003. Convoys of national guard vehicles surrounded two bottling plants in the city of Valencia, in the state of Carabobo. Soldiers in camouflage fatigues and red berets spilled out of the vehicles and pushed through picket lines of striking workers to enter the plants. At their head was a tall, powerfully built general named Luis Acosta Carles. Beret tilted rakishly over one eye, square jaw, he resembled an action hero. The general, who had diplomas in public security and human resources, was ambitious. His older brother, Felipe, had been an army officer and one of the comandante's first co-conspirators but died during the 1989 riots. Out in this regional city, Acosta Carles had had fewer chances to impress the throne, but now, as camera crews jogged to keep up with him, he sensed opportunity.

This was the latest front in a two-month-old economic war. Having failed to dislodge Chávez in the April 2002 coup, his opponents, unrepentant and angrier than ever, had launched a different assault in December: a national strike – in some ways a lockout, since it was directed by owners and managers as well as union leaders. Led by the executives of PDVSA, who feared the 'monkey in the palace' would finally wrest control of the oil company, they sought to cripple the economy and make life miserable for ordinary Venezuelans. They shut the oil industry, banks, shops, schools, restaurants, factories. What they could not shut they disrupted, triggering shortages, queues and hardship. The idea was to inflict nationwide pain and channel it into fury against the throne. It did not matter to them that the strike would destroy livelihoods and cost the country billions. Private media cast the strike as a patriotic action in hysterical, biased reports. Television bosses even dropped advertising, forfeiting revenue so they could clear schedules for nonstop assaults on the demon president.

Breweries and drink makers did their bit by halting supplies of bottled water, beer and soft drinks. Now, six weeks into the strike, Acosta Carles was helping Chávez wrest back the initiative by raiding bottling plants. The general dwarfed his men and the camera crews as he strode into the first warehouse of Panamco, Venezuela's Coca-Cola bottler, owned by Gustavo Cisneros, the billionaire who had backed the coup. It was filled floor to ceiling with bottles of Malta Regional, a yeasty drink that had disappeared from shop shelves weeks earlier. The general, sleeves rolled up over his elbows, plunged a brawny arm into a tower of bottles and took one out. He turned to the cameras and held it up. 'Malta Regional,' he barked. A clutch of microphones was thrust under his chin. The reporters were from opposition television stations – Cisneros owned one of them – and badgered Acosta Carles over his legal authority to raid the plants.

He ignored them, twisted open the bottle, tiny in his hand, and glugged it down. A young female reporter persisted, asking if he had permission from Indecu, a state regulatory agency.

'General, today the forty-eight-hour deadline that Indecu gave the company to prepare its response . . .'

She did not get to finish because the general drained the bottle, looked down at the microphones, opened his mouth into a black cavity and emitted a thunderous belch. '*Buuuuuuuurgh.*'

He finished and looked at the reporter. 'Pardon. Pardon, señorita.' Then he belched again. '*Buuuuuuuurgh.*' A hint of a smile seeped across his face.

The reporter responded, indignant: 'Isn't that rude?'

The general shrugged. 'Well, you know, it was instinct. It just came out. There was a lot of gas because it was warm.' He showed the bottle to the cameras. 'Have you seen that commercial with the football player?' he asked, turning back to the reporter. 'The one where he takes a drink' – the general mimed taking another gulp – 'and then goes "*Buuuuuuuurgh.*"' Another belch.

The reporter protested: 'This is a serious issue, and I'm asking you a serious question, General . . .'

He shrugged her off and turned to the other cameras. 'All this,' he said, indicating the stocks, 'is going to be distributed; it's for the people, for the Venezuelan people. Hoarding is against the constitution.' He spun on his heel and marched deeper into the warehouse, firing instructions at his men.

The general's expulsion of carbon dioxide from his digestive tract had immediate, enduring political impact, expressing in a way that even Chávez himself had not managed the revolution's contempt for its foes and its determination to prevail. The oligarchs could shut their factories, abuse their power, shriek and shout on their television channels and still lose. *Buuuuuuuurgh!*

Venezuelans watched the clip, played repeatedly on opposition channels, mesmerised. It made their choice stark. With the belch or against the belch. Millions called it disgusting. But millions more hailed it as comeuppance for economic saboteurs. One pro-Chávez writer called it an expression of the oppressed's collective unconscious. 'It is part of our Hispanic Arab heritage, of the reconquest.'

Within weeks the strike unravelled. Ambitious businessmen who were not part of the traditional elite helped the government to source and distribute oil, gasoline, food and other necessities. The comandante fired nineteen thousand workers from PDVSA and took complete control of the oil company. He invited Acosta Carles onto his television show to laud his role in the victory and proclaim him a hero. The general's gassy vignette became known as 'el eructo que salvó la revolución', the belch that saved the revolution.

The crises of 2002 sent the comandante ever more often to the *sala situacional,* the situation room, beneath his office. Guards at the door, infrared swipe cards, no windows, a rectangular room filled with computers and trusted military and civilian aides. Instead of the usual palace bustle, a low hum, a place to concentrate, focus and distill information. For a president accustomed to military command centers, it was a comforting, familiar environment. Control and communication hinged on information.

Restricted access meant even most ministers had no idea what it looked like, fuelling speculation about its size and influence. The comandante fed the aura, but the reality of this mysterious chamber in the first few years was rather mundane. About fifteen people reading newspapers and magazines online and in print, clipping, pasting, noting, archiving. Others seated before televisions and radios monitoring the airwaves' ebb and flow. Gossip columns, public announcements and intelligence reports were filtered to create files on governors, mayors, journalists, business leaders, trade union activists. Regional issues – cross-border smuggling in Táchira, artisanal gold mining in Amazonas, drought in Apure – were tracked and analysed for political implications.

'I loved it, there was a real buzz working down there. We had a great team, everybody with their own job and rhythm. Every day we updated profiles on the main players. Whenever Chávez visited, we were able to immediately brief him on who was doing what.' The man speaking – let us call him Andrés – had been one of the *sala*'s senior analysts and asked that his surname not be used. He was trim, with cropped salt-and-pepper hair, a dark mustache and a military-style jacket. Everything about him seemed clipped and measured.

In a low, even voice he told his story. Andrés had been a few years behind Chávez in the academy and went on to become an instructor in political science and geopolitics. Left-wing and despairing of Venezuela's 'exhaustion', he had participated in the 1992 coup – relaying information from Fuerte Tiuna – and afterward visited Chávez in jail, giving him books by the Marxist theorist Antonio Gramsci. 'Chávez had never heard of him, imagine! A supposed man of the Left.'

After Chávez's election in 1998, Andrés helped set up the situation room. It swiftly matched the mood and pace of the chief upstairs, he recalled. Working all hours, responding to requests for this and that, trying to keep one step ahead, jubilant, anxious, frenetic, in a symbiotic relationship with the comandante. And then, after the April 2002 coup, it all changed. 'It became something else.' Andrés paused. 'I can sum it up in one word,' he said, leaning forward. 'Fidel.'

Fidel Castro had long dreamed of co-opting Venezuela and its oil wealth into Cuba's revolution. He had supplied weapons and training to Venezuela's doomed guerrillas in the 1960s, then in a pragmatic switch made peace with successive presidents right up to and beyond Chávez's 1992 coup. Castro initially condemned the uprising, but two years later, when Chávez was pardoned and freed, he invited him to Havana. Fidel was in the midst of a crisis. The Soviet Union had disintegrated and with it the subsidies that had kept Cuba's economy afloat. Imminent collapse was feared. Against this background the maximum leader invited a semi-notorious Venezuelan ex–coup leader with no money, no political experience, no organised support and, it seemed, not much of a future. 'The old fox sniffed him right out,' said Andrés, admiring the prescience. 'He recognised Chávez's potential straightaway. And his weaknesses.'

The seduction was captured in a series of photographs. The first in black and white: Fidel, in uniform and cap, welcoming his guest off the plane in 1994, gripping him by both shoulders, smiling. Chávez gazing up at his bearded host with awe. Castro personally attended to Chávez for the entire visit. The pair bonded over Baskin-Robbins and marathon talks where they compared life arcs: both rural boys, talented pitchers who traded professional baseball dreams for politics and insurrection. An official photographer shadowed them, and Fidel gave his guest a photo album as a memento.

In January 1999 they met again in Havana. More photographs. Chávez, now president-elect, in a brown suit and gold tie, walking down a shiny corridor with Fidel, in olive green, deep in conversation. In the following months and years the photographs multiplied. A baseball game in Havana, Chávez in white pitching for Venezuela, Fidel in a blue jacket coaching Cuba, fifty thousand spectators cheering. Chávez declared Cuba and Venezuela were 'swimming together toward the same sea of happiness'. Here they are in a canoe in Venezuela's Canaima National Park, wearing green jungle hats, waving to the camera as a waterfall thunders behind them. Now standing in a jeep – a blurred image – inspecting hurricane damage in Cuba. Then in Sabaneta in the house where Chávez was born. A future shrine, predicted Fidel. Chávez was in ecstasy. 'Fidel had to stoop . . . it's a low door, and he's a giant. I saw it with my own eyes . . . as if it was a dream, something out of a García Márquez novel. My God!' A still image from Chávez's television show: Fidel, famously the one Cuban who doesn't sing, wearing headphones and holding a page of lyrics, crooning with Chávez. Chávez at the Caracas airport, looking wistful, blowing a kiss at the plane taking Fidel back to Havana.

Andrés watched all this from his bunker in Miraflores – the *sala* monitored Chávez himself to record reactions to what he said and did – and he worried. Like many Venezuelan leftists, he considered Fidel an anachronism, a cautionary tale of revolutionary idealism warping into totalitarian control and central-planning fiasco. But the comandante seemed to be falling deeper under the older man's spell. The 2002 coup, said Andrés, provided the final push into Fidel's arms. 'It was right after that it happened. The Cubans took us over.' He descended into the *sala* one morning to find strangers with rapid-fire Cuban accents. His new bosses. Cuba's intelligence service, G2, had thwarted countless plots against Fidel for decades. It was among the best in the business. The comandante's *sala,* in contrast, had failed to anticipate the coup. The Cubans considered Andrés and his colleagues inept or disloyal. He reciprocated. 'The mess they made! Coffee cups everywhere, always munching something, crumbs on the keyboards. That I could put up with. But then I saw their strategy: seal Chávez off from the public, manipulate him, nourish his insecurity, find evidence of assassination plots, of betrayals. Make him paranoid.'

Andrés did not last long under the new bosses. He moved to the vice president's office as an analyst, then served in the Commerce Ministry, tax agency, and PDVSA. 'I lost my faith in this project a long time ago. A lot of us have.' He sighed. 'It's a bit late now, but I regret supporting the [1992] coup. Believing the army will save us – it's a disease.' He retained a sinecure in the oil company. 'It's easy to stay inside the system if you keep your mouth shut.'

Teresita Rondon giggled too much, little, mirthful gurgles when hearing or recounting something she considered funny, which was often. The smile revealed braces on her upper and lower teeth. Rondon was self-conscious about the dentistry but couldn't help smiling. She was cheerful and attractive, with long, braided hair that swung when she walked, and had landed a well-paying government job straight out of university. She lived with her parents in Mérida, four hundred miles west of Caracas, a mecca for students, hikers and tourists ringed by icy mountain peaks. It shivered during winter nights.

She was eight years old when Chávez launched his coup, fifteen when he was elected, and now, seven years into his rule, twenty-two. Politics was not her thing. Rondon liked movies, boys and the idea of travel. She had scored high grades in her information technology course and secured a post in the mayor's office. 'The first in my class to get a job,' she said proudly. 'That's not easy in this town, believe me, there's a lot of competition.' When she was asked about her duties, the effervescent chatter turned taciturn. 'Oh, you know, human resources, personnel, that sort of stuff.' Then she would change the subject. Even on those afternoons when she came directly from the office looking distracted, vexed, she would divert conversation to another topic. Until one day, staring into her coffee, in a quiet voice, she said: 'La lista.' The list. 'That's what I do,' she said, looking up. 'The list.'

In mid-2003, opponents mounted another heave against the president: a petition to trigger a recall referendum, a mechanism enshrined in the new constitution to make authority accountable. Despite opposition leaders' complicity in the preceding year's coup and oil strike, a referendum stood a chance of success. The economy was flat, and Chávez's ratings had fallen. Even his base in the slums was restless. Organisers collected three million signatures. Chávez's allies in the National Electoral Council, supposedly an independent body, said the petition was flawed and demanded it be done again. It bought Chávez valuable months to plan a defence. As fresh signatures were gathered, he made what sounded like a threat. 'Whoever signs against Chávez will be registered for history because they are going to have to give their name, surname, identity number and fingerprint.'

After it was all over, Chávez admitted the throne had been in peril. 'An international researcher spent two months here and came to the palace to deliver a devastating message: Mr. President, if the referendum were held today, you would lose. That for me was a bombshell because you know that many people will not tell you such things and will instead soften them. That was when we began to work with the missions and ask for help from Fidel. He told me: "Look, I have this idea, attack from below with all possible force." '

The idea was to create social programmes for the poor to plug gaps in state services. They were called *misiones* – missions – and set up with speed and urgency. The timing was perfect because oil prices spiked, largely due to Iraq's conflagration, and petrodollars rained on Miraflores. Chávez had never really cared about money – in the army he barely noticed his salary coming and going – and Fidel had micromanaged his island's economy into penury. But they handled Venezuela's bounty with finesse. While Chávez sent ninety-five thousand barrels of oil daily to Cuba, shoring up its economy, Fidel sent twenty thousand Cuban doctors, nurses, and other specialists into Venezuela's barrios. They sought out the poor, sick and forgotten, treated bulging veins, infections, broken bones, arthritis, bleeding gums, stiff backs. They logged medical histories, trained community volunteers, gave courses in nutrition. It was all free – and they stayed. The Cubans lived on the upper floor of new small hexagonal clinics. This was Misión Barrio Adentro.

Teachers followed to teach the illiterate to read and write, liberating thousands from embarrassment and ignorance. This was Misión Robinson. Other teachers taught night courses to high-school dropouts. This was Misión Ribas. Its graduates were offered stipends and places at new universities. This was Misión Sucre. Credits and training were offered to small agricultural and industrial cooperatives. This was Misión Vuelvan Caras. On it went: soup kitchens, subsidised food shops, land titles, flights to Cuba for eye surgery. By the time the referendum was held in August 2004, Chávez's ratings had recovered, and he won a landslide. 'Venezuela has changed forever,' he exulted to a crowd from the palace balcony. 'There is no turning back.'

The opposition cried fraud, then collapsed. It felt cheated, crushed and exhausted. Years of marching, chanting, plotting, organising – for nothing. Chávez was more secure than ever with two-thirds of the country behind him. Opponents retreated into a cave, despairing and drained, to hibernate. The comandante could now finally ease the lever on the chair with the gold-plated sphinx and put his feet up. But then he would not have been the comandante. His power was now secure, but he was condemned to protect it, ceaselessly, endlessly. The Salón Boyacá briefers warned him the enemy – the fascist, treacherous enemy – would recover and regroup. Strike now, sir! Rout the remnants! And he did. He had warned people not to sign the petition, and now they would pay.

A digital record of the three million names was passed to Luis Tascón, a young National Assembly member and specialist in information technology. He posted it on his Web site, ostensibly to prevent the opposition from inventing signatories. Thus was born *la lista Tascón*. The Tascón list. Also known as Chávez's revenge. It formalised the country's division. Heretics this side of the ledger, believers on the other. Government and state offices used it to purge signatories from the state payroll, to deny jobs, contracts, loans, documents, to harass and punish, to make sectarianism official. People lost careers and livelihoods and went bankrupt. Fear gripped those who had signed, then it spread to their relatives. On his television show the president invited Tascón onto the stage and with mock anxiety asked: 'I don't appear on your list, do I?' By April 2005 the stories of blighted lives were creating an international embarrassment, so Chávez publicly declared a halt. 'The Tascón list must be archived and buried,' he said. 'I say that because I keep receiving some letters . . . that make me think that in some places they still have the Tascón list to determine if somebody is going to get a job or not. Surely it had an important role at one time, but not now.'

A year later Teresita Rondon confirmed the list was alive and well in Mérida. Her job was to apply it, to methodically cross-reference every municipal employee, contractor, job applicant. Teachers, street sweepers, police, doctors, secretaries, ambulance drivers, receptionists, anyone and everyone needed to be checked to determine if they were to be fired, barred or hired. Rondon's youth, energy and IT skills made her ideal. 'The list is thorough, but to run the program is slow and cumbersome, it's got glitches, it takes times to process a name.' The list, she said, had been transformed and expanded into a new software program called Maisanta, after the comandante's great-grandfather. It included all registered voters and allowed officials to check their addresses, voting stations, voting participation, political preferences and memberships in missions and other government schemes. It enabled searching and cross-referencing and rated people as 'patriots', 'opposition' or 'abstainers'. The Maisanta list was national. Chávez's order to bury it had been for the cameras. Rondon was one cog in a huge, clanking machine.

It bred a minor industry of corruption because data could be manipulated, she said. 'I've heard of people who signed paying to become patriots.' Those who couldn't afford the bribe stayed on the blacklist. 'It's not my fault. I didn't know this was the job. I can't look friends in the eye. Some of them are on the list. What am I going to tell them?' Her eyes reddened, and it seemed she would cry, but she didn't.

PALACE

★

Carefully observing the relationship between the animals you see how they avoid and fear each other. The golden age has ended. In this paradise of American jungles, as everywhere else, a long, sad experience has taught all living beings that gentleness is rarely linked to might.

— ALEXANDER VON HUMBOLDT

5

SURVIVAL OF THE FITTEST

I t was five in the morning, Caracas asleep in sepulchral darkness, and I was already late. The taxi swerved down Francisco de Miranda Avenue, for once deserted, its headlights picking out billboards for Pepsi, Polar beer, banks and the comandante's latest election campaign: '¡Ahora sí!' Now yes! The apartment blocks of Candelaria, so tatty in daytime, hulked like giant crossword puzzles, a few illuminated squares – people still partying, early risers? – amid the blackness. I opened the window to let in some breeze. It was humid. It was going to be a hot day. The taxi skirted downtown – Miraflores hid behind other buildings – and climbed the elevated four-lane highway, a dilapidated legacy of the 1950s building boom that had given Caracas, for a while, South America's most modern infrastructure. The headlights picked out fresh murals and graffiti of the comandante and the referendum slogan. '¡Ahora sí! ¡Sí, sí, sí!' We entered the first, brightly lit tunnel, the main route through the Ávila, which soared two thousand metres above us, then started the curving descent toward the sea. In the glimmer of dawn I could glimpse new, half-built shacks creeping up the Ávila's slopes. We hugged the coastline, mountain on one side, Caribbean on the other, and arrived at Simón Bolívar International Airport, a strip adjacent to the sea, just before six. National guardsmen in green uniforms and officials in red T-shirts, waistcoats and baseball caps bustled around the domestic terminal. A harried, smiling official from the Information Ministry greeted me. 'Mr. Rory, there you are, this way, hurry!' We ended up waiting an hour, then boarded a government jet. It was August 2007, and I was to be a guest on *Hello, President,* episode 291.

Chávez was at a peak of power and popularity. The opposition, exhausted from defeat in the 2002 coup and strike and the 2004 recall referendum, had boycotted the 2005 National Assembly elections. It was supposed to delegitimise the election and send a distress signal to the international community. Over here! Look! Dictatorship! The world shrugged. Venezuela's opposition was discredited, hysterical and still overreacting to Chávez's bait. The world instead gazed at Iraq, horrified at a sectarian civil war and a blundering U.S. occupation. Thus the boycott merely served the assembly on a plate to Chávez, giving him near-total legislative control for the next five years.

With oil prices soaring ever higher, money washed through barrios, banks and boardrooms. There was more of everything: chicken, beer, whiskey, motorbikes, Hummers. The only question over the December 2006 presidential election had been the margin of Chávez's victory. He did not even debate the opposition challenger, Manuel Rosales, saying that 'an eagle does not hunt flies'. He did, however, promise to fuck Rosales if he crouched. Chávez won a second six-year term with 63 per cent of the vote, the widest margin and highest voter turnout in Venezuela's history. He took every state, saturating the political map red. The only surprise was that the opposition, amid defeat, clawed back credibility. It had rallied around a single candidate, albeit an uncharismatic, husky-voiced governor from the western state of Zulia. Rather than shriek fraud, as in previous votes, it accepted Chávez's victory. Rosales even congratulated the president. 'Today we recognise that they beat us.' It was a sign the opposition was beginning to reconnect with reality. Its radical wing – those who screamed that Chávez was a vote-rigging communist dictator – began to lose ground to pragmatic moderates who said Chávez could be challenged, and ultimately beaten, at the ballot box.

Few noticed this shift, however, amid jubilant scenes at the palace, where Chávez, still only fifty-two, addressed an adoring crowd from the balcony. 'Long live the revolution! Venezuela is demonstrating that a new and better world is possible, and we are building it.' Weeks later, while the country headed to the beach with beer and whiskey for its Christmas break, he made three dramatic announcements. He would nationalise 'strategic' industries; shut RCTV, the country's most popular television channel; and seek to change the constitution to abolish term limits. His voice boomed with confidence. 'Nothing can stop the revolution!'

Eight months later, as I prepared to board the plane for his television show, Chávez had kept the first two promises and was in the midst of a referendum campaign to keep the third.

The plane soared into an azure sky and banked east, toward a rising sun. Curious to experience the show firsthand, I had lobbied hard for this invitation. Today's episode was to be broadcast from Valle Seco, a beach near the town of Guanta in the state of Anzoátegui. At a regional airport we changed for a military helicopter. The minister for indigenous affairs, Nicia Maldonado, was strapped in beside me. A captive interviewee – a surprise bonus. Ministers dodged foreign journalists. To avoid appearing uncooperative, they did not say no to interviews and instead strung us along with perpetual maybes. It made sense. There was little to gain and much to lose from exposure. Chávez was the government's sole voice. Even to parrot him was risky: without warning he could change his mind on an issue or resent sharing the limelight. Maldonado, just seven months into the job, was already under fire from indigenous groups who complained that the 1999 constitution, in theory so progressive and favourable to them, was being flouted. Ranchers, oil companies and coal miners were occupying their lands in the west, and a proposed government gas pipeline would cleave their land in the east. After exchanging pleasantries with Maldonado over the rotor's blades – we agreed it was going to be hot – I asked about the pipeline controversy. She looked blank, and I repeated the question. She smiled and pointed to her ears.

'Can't hear. Helicopter. Too loud.'

'The pipeline,' I bellowed. 'Going ahead?'

She shrugged. '*Disculpa*. Can't hear.'

After a few more attempts I gave up, and we both gazed at the coast passing below. After landing at a small, dusty military base, the minister skipped into a car and disappeared. We drove in convoy – the *Hello, President* entourage included dozens of technicians as well as officials – on a winding road past run-down fishing villages with bare-chested men on doorsteps sipping their first beers of the day, until we came to Valle Seco, a hamlet with a golden beach and handsome wooden jetty perched over limpid water. An advance team had set up a large white tent, portable toilets, rows of white plastic chairs and a desk planted in the sand. It had a pile of books, maps and notepads. Cameramen were busy with cables and lenses. I noticed audience veterans – ministers, governors, and mayors – gulping coffee, tucking into empanadas, and queuing for the toilets, fuelling and preparing for the marathon. Local women and children who were not allowed into the official cordon waded out into the ocean, waist-high, to watch from there. They joked and laughed, looking forward to the show.

Ten minutes before 11:00 a.m., the comandante appeared. Wearing black trousers and a red shirt, he walked to the end of the jetty and looked out at the ocean for several minutes, a picture of reflection, then took up position at the desk, flashing a wide grin. 'How are you all? Here we are, look, how marvellous! By the sea, so inviting it makes you want to plunge in. Here we are. Greetings to all the people of Anzoátegui and all the people of Sucre state. We are on the border between Anzoátegui and Sucre. A pretty and clear day, a clear day. Here is the Caribbean, the Caribbean Sea. What a beautiful land! It's been quite a while since I've been here. Greetings to the fishermen, to the children, to the boatmen for the tourists. Ah, over there is Mochima, Mochima National Park, what beautiful water, what a gorgeous bay . . . Look there, the little ones in the water, a kiss to you boys and girls, may God bless you, a hug to the boys and girls of Valle Seco. How lovely is Venezuela! How lovely is my country. *Hello, President* number 291. And today we are going to speak of something marvellous. But you already know that.'

The program's focus was to be the constitutional referendum due in December 2007, four months hence. When the constitution was adopted in 1999, the comandante said it would last a thousand years, but now he said it needed urgent changes. It would 'restructure the geometry of power' by empowering grassroots assemblies, known as communal councils, curbing the authority of mayors and state governors and, most important, abolishing term limits for the president, allowing Chávez to run for a third term in 2012. Since winning his

second term the previous December, the comandante had accelerated the revolution, obtaining an enabling law from the National
Assembly so he could rule by decree, amending history textbooks to
recast his 1992 coup as a heroic uprising, and, most controversially,
closing RCTV. It was the country's oldest, most-watched channel, a
producer of quiz shows and soap operas whose popularity cut across
class and political lines. It was also one of the four private channels
that had backed the 2002 coup against Chávez. Two of the channels,
Televen and Venevisión, had made peace with the president by dropping their attacks, shunting neutered news broadcasts to graveyard
slots and abandoning political commentary. Their licences were re-
newed. RCTV's rabid anti-Chávez owners continued their attacks,
and so in May 2007 the government refused to renew its terrestrial
license, banishing it to a remote satellite slot where it ailed and died.
The decision was unpopular even with government supporters, who
lost their favourite programmes. It triggered student protests that
rolled across campuses and cities and breathed life back into the
moribund opposition. With record oil prices pumping the economy,
however, Chávez was still expected to easily win the referendum.
Today's broadcast was to mobilise his supporters to vote yes.

Eyeing the crowd, sipping a little tumbler of coffee, the comandante pitched the communal councils as the referendum's center-
piece. 'What is the essence of the proposal I have made to the
Venezuelan people? Popular power ... from the bases, from Valle
Seco, from Guanta, from these communities, from this sea, from
these waters, from these mountains; that is how we start building the
new democracy, the Bolivarian democracy ... something that has
never been done here in Latin America.' He then greeted by name – I
lost count after thirty-five – audience members, almost all ministers,
governors, mayors, assembly members, military officers and local

officials. He punctuated the list with personal asides. He peered at the last seated rows.

'Are you hearing me at the back?'

'No,' replied a chorus.

The president laughed. 'How can they answer if they don't hear? Are you eating empanadas down there?'

Laughter. 'No.'

The president went along with the joke. 'It seems there is a sound fault, from here I can sense it. I've been doing this nine years and can sense when there are faults.' He reminisced about being a cadet seeing the sea for the first time, then chatted to small children ushered to his desk. Dark-skinned like most people from this community, they hovered shyly.

'What's your name, girl?'

'Nairobith.'

'Nairobith. And you're from Valle Seco? Look at those mosquito bites' – with concern he examined red marks on her arm – 'you need to put some cream on that, Nairobith, that's serious.' He blew her a kiss, and she scampered off with friends, carrying her flip-flops.

'May God bless you . . . Hey, my shoes? Where are you taking them?' The children hesitated, and the audience laughed.

'Ah no, I've a very big size, look' – he bared a foot – 'I take 44; they called me Goofy when I was your age.'

The warm-up continued. He encouraged a boy to take up base-ball, blew kisses at the women standing in the ocean, reminisced about his boyhood.

After an hour, shuffling through notes, he came to me. 'Here we also have a British journalist, Rory Carroll . . . from the newspaper the *Guardian*. Rory, do you speak Spanish?'

Yes, I replied, though I was still taking lessons.

'What brings you here, to Valle Seco, you who are from Great Britain?'

'I'm Irish, in fact, but . . .'

'Ah! You're Irish. So what brings you to these Caribbean shores? How long have you been living here among us?'

'Almost one year.'

'Almost one year.'

'Yes.'

'And where did you study journalism?'

'In Dublin. I've been with the *Guardian* ten years.'

'The *Guardian,* from London, right?'

'Yes.'

'What's your purpose? What question do you have for me? Do you have a question? Usually, journalists come with lots of questions.'

The audience tittered, the camera zoomed in, and I drew breath. I'd expected to get a private chat with Chávez later that evening, after the show, not a public exchange now. In halting Spanish, I asked the first question that popped into my head. Why should the president have the exclusive right to indefinite reelection while denying that to governors and mayors on the grounds they could become regional caudillos? Was there not a risk the president himself could become a caudillo?

The question landed with a thud on his desk. His nose wrinkled. He paused and squinted. 'Well. That is the question that Rory Carroll brings us.' The jovial atmosphere evaporated. From the corner of my eye I detected some red-shirted neighbors inching their seats away from me. Then it began. He flung the question back out to sea, beyond the horizon, and turned it into a harangue against the evils of biased media, European hypocrisy, monarchy, the British queen, the Royal Navy, slavery, genocide and colonialism.

'There is much cynicism in Europe, Rory, eh? There in Europe, where you're from, I think that Europe competes with the United States. It's older and more cynical, it's had more years to practice cynicism, and I think the United States has learned a lot from European cynicism . . . which celebrates the discovery of America, for example, while denying the African holocaust.' What this had to do with the question I did not know, but he continued. He extolled the African blood that ran in Venezuelan veins and lambasted Europe's history of war and conquest. He ordered the camera to focus on his brown skin to illustrate the point.

'In the name of the Latin American people I demand that the British government return the Malvinas Islands to the Argentine people.' Then, after another riff on colonialism: 'It is better to die fighting than to be a slave!'

He directed the camera back at me, and I adopted what I hoped was a poker face. The mobile phone in my shirt pocket was continuously vibrating with messages from colleagues watching on television. Chávez continued, glowering. 'Never has a European journalist asked our opinion about the arrival of Christopher Columbus. Cultured Europe and us the barbarians. What cynicism!' How dare Britain, whose unelected queen reigned over Caribbean territories, criticise Venezuelan democracy, he said. 'There they say Chávez wants to perpetuate himself in power, just because I'm proposing that the people decide about the possibility of continuous reelection for the head of state.'

On and on. Europe the monarchist. Europe the queen of cynicism that had oppressed Latin America for centuries. Europe with no term limits for prime ministers. The audience punctuated each accusation with applause. An aide slipped him a piece of paper with the names of European states that had no term limits for leaders. He read each one like pulling a trigger. Italy! Portugal! Slovakia! Estonia! Cyprus!

He resumed assailing British monarchy, then demanded my opinion. The microphone was passed to me in silence. By now my neighbours had edged quite a bit away, leaving me a little oasis of space.

'I repeat, I am not only Irish but also a republican, so this system [of monarchy] I don't defend . . . but that doesn't matter, because the question was about your country, and you, and my question was: If the mayors and governors don't have the right [to reelection], why should you?' It was an attempt to stress the fact I was from a country that had suffered more under British colonialism than most, that in any case my opinion on such things wasn't relevant, and that the president's tirade had dodged the original question.

The microphone disappeared, and Chávez resumed the onslaught, turning my phrase 'doesn't matter' into a rhetorical stick, implying I'd said he didn't matter, that Venezuelans didn't matter. 'It matters to us, *compañero,* it all matters to us, the destiny of the people of Europe, of the people of Africa . . . because we all share this planet, Rory.'

Eventually, ire spent, he moved on to other topics, leaving me to stew in my puddle of old-world vice and cynicism. The hours passed quickly after that. The comandante drew diagrams and maps setting out the new 'geometry of power'; quoted Mao, Gandhi, Christ, Marx, Engels; read out extracts from Gramsci (first flicking an insect that had landed on the book); patted a dog that trotted up to his desk; railed against capitalism, Venezuela's private media and Catholic cardinals. When a makeup woman dabbed sweat from his face, the cameras would point at the audience. Chávez never stopped talking, not even while she rubbed tissue over his lips. Proclaiming a golden age of sport, he donated tickets for a trip to Cuba to a baseball team and a bus to a group of female athletes.

Somewhere amid all this he unexpectedly returned to my question. Catching my eye, the voice softer, he answered with an analogy. 'I have to finish this picture. That another person could finish it is true, but nothing more than a line. If I give the brush to someone else, they would start to change the colours because they would have another vision, start to alter the contours.' Other officials were not responsible for the big picture and so did not need indefinite reelection, he said, looking at the seated governors and mayors. 'Nothing personal.' They smiled wanly and applauded. Seven hours later it was dusk, and the show ended in applause and cheers. Officials kept a distance from me, the toxic interloper, until Chávez shook my hand. A firm grip, a smile and a pat on the shoulder. The eyes were glazed – a normal human would have collapsed hours earlier – and he moved quickly to his trailer. Ministers shook my hand after that. The flight back to Caracas was the worst of my life. A lightning storm filled the night sky and sent the jet into sickening plunges and rolls. We landed in pitch-black driving rain. I thought of Gabriel García Márquez, landing on this same spot after his flight from Havana, eight years earlier, and his wondering if the comandante would turn out to be a saviour or an illusionist.

The Amazon rain forest seethes with a ceaseless, merciless struggle for life and death. Venezuela's rain forest was hundreds of miles south, but its relentless, silent combat was replicated in the glass and concrete ministry buildings that ringed Miraflores. At first sight the honking cacophony of El Silencio, the government district, bore no comparison to the Amazon. It took just fifteen minutes to walk the six-block radius that contained most ministries and state institution headquarters. Turning right onto Urdaneta Avenue as you exited the palace brought you to the Finance Ministry, a brown opaque cube that towered over the neighbouring Central Bank and National Budget Office. One block down was the colonial facade of La Casa Amarilla (the Yellow House), the Foreign Ministry. From there it was four minutes to MinCI, the tattered tower housing the Ministry of Communication and Information. Salsa music blared from clothes shops lining the route. A few blocks north clustered Plaza Bolívar, city hall, a pro-Chávez militia headquarters and the Education Ministry. South was the National Electoral Council. In between were the Energy, Planning, Transport, Justice and other ministries. On every corner the comandante gazed from murals and billboards. Slogans from election campaigns – '¡Vota no!' (the 2004 recall referendum), '¡Ahora sí!' (the 2007 constitutional referendum) and 'Viva Chávez' (any year) – jostled with graffiti. Every few steps along the sidewalk you encountered stalls selling clothes, pirated DVDs, batteries, mangoes, bananas, hot dogs, mobile phone chargers, government-issued pale blue booklets of new laws. Crossing streets meant navigating motorbikes that raced past trucks, buses, SUVs and old Chevys. By day El Silencio teemed with sound and movement. By dusk it emptied. Muggers owned the night.

Within and between ministry offices there unfolded pitiless competition for the palace's nourishing rays, a remorseless process of adaptation and accelerated evolution that condemned ministers, vice-ministers and ambitious aides to never-ending combat. The winners who broke to the surface basked in the comandante's approval and patronage, but they continued fending off rivals who swarmed in the shadows below, forever pushing upward, grabbing, straining, stretching. The losers were those who lost their strength, failed to adapt and atrophied in the gloom.

Upon taking office, the comandante had inherited twenty-one ministries and in the name of efficiency and lean government reduced that to fourteen and said the target was nine. This hacking did not last long. His impatience to change and create things, his riot of ideas and initiatives and schemes, nurtured bureaucratic abundance. Ministries sprouted new branches and new departments that divided, subdivided, fused, split. The Ministry of Transport and Communications became two separate ministries. Then Transport merged into Housing to make the Infrastructure Ministry. Transport separated again and merged back into Communications until each split again into individual ministries. Transport further split into the Ministry of Ground Transportation and the Ministry of Air and Water Transportation. Chávez's solution to a problem – a series of air crashes or complaints over a ferry service – was to create a ministry. The cabinet reproduced and multiplied to fifteen, twenty, twenty-five, thirty ministries, until even the comandante lost count. Thirty-one, thirty-three? The United States had fifteen. A bigger oval table was brought into the cabinet room, but still ministers could not all fit around it. The government Web site could not keep up with the changes. A new ministry would be announced – for instance, the Ministry of State for the Revolutionary Transformation of Greater Caracas. It would issue a press release, as if waving a tendril, then disappear back beneath the canopy, invisible, not answering the phone, its existence uncertain until an announcement a few months later that it was officially split or merged into something else.

Ministers rose and fell even faster than ministries. The comandante went through more than 180 ministers in over a decade.

Ministers and courtiers battled for favour and advancement. Some lasted just a few weeks, snapped twigs quickly forgotten. But the nimblest and most versatile survived year after year. With faces turned permanently toward the palace, they sank roots and colonised El Silencio, made it their habitat, establishing contours to the revolution. Over a decade of evolutionary ferment those who learned to survive and thrive formed three distinct species.

The disciples invested everything in submission. All categories had to show loyalty – it was the first condition of ascent – but the disciples went further by making instant, complete obedience their speciality. They brought no ideas or special talents, controlled no constituencies. They offered themselves as reliable fillers of any role, any post, no questions asked.

Nicolás Maduro thrived this way. A tall man with a thick, dark mustache and black hair, he had no qualifications or education beyond high school but had an easygoing demeanor and instinct for advancement. He started his career driving a bus in Caracas and soon after obtained a doctor's certificate saying he had a disability, allowing him to pursue an alternative career in the union while keeping a company salary. Chávez was suspicious of union agitators – they tended to be headstrong – but Maduro, elected to the National Assembly, was pliant. Whatever hour Chávez phoned, whatever law he wanted amended or revoked, Maduro assented. He became head of the assembly in 2005 and then, despite not speaking any foreign languages, foreign minister in 2006, a post he held for six years. He crisscrossed the world following Chávez's orders and reading Chávez's script, never deviating, never ad-libbing, never proposing his own initiatives. Break ties with Bogotá, fix ties with Bogotá, assail Washington, schmooze Beijing, nurture Tehran, insult Madrid, whatever the order, he complied. When the comandante patronised

Maduro in public – 'Look at Nicolás there, handsome in his suit, not driving a bus anymore' – he just smiled. Foreign ambassadors said the foreign minister grew into his job but that he never took a big decision. Only Chávez was allowed to shine, so Maduro did not shine. And thus he prospered. He acquired an extensive wardrobe, put on weight, grew thick around the trunk. The disciples came from varied backgrounds but shared an instinct for adopting the attitudes and rhetoric of power. Those from privileged backgrounds changed their accents, dropping lisps and other posh giveaways for local colloquialism. They acquired red T-shirts and baseball caps for party events and attending the president's television show. When Chávez made an announcement, the disciples were the first to seek microphones to praise it. Shallow political and ideological roots let them sway and bend to the wind from Miraflores.

The utopians relied on tapping the comandante's imagination, on making blueprints of his dreams of revolution. Their leader was Jorge Giordani. An unusual-looking man, he was thin as a whip with large blue eyes, thick spectacles and a wide, pale face fringed by a straggly white beard and bald head. An anorexic Santa Claus, went the joke, but for his austerity he was nicknamed the Monk. He wore dark, shapeless suits and scuffed shoes and carried a battered briefcase that seemed to have been slept on by a cat. Giordani cared little for appearances in this world because he was busy perfecting the one in his head. He illustrated it at press briefings by drawing charts and diagrams so elaborate they resembled space shuttle designs. If someone suggested his designs weren't working in this world, he would redden, massage his fingers and suggest that perhaps the questioner had not understood the model. Giordani was one of the very few ministers who spoke English but did so only in private. His wife, who ran a school, was a close advisor. It was while studying electrical engineering in Italy in the 1960s that Giordani had had his epiphany: just like circuit boards, humanity could be rewired, its currents conducted to make a new society. He infused this idea with Marxism during postgraduate studies in urban planning at England's University of Sussex. He thrilled to theories about making order out of chaos. After Chávez's 1992 coup, Giordani, by now a professor at the Central University of Venezuela, tutored him in jail on how to turn the Bolivarian movement into a government. Armed with charts and maps and formulas, he spent a decade as planning minister. A professor can spend a lifetime polishing ideas without anyone caring. Chávez exhilarated such men – there were no women in this category – with the promise of putting theory into practice. In return they promised him a new world.

The fixers formed the third category. They were the most dynamic and grew tall by resolving, or appearing to resolve, problems. When the comandante encountered economic turbulence or dissent in his ranks, a squall that needed calming, he would turn to fixers, many of whom came from the military. The most ambitious was Diosdado Cabello. His name literally meant God-Given Hair. Born into humble means in Monagas state, a scorched terrain of plateaus and savanna in the east, he had cropped, military hair when he studied at the academy under Chávez, who by then was an instructor. Diosdado, as everyone called him, even enemies, joined the 1992 coup, served time in jail and started to lose his hair upon entering government. He skipped from post to post. A leader of the MVR party, the state telecommunications regulator, infrastructure minister, the president's chief of staff, vice president, governor of Miranda state. Diosdado's gift proved to be not his hair but an ability to influence multiple institutions and organisations, nurturing allies, placing lieutenants in key posts, co-opting successors, spinning a web of patronage that included factions of the military, half a dozen ministries and pro-government radical civilian militias. He was nicknamed the octopus: tentacles everywhere. The comandante allowed Diosdado and other fixers – all calculating, pragmatic bruisers – to amass wealth and patronage because he could deploy them, when needed, to assert presidential authority. A visit from a fixer was enough to make a rebellious governor, banker or party faction kneel and pledge loyalty to the comandante. Diosdado was said to have acquired so much wealth and so many secrets at the Infrastructure Ministry that when he was shuffled to another post in 2004, a legend grew that he had burned the headquarters to hide the evidence. It was in one of the city's twin fifty-six-storey Parque Central Towers, once South America's tallest skyscrapers and monuments to the 1970s oil boom. The inferno's cause was never fully established, and there was no real evidence that Diosdado had done it. But many considered the blackened ruin, which loomed over Caracas abandoned and unrepaired for years, as Diosdado's work. When he vacated the Miranda governorship four years later, for reasons unknown he took all the computers, files, security cameras, even the furniture and fittings.

A centimetre of Miraflores is worth more than an estate in the Great Savanna.' It was an expression coined long before Chávez, but the oil boom that gushed ever-increasing torrents of petrodollars from 2004 gave a giddy air to ministers and courtiers at the palace. It inflamed ambition and insecurity. It dangled the promise of influence, status and wealth with the dread of banishment. Attract the president's eye and elevation would be swift. Yesterday a nobody, today you beheld a fiefdom of influence and patronage.

Bodyguards in armoured SUVs picked you up from home. Civil servants flapped around your desk. Mayors and businessmen queued outside your office, clutching petitions. The palace requested your attendance at this and that. A heady existence. But the air was thin, the ledge slippery.

In public, ministers all sounded the same. 'The Bolivarian process is an organic process of deepening revolution through popular empowerment. We have a strategic plan, systematised and endogenous.' That was Lídice Altuve, the information vice-minister, but it could have been any of them, all speaking quasi-military corporate jargon. They would appear onstage, flanking the comandante, clapping and smiling in unison. They loathed and mistrusted each other. Alexander von Humboldt, a German naturalist who explored Venezuela in the early nineteenth century, noted how wildlife along the Orinoco would twitch and quiver. 'Carefully observing the relationship between the animals you see how they avoid and fear each other. The golden age has ended. In this paradise of American jungles, as everywhere else, a long, sad experience has taught all living beings that gentleness is rarely linked to might.'

Giordani, the ascetic, soft-spoken Monk, had shown his mettle in agreeing to tutor Chávez in jail in 1992. University colleagues had blanched at the invitation to give courses to coup plotters at their grim, mosquito-filled jail in Yare, but Giordani did not hesitate and forged a bond with the future president. He was rewarded with a ministerial post in 1999, but instead of applying his blueprints for a new society, he found himself just another voice at a long cabinet table filled with ambitious colleagues pitching their own, different ideas.

One by one, the Monk eliminated his rivals. He did not trust his inherited Planning Ministry officials, who predated Chávez, and installed a parallel team of academic protégés from the university. These former Ph.D. students had studied under him, shared his ideas and were utterly loyal. The flux of instructions from Chávez spawned instant committees, tight deadlines and shifting targets. Some ministers lost their bearings amid the churn, but Giordani, methodical and strategic, identified key posts in newly created departments and committees and filled them with acolytes, a skill acquired at university. They steered meetings certain ways, delayed or accelerated discussions according to necessity, promoted allies, blocked outsiders, brought information and drafting documents back to base at the Planning Ministry. He set up a special academy at Los Teques, on the outskirts of Caracas, to train his protégés for government. Thus Giordani was able to ambush colleagues at crucial moments. Gustavo Márquez, head of industry and commerce, slaved over a new law only to find it, in the space of minutes at what he thought was a routine meeting, rejected and replaced by a Giordani draft. Márquez then found his department abolished and himself packed off to run Venezuela's pavilion at an expo in Hannover.

Guaicaipuro Lameda proved a more formidable adversary. As national budget controller, he openly challenged the Monk's estimates and mocked him when he turned up at meetings with rolled-up blueprints under his arm. 'Is that your bazooka to kill us all, Jorge?' Once, when sharing a limousine in Moscow, Lameda teased his Marxist colleague by pointing out numerous neon signs for McDonald's, a sign of capitalism's triumph. 'Look at all those yellow Ms, Jorge. Do you think they stand for "Moscow"?' The Monk had his revenge. After being promoted to head the state oil company, Lameda found himself blindsided by an eleventh-hour Giordani draft of a new hydrocarbon law. Lameda noted a decade later, 'But you know what? The irony is things are even worse when Giordani is not there. Everything sags, disperses. While Giordani runs things, there is at least coherence and organisation.'

The Monk's key advantage, besides his team of acolytes, was access to Chávez. He sought contact with the comandante at every opportunity. While other ministers used the grand salons of Miraflores for meetings, Giordani lurked in the annex outside the president's office, waiting for a chance to murmur into the chief's ear. Those without access were vulnerable to rumour and smear. In a twinkle they could find their department abolished or folded into a rival's domain. When the comandante started skipping cabinet meetings in 2004, jostling for the ear intensified. Ministers could spend weeks or months vainly seeking an audience. Desperate to know what the comandante was thinking, ministers strained to pick up gossip, glean rumour, catch fragments. They would hiss to one another: Amigo, what have you heard? The privileged, such as the Monk, were invited to visit the comandante's office or to stroll with him around the adjacent patio of loquat trees, where a bronze jug cascaded water into a pond.

Twice Giordani fell. Chávez's mercurial personality and work rhythm drained him, and he could not abide the 3:00 a.m. calls. He defiantly turned off his palace-issued mobile phone before going to bed. Chávez became so angry he ordered Diosdado, then his chief of staff, to drag the Monk from his home and escort him through darkened, deserted streets for a tense predawn meeting at Miraflores. Chávez clashed with and fired all his ministers at one time or another but forgave and reinstated his favourites. The utopian professor appealed to the comandante's yearning to reengineer society. And he imbued the cabinet with a cerebral gravitas it otherwise lacked. Half the ministers had no college degree.

Nine finance ministers fell in succession until finally, in 2010, Giordani achieved his goal: the Planning and Finance ministries were merged under his leadership, making him the revolution's undisputed economic czar. To what extent he engineered colleagues' downfalls remained unclear. It was palace custom not to give reasons for axing. Chávez, or his private secretary, would phone the marked one to say thank you but your services are no longer required. Goodbye. The victim was left guessing. Did someone whisper to the comandante? Who? Richard Canan, a young, rising commerce minister, was fired after telling an internal party meeting the government was not building enough houses. Ramón Carrizales was fired as vice president after privately complaining about Cuban influence. Whatever the cause, once the axe fell, expulsion was immediate. The shock was disorienting. Ministers who used to bark commands and barge through doors seemed to physically shrink after being ousted. They would speak softly and shuffle into a room, meek and hesitant. They haunted former colleagues at their homes, seeking advice and solace, petitioning for a way back to the palace. 'Amigo, can you have a word with the chief?' One minister, one of Chávez's favourites, laughed when he recounted this pitiful lobbying. 'They know it as well as I do. In Miraflores there are no amigos.'

Chávez's gaze seemed to follow ministers every waking minute. From their mantelpieces and living room walls (it was wise to have portraits at home), from murals and billboards on their way to work, from the elevator (where posters said, '¡Adelante Comandante!', Forward, Comandante!), from their offices (multiple posters of Chávez in different poses), from their desks (he adorned little calendars), from the T-shirts of waiters who brought coffee ('¡Viva Chávez!'), from the covers of newspapers, magazines, and government reports. The instantly recognisable tenor voice exulted, scolded, accused, joked and reminisced from radio and television several times a day. This was why caricaturists in opposition newspapers focused on his eyes and mouth – exaggerating the squint, puffing the lips, protruding the tongue. But for ministers the most relevant parts of Chávez's physiognomy, the ones that kept them awake at night, made their hearts pound and halted them mid-sentence, as if struck dumb, were his ears. Physically, they were unremarkable. Not petite or oversized, not flappy or pointy: regular ears. What did the comandante hear?

That enemies could whisper intrigues against you was bad enough. But the principal source of paranoia was fear over what you said yourself. That somewhere at some time to someone you would say something you should not. It could be anything. A grumble about the government. A reference to a bank account. A joke about the president. And that could be enough. The scythe could swing. Aides, secretaries, drivers, all were potential informants for Cuba's G2 intelligence service and Venezuela's DISIP, later to become SEBIN (Bolivarian Intelligence Service). Home phones, office phones and above all mobile phones were assumed to be tapped, and choice conversations played to the comandante. This, many believed, accounted for the otherwise inexplicable fall of so many ministers. It was the reason high-ranking officials treated their phones as radioactive.

The eavesdropping was real. And, to an astonishing degree, open. Selected clips played five nights a week, Monday to Friday, on the *Razorblade* talk show. Mario Silva heaped abuse on government opponents. 'Hey, Otero [a newspaper owner], I know you're watching, so I'll say this slowly. You're. A. Son. Of. A. Bitch.' When he

Here, pardoned and freed after a 1992 coup attempt,
Hugo Chávez is a civilian, a celebrity, and soon
to be a presidential candidate.

Personal contact cements the bond between leader and followers. Security concerns and illness would curb such contact in later years.

The master communicator directs his own television shows, even selecting camera angles, and reviews footage after each broadcast.

Foes call him a clown, but Chávez uses props—in this case a parrot with a beret—to stay at the center of attention.

Chávez reveres Fidel Castro as revolution incarnate and casts himself as his heir.

Chávez appointed Guaicaipuro Lameda, a number-crunching general, as national budget controller, then as head of the state oil company.

Happy days at the palace around 2001, but Chávez's second wife, Marisabel Rodríguez, *center,* and Lameda would soon turn against him.

Lameda leads a march on the palace on April 11, 2002. Hours later, gunfire would kill at least nineteen people, and Chávez would fall—briefly—from power.

María Lourdes Afiuni, a judge who angered Chávez, poses for a smuggled smartphone photograph with daughter Geraldine in the judge's jail cell.

Chávez called Eva Golinger, his American courtier, Venezuela's sweetheart. Critics dubbed her the bride of the revolution.

General Raúl Baduel, Chávez's lifelong "brother" and his savior in the 2002 coup, was convicted of corruption and jailed after turning against the chief in 2007.

As bookworm cadets, Baduel devoured Asian mysticism; Chávez, Venezuela's legends. Both applied Sun Tzu's ancient text, *The Art of War*, to politics, Chávez with more success.

Richard Nuñez, leader of the Cementerio gang, keeps a pistol since he was ambushed and shot by a rival gang in 2010.

Richard Nuñez's gang buys bullets from police and rules its neighborhood like a fiefdom.

Police patrol a barrio in Caracas, one of the world's most murderous capitals, in 2010.

Accused kidnappers paraded before the media. Fear of abduction afflicts all classes. One impoverished mother sold her fridge to pay her daughter's ransom.

Jorge Giordani outfoxed cabinet rivals to become economic czar. His web of controls and special funds augmented Chávez's power but strangled the economy.

After a decade in power, Chávez uses a campaign caravan to fill the streets with noise and passion.

Oil Minister Rafael Ramírez, *left*, Foreign Minister and future vice president Nicolás Maduro, and Minister of the Presidency Erika Farías receive instruction from a convalescing Chávez.

leaned forward, gazing intently at the camera, a smile curling his mouth, you knew he was about to hurl 'scum', 'faggot', 'limp dick', 'fascist' or another of his favourite epithets. Offscreen, with friends, Silva could be warm and cerebral (he was well read and played chess), but on-screen he spat abuse.

The president often appeared on the show, or phoned in from the palace, for jokey banter. He urged everyone to tune in. 'Did you see *The Razorblade* last night?' he would ask supporters at a rally. 'Magnificent. And I understand Mario has something special lined up tonight. Don't miss it!' The something special was invariably intercepted phone calls. Silva was coy about the source, but everyone assumed it was state intelligence services. 'A banquet tonight, folks!' he would say, tapping his nose. 'Three clips. Three different recordings. Go grab your popcorn, the first will be rolling in a few minutes.'

The programme did not air the revolution's dirty linen – only the opposition's – but still chilled ministers and courtiers. They assumed the palace was listening to their phone conversations as well. And that informants made clandestine recordings. A tape of a Chavista mayor enjoying what appeared to be an orgy at his official residence in east Caracas became infamous, though never made it onto *The Razorblade*. It was widely believed the intelligence services targeted victims' wives on the assumption they gossiped more freely. A muckraking newspaper, *Las Verdades de Miguel* (Miguel's Truths), which sold out in El Silencio every Friday, fuelled the paranoia with character assassinations. 'Watch out, Comandante! A spy in the heart of government', read one typical headline, citing a minister's supposed intrigue. The paper also specialised in gnomic warnings. 'Worse than treason is loneliness. Once again the swords sharpen.' The impression grew that the palace had ubiquitous ears and that every morning the situation room supplied eye-opening transcripts and clips to the comandante.

The irony of advancement in El Silencio's ministries and state agencies was that success, landing a coveted position, brought misery. Meals at the palace offered a cruel juxtaposition. Oil paintings in the Parnassian style lined the walls with scenes of bacchanal and indulgence. Nymphs and deities gorged in sensual ecstasy on tropical fruits, juicy meats and foaming champagne. Veuve Clicquot so liked this spirit of gaiety it had paid for the works' restoration under a previous administration. But the tables where visiting ministers ate had no munificence, no joy. 'I have watched them eat. They are so rigid. They don't smile or show any sense of enjoyment; they can't loosen up,' said Helena Ibarra, a chef who accompanied the comandante's entourage on early foreign trips and later served ministers in her Caracas restaurant. It was not the fault of Miraflores's kitchen. At the comandante's behest it served traditional fare, corn bread arepas, beans, minced beef, hard, salty cheese, as if outside the palace stretched the plains of his youth. The ingredients were fresh, the dishes tasty, but ministers did not savour them. They were too nervous.

The tension originated in the comandante. On television he seemed to relish food, munching a tortilla in a market, crunching an apple on a farm – always little bites, so he could keep talking – and would reminisce about the fried plantains of Barinas, or the fried sweets his grandmother used to make. The cameras did not show that he had a personal taster, lest someone try to poison him, or that he ate to allay stress, binging at all hours. Shrill accusation he shrugged off, but mockery, betrayal and fear of assassination stoked a ravenous appetite. The comandante especially adored *hallacas,* a type of tamale, and the caramelised sugar of *dulce de leche.* In office his weight ballooned. It did not help ministers' nerves that alcohol and tobacco were banned in the palace and on the presidential jet. Chávez had forsworn such vices and expected officials to do the same in his presence, though everyone knew he sneaked the odd smoke.

How nice it would have been for ministers released from palace duty to climb into the ministerial SUV and tell the driver: Casa Urrutia in Las Mercedes! To sit at the best table, sip an aperitif, choose between the bisque and the seafood platter and lean back, an illustrious personage of respect and power. A minister who dared enter a plush restaurant in Las Mercedes, Altamira, La Castellana, or any other part of well-heeled eastern Caracas, the opposition's heartland, was greeted with the clink-clink-clink of diners tapping glasses with spoons in protest. Insults compounded the humiliation. Thief! Liar! Son of a whore! Some ministers would slip into Ibarra's Palms restaurant because it had a refuge, a secluded upper section, but most gave up dining out. It was the same at malls, cinemas and supermarkets in wealthy neighborhoods: scorn, abuse, hisses. When not at their desks or public events, ministers retreated to their homes. They would shut the gates, bolt the locks and close the curtains, sealing off, as best they could, the contempt outside. Even then there was no respite. The comandante might appear on television at any moment and drop a bombshell. Sleep would be invaded by the palace-issued mobile phone.

When things got to be too much, some courtiers sought counsel from a small, wiry fortune-teller known as Rey David. King David. His full name was David Goncalves, and he had learned his trade, he said, from a Portuguese gypsy. He had his own radio show and became famous during the Ávila mudslide disaster by giving thousands of free consultations to people seeking missing relatives. By the time Chávez won the 2006 election, senior government officials were among those summoning 'El Rey' for private home visits. Many Venezuelans are superstitious and blend Catholicism with a semi-clandestine jumble of astrology, mysticism and Santeria, a type of voodoo imported by slaves from western Africa. Rich and poor alike believe it. Judges, bankers and politicians privately attribute misfortunes – illness, car accidents, career setbacks – to malign spells. They wear amulets and pay Santeria priests to reverse the spells and, in some cases, curse their enemies. Others ask the likes of Rey David to read tarot cards. So many anxious officials unloaded their troubles onto him he acquired inside knowledge of El Silencio's power struggles to the point he really could, in some ways, predict the future.

Goncalves just as often got things wrong. His main value was in conveying his clients' mood. 'Those who have a lot of power have a lot of enemies. There is a lot of anxiety and fear. They don't trust their own bodyguards. They all want to know how to keep their money and power. That's their struggle. They feel persecuted and worry about blackmail. A lot of it comes down to this,' he said, rubbing his fingers under the table. Prominent clients did not want to be seen visiting Goncalves, lest it suggest intrigue, so they invited him for discreet home visits. One client was so wound up that the consultation lasted ten hours, he said.

A minister needed to master three skills. The first was the balance between stillness and motion. Most of the time a minister was stone. He or she was not supposed to suggest an initiative, solve a problem, announce good news, theorise about the revolution or express an original opinion. These were tasks for the comandante. His fickleness encouraged ministers to defer implementation until they were certain of his wishes. In any case they spent so much time on stages applauding – it was unwise to skip protocol events – there was little opportunity for initiative. Thus the oil minister Rafael Ramírez would lurk, barely visible, while the comandante signed a lucrative deal with Chevron. Or the information minister Andrés Izarra would stand, mute, while the comandante gave a press conference.

But upon command the stone would transform into a whirling dervish. We are nationalising the steel company, draft a declaration! We are flying to Tehran, pack your bags! Form a new police force, quick! The comandante's impulsiveness demanded instant, urgent responses. He would become consumed by a theme. Rice! Increase rice production! The order would ricochet through El Silencio. The agriculture, planning, transport, commerce, finance and infrastructure ministers would work around the clock devising a scheme of credits, loans, cooperatives, mills and trucks to have it ready, at least on paper, for the comandante to unveil on his Sunday show. Thus was born the Mixed Company for Socialist Rice. Then, the next week, chicken! Cheaper chicken! The same ministers would forget about rice while they rushed to squeeze farmers, truckers and supermarkets so the comandante could say, on his next show, that chicken was cheaper.

The second skill was flattery. Those who mastered the game were handsomely rewarded. Tarek Saab, a human rights lawyer and poet, wrote an ode about the comandante's rebel great-grandfather, Maisanta, which he dedicated to the comandante and his mother. He was named poet of the revolution and catapulted into the governorship of Anzoátegui state. Jacqueline Farías, a hydro-engineer, proclaimed the comandante a gift of history. 'It is a privilege to have Hugo Chávez as the leader of this process. He has an ability to communicate and touch your heart and soul. We haven't had this since Simón Bolívar.' Asked if he had any defects, she pondered a moment. 'He never rests.' She became a cabinet star, then administrator of the capital district. Others seized their moment when Chávez, viewing an art fair, assessed an elderly woman's landscape, picked up a brush and added a tree 'for balance'. His entourage laughed and clapped.

Addressing Chávez contained its own code. Simplest was 'Presidente', a term from the early days, when holding the office seemed marvel enough. 'Comandante', a rank equivalent to lieutenant colonel that emphasised submission, gradually rivalled 'Presidente' for frequency. Someone – many claimed authorship – fused the terms to make 'Comandante Presidente', linking military and constitutional authority. To emphasise a personal bond, some inserted a possessive adjective so he became 'Mi Comandante Presidente'. The risk, moving up the scale, was that too-obvious sycophancy would sabotage rhetoric about equality. Ministers who bowed and perspired while they said 'Mi Comandante Presidente' crossed that line. Those who said it with a relaxed smile were fine. It was a question of tone. Using the comandante's full name, Hugo Rafael Chávez Frías, earned extra points. Clothing was another medium to express obedience. The comandante liked red, so ministers wore red baseball caps, red T-shirts, red guayaberas, red skirts. State garment factories produced mountains of the stuff. Then one day the comandante appeared on the palace balcony sporting a yellow shirt and said, without elaboration, there was too much red. Consternation around the palace. What to do? Some ministers hesitantly abandoned the colour, worrying it was a trick. Others flashed just a bit of red, trying to gauge the correct level. When, a few weeks later, the comandante resumed wearing red, again without elaboration, the crisis passed, and ministers reverted to red.

The third ability was to mould their faces into masks: to arrange features into appropriate expressions when on camera or in the comandante's sight line. This was tricky when the comandante did something foolish or bizarre because the required response could contradict instinct. Thus a grimace would have to become a smile, or vice versa. Missing a cue could prove fatal. During a show the comandante's laser-beam gaze swung from face to face, spotlighting expressions, seeking telltale tics. Immediately after a broadcast, Chávez reviewed the footage, casting a professional eye over the staging, lighting, camera angles – and audience reaction. The advent of You-Tube in 2005 intensified the scrutiny because a misjudged grin or scowl could be picked up by foes and splashed over the Internet.

The comandante's occasional lapses into ridiculousness were inevitable. He spoke up to nine hours at a time live on television, without a script, and punctuated the marathons with unexpected gestures and topics. This way he kept the political initiative and dominated media coverage. Being capricious and clownish also sustained interest in the show and underlined his authority. No other government figure, after all, dared show humour in public. But on occasion this dissolved into absurdity. Who tells a king he is being a fool?

In November 2005, Chávez announced a change to the national coat of arms so the white horse would gallop to the left – in keeping with his politics – rather than to the right. 'It's a reactionary symbol,' he told his audience, gathered by the banks of the Orinoco in Puerto Ordaz, a steamy city on the edge of the Great Savanna. The horse was not Venezuelan but 'imperial' because its rightward gallop and backward gaze were designed during the 1908–35 dictatorship of Juan Vicente Gómez, who had 'sold out to U.S. imperialism'. The camera panned over the seated officials who swiftly applauded. The idea, the comandante added, came from his eight-year-old daughter, who had asked why the horse galloped one way and looked the other. 'Rosinés said, "Daddy, why does that horse look backward?" ' Chávez beamed in pride. If the audience felt Venezuela had just officially become a banana republic, it did not show it. The applause swelled. Weeks later the compliant National Assembly approved a bill changing the coat of arms.

Ministers faced another test of the mask in September 2007 when the comandante announced clocks would go back half an hour. The aim was to let children and workers wake up in daylight, he said. 'I don't care if they call me crazy, the new time will go ahead, let them call me whatever they want. I'm not to blame. I received a recommendation and said I liked the idea.' Chávez wanted it implemented within a week – causing needless chaos – and bungled the explanation, saying clocks should go forward rather than back. If ministers realised the mistake, they said nothing, only smiled and clapped. On another occasion, when Chávez misspelled a verb on a blackboard while preaching literacy to children, the education minister, Aristóbolo Istúriz, squirmed and coughed, looking tormented, before finally murmuring a correction. Chávez took it well and rewrote the word. Another time ministers sat with rictus smiles while the president jovially revealed a battle with his sphincter during a previous televised event. 'Nobody knew it, but I had colic . . . Yes, I had diarrhea! I'm a human being just like the rest of you; at times people forget that. My God, *ooof*! I was sweating so bad.' The camera panned over faces apparently delighted with the anecdote.

On rare occasions the correct response was not obvious, sowing panic. In a speech to mark World Water Day in 2011, the comandante said capitalism may have killed life on Mars. 'I have always said, heard, that it would not be strange that there had been civilisation on Mars, but maybe capitalism arrived there, imperialism arrived and finished off the planet.' Some in the audience tittered, assuming it was a joke, then froze when they saw neighbors turned to stone. To these audience veterans it was unclear if it was a joke, so they adopted poker faces, pending clarification. It never came; the comandante moved on to other topics.

Nuris Orihuela, the former head of the comandante's space program, had been a serious, competent minister. A university physics professor with left-wing credentials, she had entered government soon after Chávez came to power and served as head of the state seismology institute. Promoted to vice-minister of science and technology, she had presided over the successful launch of a Chinese-made telecommunications satellite called Simón Bolívar. In person, Orihuela was the antithesis of a Venezuelan woman: boyish, short hair, no makeup, jeans, brogues. A confident woman, not afraid to be different, who exuded professionalism. In her passion for technology and social progress, she was clearly, in the best sense, utopian. Even academics outside the government who loathed Chávez respected Orihuela. She left government in 2009 – she had an unexplained dispute with Chávez over Iran – and two years later occupied a small, windowless university office at the end of a dingy corridor. She was qualified to interpret the president's Mars comment, one of his most bizarre, and had nothing to lose in doing so. She seemed beyond the cloying sycophancy of El Silencio.

'You must understand that the president is very, very intelligent,' she said. 'He understands the transcendence of technology and space. He absorbs information very quickly.' She paused, selecting her words carefully. 'But it needs to be given to him in a responsible way. A considered way. The problem is some people give him information that is incomplete and not in context. That is unfortunate because a huge intelligence such as his may make rapid connections that are not' – she paused again, weighing the words – 'that are not necessarily correct.' Shortly before the president made his comments, there had been a report about water on Mars, she said. 'So you see, conclusions were made . . . The president is a good man, he speaks from the heart and looks you in the eye. He tells the truth. So really, there is no reason to worry.'

6

THE ART OF WAR

On 2 December 2007, something unexpected happened. Chávez lost the referendum. By a slim margin voters rejected the proposed sixty-nine articles amending the constitution. The invincible soldier who had won vote after vote year after year was defeated. The country was stunned. A victory party in front of the palace was cancelled, and tearful supporters went home. As workers dismantled the stage, a giant Chávez doll was deflated with a long, sharp hiss and left facedown on the concrete. Just a year earlier Chávez had been reelected in a landslide, but instead of accelerating, the revolution was now braking. Partly it was that the opposition, infuriated by the RCTV closure and mobilised by students, turned out its core vote. But mainly it was that half his own supporters – the so-called soft Chavistas – abstained. The economy was booming, but they were annoyed that government policies were distorting the supply chain, causing shortages of milk, coffee, sugar and toilet paper. The other reason was that Chávez's mayors and governors campaigned half-heartedly. The referendum would not abolish their own term limits, so they had nothing to gain from a yes vote. The comandante accepted defeat – disproving suspicions he would cancel the result – but bared his fury. At a press conference he said the opposition had won a 'victoria de mierda', a shitty victory. Previously, he had avoided swearing in public but now wallowed in it, repeated it, drawing out the word. 'Mieeeerdah.' He lambasted supporters who had abstained. 'You have no excuse, you have no consciousness, you have no resolve for the fatherland.'

He blamed his defeat above all on a single man, a Judas whom he had once called brother. He would have his revenge.

When Raúl Baduel was a teenager growing up in Maracay, a garrison town sixty miles west of Caracas, he would spend entire afternoons clutching the airfield fence and gazing up, mesmerised, at paratroopers. The idea of standing at the door of a McDonnell Douglas and launching into the void thrilled and terrified him. 'I knew then that was what I wanted to be more than anything in the world. A paratrooper,' he recalled decades later. After finishing high school, he enlisted in the academy in 1972 and there befriended Chávez. On the surface there was little reason for the two cadets to become close. Chávez was a year ahead, which made him senior, and a typical *llanero* extrovert full of jokes, proverbs and chat. Baduel was taciturn and serious with a soft, husky voice. They both liked books, but whereas Chávez devoured Venezuelan history, Baduel was drawn to Eastern philosophy and mysticism. Yet they became, in their own words, brothers. They both adored the army, and Chávez, in his freewheeling way, treated the younger cadet as an equal.

He even called him by his chosen nickname, Papa – taken from a character in a U.S. television series about U.S. fighter pilots in World War II – which implied deference.

As the two men moved up the ranks, differences in their personalities became marked. Baduel, formal and polite, blended Catholicism with Buddhism and acquired a lifelong love of incense and Gregorian chant. He preached the samurai code. He also married Cruz María, with whom he would go on to have twelve children. Chávez blended Catholicism with his own syncretism – he told comrades he was the reincarnation of Ezequiel Zamora, the nineteenth-century *llanero* general – and became more gregarious and theatrical. He had three children with his wife, Nancy, who lived in Barinas, and started a decade-long affair with a historian, Herma Marksman, in Caracas. Both men, however, shared increasing disgust with Venezuela's oil-boom bloating and institutional decay.

On 17 December 1982, the anniversary of Bolívar's death in 1830, Chávez was the chosen orator for a barracks ceremony. He told the assembled soldiers to picture the Liberator in the sky, watchful, frowning, because what he had left undone remained undone. Afterward, Chávez, Baduel and two other captains, Jesús Urdaneta and Felipe Acosta Carles, jogged six miles to the Samán de Güere, an acacia tree under whose shade Bolívar used to rest. It was a humid, sticky day, and the friends arrived drenched in sweat, Chávez last. There they plucked leaves, a military ritual, and Chávez improvised another speech, this time paraphrasing Bolívar's famous 1805 oath: 'I swear to the God of my fathers, I swear on my homeland, I swear on my honour, that I will not let my soul feel repose, nor my arm rest until my eyes have seen broken the chains that oppress us and our people by the order of the powerful.' The others echoed his words, and a conspiracy was born. A decade later, when Chávez led the failed 1992 coup, Baduel remained undetected as a conspirator and stayed in the army. His involvement became public knowledge only when Chávez, on the eve of his inauguration, revealed him as the 'fourth man' to García Márquez on the flight from Havana. Baduel was seated just behind the writer and the president-elect. 'Márquez wanted to interview me there and then,' Baduel recalled later. 'But Chávez told him that wasn't the time. Márquez never did get to interview me.'

Baduel served as Chávez's private secretary in the palace in 1999, then returned to Maracay as a general to fulfil his boyhood dream: command the city's paratroop brigade. It was from there he unravelled Pedro Carmona's usurpation in April 2002 by rallying not just his brigade but the entire Fourth Division against the coup. It was Baduel's commandos who rescued Chávez from his island prison and returned him in triumph to the palace. Baduel became the revolution's hero, his bond with the comandante the stuff of legend. Chávez, confronted by new threats in the form of the 2002–3 national strike and the 2004 recall referendum, needed loyalists in key posts, so he brought the general back to Caracas. He promoted Baduel to head of the army, then defence minister. The president continued to call him Papa and became godfather to his youngest daughter. With his incense and chants, Baduel was an unusual but respected, powerful figure in government.

And then something stirred. It began with small things. Guaicaipuro Lameda remembered phoning Baduel in January 2003 to complain about Luis Acosta Carles's televised belch. 'He was just as indignant as I was. He said it was an affront to military dignity.' Yet a few days later Lameda watched Baduel applaud the belcher on the president's television show. 'Chávez told everyone to clap, and Baduel went along with it.' In January 2005 the president declared himself, for the first time, a socialist and married the Bolivarian revolution to what he termed 'twenty-first-century socialism'. Everyone in government parroted that they too were socialists. Baduel talked about Scandinavia-style socialism.

Chávez herded his political coalition into a single socialist party, the PSUV, but also wanted the armed forces, the state's most venerable and respected institution, to embrace socialism. This was consistent with his long-held belief that the military was the sacred heir of Bolívar's liberation armies. The constitution banned the military from political activity, but for Chávez it could not simply stand to attention, neutral, as Venezuela advanced toward a new destiny. It needed to lead. To mould society just as it had moulded him. More pragmatically, he wanted military men in government because they understood discipline, obedience and the chain of command in a way state bureaucracies and civilian leftists did not. Thus he fast-tracked selected officers up the ranks and brought others into government. About a third of senior officials had epaulets. Baduel's mission, as defence minister, was to steer the armed forces down their new ideological path.

The first public hint of a breach came on a hot, humid night on the eve of the president's December 2006 reelection. He was addressing a rally in front of the palace and summoned Baduel, wearing green fatigues and black beret, to join him onstage. Here, said the comandante, wrapping an arm around him, was an embodiment of revolutionary passion and faith. He thumped the stage. 'Long live General Baduel! Long live the Bolivarian armed forces! Long live the revolutionary people. Here we are, lifelong brothers!' The crowd roared. Chávez hugged Baduel closer and shouted: 'Let us proclaim the eternal motto: Fatherland, socialism or death! We will prevail!' It was a recent import from Cuba, where Fidel's soldiers and young communist pioneers had long cried, 'Fatherland or death. We will prevail.' To emphasise Venezuela's ideological turn, Chávez inserted the extra word. Baduel froze. He did not smile or wave or punch the air; instead, stood motionless, arms dangling, expression hollow. He bit his lower lip and gave a brief, awkward salute when the comandante swallowed him in a hug, then scurried offstage. Chávez waved to the crowd as if all were well. But his minister had just failed a test.

Years later Baduel would explain the moment in terms of principle. He wanted to keep the armed forces out of politics out of respect for the constitution. He was alarmed by the comandante's version of socialism, which sounded more Cuba than Scandinavia. And he loathed the comandante's idea of creating armed civilian militias. 'I didn't want to go to the rally,' recalled Baduel. 'The constitution banned us from such events, but it was a direct order. I tried to hide in a corner, but the president brought me onto the stage. He wanted me to shout the motto, but I kept my mouth shut and just saluted.'

Relations between the two men began to cool. Palace tongues noted Papa no longer had ready access to the ear, in fact was no longer Papa, only Baduel.

The next test came in February 2007 when Chávez ordered a military parade to commemorate his 1992 uprising. Baduel protested, in vain, that it was inappropriate to honour a coup. 'The day before the parade he requested the protocol arrangements. I knew he was planning something, and during the ceremony it happened.' An officer on the parade ground shouted the new motto – the first time it was used at an official army event. It ricocheted around the country, a warning the armed forces were becoming openly political. Baduel was furious and told the media he had not approved it. Chávez shrugged, saying the shout reflected a spontaneous revolutionary spirit within the ranks.

Baduel felt trapped. How much easier it was to leap out of a plane. In free fall he could turn and roll, but as defence minister he felt tangled and trapped. He was still in government, still with influence over the armed forces, but mistrusted by Chávez.

The comandante had noted political ambition in his old friend. Baduel acquired economic advisors and began expressing opinions on oil policy. Privately, he criticised the government's nationalisations, saying they would lead to ruin. Guessing his intentions became a new political parlour game around El Silencio. Supporters in the armed forces and media whispered he should be the next president, that his calmness and moderation would soothe and unite the nation. Chávez, however, could not fire him without exposing division in his ranks, something to avoid in the middle of the 2007 referendum campaign.

Baduel increasingly sensed a heaviness when he entered the palace. He had no doubt his phones were being tapped and suspected he was under physical surveillance. He sensed a sword being sharpened. When it swung, it broke the last rule left in Venezuelan politics: private lives remained private. Around the palace and El Silencio everyone gossiped about who was sleeping with whom. There were bountiful rumours of adultery among ministers, opposition leaders and their spouses. It was taboo, however, to publicly use the ammunition. Until Baduel.

One morning an anonymous source sent a series of excruciating photographs to newspapers. Then, in case anyone missed them, they were hacked onto the National Assembly Web site. First, here was the general, naked, brushing his teeth over a blue-tiled bathroom sink. Unshaven, with a hairy chest, he looked at the camera, his groin partly obscured. Next, sprawled on a bed with a pink blanket, apparently asleep, wearing only a white T-shirt, his penis seemingly semi-erect.

Then the coup de grâce: naked on a different bed, obviously awake, apparently masturbating with a doll. Beside him a yellow pillow in the form of a Japanese cartoon character called Pikachu. It was as if Baduel's dignity had been taken out and shot. A former mistress – a female officer – had taken the photographs some years earlier as a joke. But who disseminated them now? Baduel felt sure it was intelligence services trying to sabotage his credibility. He was branded the Bolivarian Pikachu. His wife stood by him, and he continued as defence minister, but the humiliation burned.

In July 2007 his term as minister expired, and he let the veil slip. At an elaborate handover ceremony at Fuerte Tiuna, he said the country needed not Marxism but democratic checks and balances. He warned of dark clouds ahead and said he would retire to his farm, like the Roman consul Lucius Quinctius Cincinnatus, who renounced power after saving the republic, and reflect on a return to public life. The comandante, looking shaken, thanked the general for his services. But after the ceremony, away from microphones, he hugged his old comrade for the last time. Baduel later recalled: 'He pushed his face very close to mine and whispered: "Now you will have plenty of time to enjoy your *latifundios*."' In ancient Rome latifundia were landed estates worked by slaves. In Venezuela it was a pejorative term for farms and businesses ripe for expropriation. It was a threat.

Baduel was not intimidated. He revered Sun Tzu's ancient text, *The Art of War,* and would cite its axiom: 'Let your plans be dark and impenetrable as night, and when you move, fall like a thunderbolt.' On the eve of the December 2007 referendum, with polls giving the comandante a narrow lead, Baduel held a press conference. Vote no, he told the nation, or tyranny will reign. It had a dramatic, immediate impact. Here was the president's saviour, his brother, tolling a bell of warning. Moderate Chavistas who had misgivings about the referendum felt emboldened to abstain or even vote no. The opposition, which had not really believed it could win, felt an eleventh-hour surge of energy. It tilted the vote against the coman-dante. Baduel now had the satisfaction of watching a giant inflatable Chávez hiss and deflate in front of the palace. In the war of the dolls the score was even.

Throughout 2008, Baduel gave more press conferences, sur-rounded himself with political advisors, and published a book, *My Solution: Venezuela's Crisis and Salvation*. But he miscalculated. The opposition did not invite him into its ranks, leaving him isolated. More gravely, he underestimated his old friend. Chávez rallied his followers against Baduel and denounced him as a traitor, a stooge of the extreme right. He directed chants for the general to be taken to the 'paredón', the execution wall. In November 2008 military prose-cutors charged Baduel with stealing $14 million from the defence budget. A few months later he was arrested. State agents forced him into a car, put a gun to his temple, and said: 'You don't talk.' The paratrooper had jumped without a parachute. He was sentenced to eight years for corruption and jailed in Ramo Verde, a military prison on a hilltop outside Caracas with three layers of guards.

A Sunday morning in March 2011. Cruz María Baduel, an attrac-tive woman with blond hair and a confident manner, made her weekly visit to the prison. Baduel stood up to greet her. A burly fig-ure, ramrod posture. The hair had greyed in the two years he had been here. He wore a short-sleeved shirt tucked into ironed jeans, a Tommy Hilfiger belt and polished black shoes. The cell was dark and windowless but big, with its own kitchen and bathroom – a sign of the prisoner's status – and adorned with posters of Gandhi, Martin

Luther King, Nelson Mandela and religious icons. Gregorian chant seeped from the stereo. Books on politics, religion and philosophy lined the shelves. A pile by his bedside was topped by a tome on military history: *The Audacity of Icarus: Venezuela's Paratrooper Pioneers, 1949–1979.* Newspapers were stacked in the corner. They had stopped mentioning Baduel some time ago.

Sunday was visitors' day, and other members of his family – his father and several children – arrived, as well as an evangelical pastor. They gathered around a table to hear an ululating, melodramatic peroration about salvation and sin. 'May Jesus hear his children's prayers! May Jesus show his divine mercy! May Jesus smite the chains of injustice!' The sermon's length seemed to test the family's patience, though nobody said anything. When the pastor finally finished, his face wreathed in perspiration, tears in his eyes, he was profusely thanked, embraced and shown the door. This being Sunday, the comandante was at this moment hosting his show, episode 373, but the Baduels kept the television off. Their four-year-old daughter also asked for the Gregorian chant to be turned off. 'She can't stand it,' Baduel said, shrugging. She sat on his lap and nuzzled his neck. 'People say I asked Chávez to be her godfather,' he said, nuzzling back. 'But he asked me.'

They drank sweet black coffee from little plastic cups while the family prepared a lunch of arepas, Orinoco whitefish, shrimps and salad. Baduel told an anecdote about his time as head of the army. 'One day Chávez summoned me to La Casona [the presidency's private residence]. He was upset because in Moscow the previous week the Russians showed him a case with $20 million, which they said General Carneiro [the then defence minister] had tried to skim from an arms deal. The president was furious and used a vulgarity . . . It starts with *a,* but I'd rather not repeat it. Anyway, we were walking around the pool discussing who should replace Carneiro when the former Argentine president, Duhalde, comes up. Chávez had forgotten he had invited him to lunch. He decided to play a trick. He gripped my arm and said loudly, "Yes, your divisions attack Colombia from the west, and the rest will swing around in a pincer movement." You should have seen Duhalde's jaw drop. Chávez burst out laughing. It was his way of breaking the ice. He told me we should finish our conversation later that night with Diosdado over a game of *bolas criollas*. That's how he was: angry one moment, joking the next.'

Power changed Chávez, continued Baduel. 'When I was his private secretary in 1999, he attended cabinet meetings, but by the time I was a minister in 2005, he had lost interest. For him it was small potatoes. He preferred to be elsewhere saving humanity. Our purpose as ministers was to rubber-stamp things he had already decided . . . unilateral decisions based on things he had been reading the night before. To me that was capricious, an insult to the Venezuelan people.'

The politicisation of the armed forces, he said, was the breaking point. 'It became obvious the only thing Chávez cared about was being president for life. The mask kept slipping. I was told that Fidel warned him about me, said I wasn't to be trusted.' Baduel considered himself a martyr who stood up to a tyrant. Why did he serve him faithfully for so long? Baduel shifted in his seat. 'I never called him comandante, you know. I referred to him as president, nothing more.' His opposition, he said, began earlier than people realised, in subtle ways. 'I didn't smile during those ceremonies when they shouted out, "Fatherland, socialism or death." You could see I did not approve.' Resistance through scowling: not exactly the samurai code. Still, Baduel had paid a heavy price in the end.

He called the corruption charge a judicial farce. With the courts under palace control, his conviction was clearly political – even Chávez's allies admitted that in private. That did not mean Baduel was necessarily innocent. There was no way of knowing.

'I am tranquil. They can jail my body but not my mind. That remains free. We have become a dictatorship with a facade of democracy. I know I will leave this prison only when Chávez leaves the presidency of Venezuela.' The general walked me to the end of a passageway with grilled windows; the only spot where he could observe his beloved sky.

Locking up Baduel was one thing, containing the consequences of his revolt another. Losing the December 2007 referendum left Chávez suddenly vulnerable. As 2008 began, two shoals threatened Chávez. With finely honed survival instincts, he rolled and rebuffed each one.

The first was the military. As a fighting force, Venezuela's armed forces were feeble, but they were potentially lethal to their commander in chief. In theory, the military was Chávez's bulwark. The army, navy, air force and national guard, encompassing 113,000 men and women, all swore an oath of allegiance, and after Baduel he entrusted only his most loyal lieutenants to the Defence Ministry. But he still could not completely trust the institution. For half a century its top brass had considered itself the United States' Latino cousin. Officers played baseball, drove Chevys, drank scotch and trained at the U.S. Army's School of the Americas. Chávez purged many generals after the 2002 coup but still worried about revolt over the military's radical new path.

Many officers were affronted by the incorporation of an estimated five thousand Cuban military and ideological specialists in government offices and military bases. Others were appalled by the tacit cooperation with leftist guerrillas waging a cocaine-funded, decades-long insurgency against the Colombian state. Officially, Chávez was neutral but in reality adopted a fickle policy toward the guerrillas. He turned a blind eye to their incursions along the thirteen-hundred-mile porous border and appointed his interior minister, Ramón Rodríguez Chacín, to act as liaison. There was evidence he funnelled weapons and money. Then, during diplomatic thaws with Colombia's government, he would have guerrillas arrested and deported. 'He has an enormous muddle in his head that nobody understands,' one exasperated FARC operative wrote in an intercepted e-mail. Chávez was a 'deceitful and divisive president who lacked the resolve to organise himself politically and militarily,' complained another commander.

Many Venezuelan officers were just as angry because of the rupture in traditional military policy. Two centuries of Venezuelan history had been written through military coups, and Baduel's rebellion could have triggered another. But it didn't. First, Chávez deliberately jumbled the hierarchy, shuffling and leapfrogging promotions so that officers tangled with each other and new rules in efforts to climb the career ladder. (Efficiency suffered. When the comandante abruptly ordered ten battalions to Colombia's border, tanks got lost, helicopters failed to show up and troops went AWOL. It was the Keystone Kops. But since the mobilisation was political theatre – a periodic, fleeting 'crisis' – the farce did not matter.)

Second, he forged personal bonds at every opportunity, asking privates and generals about their schooling, memorising their parents' names, inviting them to play softball. He played the role of teacher, father, commander.

The comandante had an additional means of keeping the

military in line: civilian militias. Specifically, Lina Ron. She was the raspy-voiced, platinum blonde leader of a militia that roared around Caracas on motorbikes. Her motto was 'With Chávez, everything; without Chávez, bullets'. A medical-school dropout and left-wing radical, Ron wore red lipstick, but the prematurely lined face bespoke a life of struggle. She accused Venezuela's elite of looting oil wealth and siding with U.S. imperialism. Ron became a celebrity by burning the U.S. flag after the September 11 attacks, saying the Yankees had received a taste of their own medicine. She based her small political party and militia in a three-storey house a few blocks north of Miraflores. Hair streaming from helmet, she led her squadron on missions around the city, storming the archbishop's office, a television station, an opposition party meeting, any institution that opposed the revolution. The members of her squadron made for loud, colourful additions at Chavista parades, revving their bikes in slow procession, an unofficial praetorian guard for the president, following behind on a truck. Ron also championed poor families who petitioned her for help securing state jobs and welfare. Woe betide any official who said no to Ron. Change, she said, came from the street. About half a dozen such militias carved fiefdoms around the city, marking territory with murals, slogans and sentries. The comandante encouraged them and said, were he to be toppled, 'five hundred Lina Rons would appear' and the country would face 'chaos, violence and death'. After her antics generated negative international headlines, he distanced himself, and she died of a heart attack, aged fifty-one, in March 2011. In death he rehabilitated her. 'She was a complete revolutionary. Let's follow her example!' By then he had formed the Bolivarian Militia, a supposedly 120,000-strong volunteer force of students, civil servants, housewives and pensioners that answered directly to the palace. They marched in ragged formation through Caracas, shouldering rifles and shouting fealty to the comandante. 'If I fall, unleash a whirlwind,' he told them. 'You know what you would have to do: Simply take all power in Venezuela, absolutely all! Sweep away the bourgeoisie from all political and economic spaces. Deepen the revolution!'

Upon losing the referendum a second threat loomed. This was the opposition. Dormant since the 2004 referendum, it suddenly sensed blood in the November 2008 local and regional elections. It swarmed around the comandante, jaws snapping. The sharpest teeth belonged to Leopoldo López. He was mayor of Chacao, the richest district of Caracas. He was young, charismatic, ambitious and movie star handsome. He was also, as it happened, the great-great-grand nephew of Simón Bolívar. His plan was to become mayor of greater Caracas – polls made him the favourite – and use that as a platform for the 2012 presidential election. Warning lights flashed in the Miraflores situation room. Leopoldo, as everyone called him, was dangerous.

The comandante batted him out of the water. The comptroller general, a compliant ally, declared the mayor 'inhabilitado' – disqualified from seeking public office – over accusations of misusing state funds. The fact he was not formally charged made the case virtually impossible to fight. Around three hundred other politicians were also disqualified, but the main target was Leopoldo.

The comandante calculated that the disqualifications would split the opposition into its habitual bickering factions. Instead, disciplined by desperation, it rallied around unified candidates and won key states and cities, tearing strips of power from Chávez. Its stand-in for Leopoldo, a balding, bespectacled old-timer called Antonio

Ledezma, even won greater Caracas. 'Today is a sublime day of hope,' he told cheering supporters. 'But there is no time to celebrate. Let us work!' Ledezma was right not to celebrate. The comandante quickly swatted the mayor into irrelevance. Lina Ron's followers occupied city hall, a handsome colonial-style building on Plaza Bolívar, banishing Ledezma to a cramped, nondescript office several blocks away. They daubed the city hall facade with graffiti, installed themselves in its offices and loafed around the entrance, unmolested by the police and national guard. Chávez formalised the usurpation with a law creating a 'capital district', a new administrative designation that let a loyalist run Caracas and occupy city hall. Ledezma, stripped of powers and budget, remained mayor in name only. Chávez used a separate law to emasculate other mayors and state governors. A few were threatened with jail. Soon after being elected mayor of Maracaibo, Manuel Rosales, Chávez's challenger in the 2006 election, was charged with corruption. He fled to Peru in April 2009.

Chávez controlled the armed forces and neutralised opponents but remained vulnerable. Because he was barred from running again, a forbidden question was whispered in the palace. Who would succeed the chief after his term ended in 2012? Ministers and courtiers watched each other like cardinals around an ailing pope, gauging power's ebb against the tick of the clock. Untended, it would become a weed whose pathogen contaminated the comandante's authority. In 2008 a murmur spread through El Silencio: Chavismo without Chávez. The only solution was to abolish term limits. The comandante chose his moment. Having subverted the results of the local and regional elections, he promptly announced a new constitutional referendum to abolish term limits. Allies on the National

Electoral Council rubber-stamped an early date, February 2009, before the opposition could catch its breath. Chávez plundered the best managers from PDVSA and other state companies to run the campaign and mobilised his own mayors and governors by offering them, this time, the promise of abolishing their own term limits. The 'red machine' went into high gear. Honking, cheering cavalcades toured the barrios. Platoons of red shirts distributed free mattresses, fans, fridges and stoves. They handed out flyers with ten reasons for voting yes. Number one: 'Chávez loves us and love is repaid with love.' Number two: 'Chávez is incapable of doing us harm.' Chávez won the referendum with 55 per cent of the vote. He pumped the air from the palace balcony and vowed to rule until 2030, when he would be seventy-five. The crowd cheered.

7

THE DEVIL'S EXCREMENT

I was at university and dating a very rich girl, the daughter of a banker. She had a BMW when nobody had a BMW. And this Italian friend of mine told me if you're going to get married for money, you need to have three conditions. The first one: the father must not have a son. Second, he has to be old and weak and tired. If he's young, he won't let you in. And finally, he has to be generous. If the three elements fit, you can marry that woman for money. Otherwise, you shouldn't marry her for money, because you're not going to get any.' Baldo Sansó leaned back in his seat, smiling at the cunning. 'Of course,' he added, 'it's completely cynical. And the likelihood that you're going to be miserable if you marry for money is enormous. Tsk, a man marrying a woman for money – a miserable life.'

It was March 2011 in the penthouse office of the headquarters of the state oil company, PDVSA. A realm of black leather sofas and corporate abstract art in a glass tower insulated from the cacophony of the city below. The only sounds were the hiss of sliding doors and the click clack of young secretaries in high heels and tight trousers walking on tiles. It was evening and executives were heading home, all save Sansó, who remained in his office gazing at the panoramic view. As the sky darkened, his own reflection looked back from the window. Lean, black hair swept back over a high forehead, a long nose, alert eyes. He wore a blue Versace suit, purple tie and pointy black slip-on shoes. A dapper eagle ready to swoop. Few knew what he looked like – Sansó kept his picture out of the papers – but his name was whispered across boardrooms and ministries. He was one of the architects of Chávez's oil policy, a PDVSA prince associated with huge bond issues, currency swaps and other high-finance deals. Sansó, fairly or unfairly, was a byword for venality. The opposition included him in its list of the ruling elite's 'ten most corrupt'. Even some pro-government sources singled him out as an alleged dark lord of Mammon. He was well aware of his reputation and saw our interview as an opportunity to set the record straight.

His office was big enough to play volleyball in. On the bed-sized desk sat two BlackBerrys, a lacquered Chinese box of Cross pens, and a framed black-and-white portrait of his blonde wife (a college girlfriend whose father, apparently, was not especially well-off) and infant son. A red baseball-style company jacket hung from a hanger. It was difficult to envisage Sansó wearing anything that garish. 'I wear it when I attend [pro-government] demonstrations,' he said, smiling. 'I enjoy going. There's so much diversity there. For a guy like me that's fascinating.' He made it sound like a safari. 'If I go to an opposition march, it's just to see how beautiful the girls are.'

Sansó had a privileged background. His mother was a former Supreme Court judge whose legal firm represented PDVSA, among other lucrative clients. He had studied in Venezuela, Canada and the United States. 'I consider myself a left-wing guy. At college I was into leftist causes.' Afterward, he worked at a New York law firm, then as a consultant in Rome and Milan for Bain & Company, a Boston-based management consultancy. 'These strategic consultancy firms are very competitive, like investment bankers. Working for them in Italy was very tough. There they have this idea of manipulation. They really know how to get you to do things for them. They're much, much tougher than the Americans. They have knives in their mouths.' Sansó moved back to Caracas in 2003 and joined PDVSA just as Chávez was defeating the oil strike and wresting control from the company's old guard. 'Man, those guys were so arrogant,' said Sansó. 'They were convinced they were indispensable. When Chávez fired twenty thousand of them, almost all white-collar, they thought there was no way we could keep the thing together. They thought Chavistas were all stupid, corrupt, black, incompetent. Well, we showed them.'

Sansó defended Chávez's energy policy, saying the comandante had helped revive OPEC, sending prices rising even before the Iraq war, and had had the vision to recognise Venezuela's oil was not just around Lake Maracaibo, in the west, but also in the center of the country along the Orinoco in a smiling arc known as the Faja. The same wilderness that had swallowed gold-seeking conquistadores contained enormous deposits of extra-heavy crude. The black ooze had long been written off as tar, a costly-to-extract type of liquid coal, and the old PDVSA gave foreign oil companies a virtual free hand to develop it. Chávez insisted it was oil, and eventually even the U.S. Geological Survey agreed. The zone contained an estimated 220 billion barrels – making Venezuela's total reserves vaster than Saudi Arabia's. Chávez partly nationalised the Faja in 2007, taking majority shares in the operations, an audacious decision that infuriated the foreign oil companies working there. 'For that alone Chávez was worth it,' said Sansó. 'He was crazy enough to do it. Any reasonable guy wouldn't have had the guts. He would have said it's not possible. A century from now Chávez will be remembered and thanked for this, no matter what else happens.'

The comandante, said Sansó, had also proved shrewd in milking foreign oil companies. Squeeze too hard and they would leave, taking their equipment and checkbooks, too soft and they would dribble just a pittance of revenue to the state. Chávez squeezed so hard some left and sued in international courts, but most stayed and paid higher taxes, royalties and signing fees, gushing extra billions into the treasury. His enforcer was Rafael Ramírez, a tall, pale man from the Andes, who doubled up as oil minister and head of PDVSA. He was also Sansó's boss and, having married his sister, family. 'I don't agree with everything my brother-in-law has done here, but he calculated the companies' greed to perfection. Geology was on our side.'

It was no secret PDVSA's politicisation and myriad tasks – as funder and administrator of the social missions it operated as a parallel state – had enervated its ability to pump oil and find new wells. By 2010 it had spent an estimated $23 billion on social programmes. Analysts said the company was in crisis and produced far fewer than the three million barrels it claimed to pump daily. Sansó admitted there was decay but made a version of the old industry joke that the second-most-profitable business in the world, after a well-run oil company, was a badly run oil company. 'Oil is not so complex. There is no other product in the world that costs you $4 and you sell for $100. The margins are ridiculous; it makes it easy. The real art is exploration. Once you've found it, you pump it. It's pretty simple.'

Up to now Sansó had given a conventional defence of the economic policies that had nourished the revolution for a decade. But as night seeped across Caracas and his headquarters emptied – there were no more footsteps or hissing doors – he edged toward transgression. He was convinced a recent newspaper article in which he said . he was misquoted criticising the government – 'they screwed me, completely screwed me' – had shredded his goodwill at the palace and that he was about to be fired. Cast off the ledge. Thus there seemed little to lose from plain speaking.

'Where does Chávez fail?' he asked. A question clearly on his mind. 'Dutch disease.' It was a technical term about how revenues from natural resources can strengthen the exchange rate, making it cheaper to import everything rather than grow or manufacture it at home. How a country, in other words, can become a bloated sloth. The phenomenon was named after the Netherlands, whose productivity fell after a gas boom in the 1960s, but would have been better called third-world disease. 'I've broken my brain trying to solve it here,' said Sansó. The economy, he despaired, had become a parasite. Chávez's initial pragmatism in fostering private and state enterprise meant Venezuela could have thrived and built a broad-based, sustainable economy. But the 2002 coup and strike changed that.

'Chávez was radicalised by the private sector's repeated betrayals . . . He came to understand socialism as political socialism. He started talking about the new man and creating a new society.' He shook his head. 'It was a historic opportunity that was wasted. This is all Chávez's fault. He doesn't understand economics.' One never heard a senior Chavista so bluntly criticise the comandante. Sansó was just getting warmed up. 'It's a pity no one took twenty minutes to explain macroeconomics to him with a pen and paper. Chávez doesn't know how to manage. As a manager he's a disaster. I'm fed up with Chávez . . . I'm not a Chávez fan.' Coming from a member of the revolution's economic elite, this was heresy.

The oil prince surged on. Having lambasted incompetence, he

plunged headlong into the revolution's other unspoken taboo. Vice. 'There are corrupt people who see opportunities to make a lot of money here,' he said. The tone was acrid. 'There are all these people who hate you and yet come here looking for favours.' These were things everyone knew but never said. Sansó was angry now, defiant. 'Everyone thinks I'm a crook. A corrupt guy. And yes, I want to make some money. But I don't need to steal. Before coming here, I was making 200,000 euros. I'm living very well; that's why I'm not corrupt.'

Whispers said otherwise. Sansó had been involved with the country's biggest brokerage firm, Econoinvest, whose offices investigators raided in 2010.

'A whole mafia. Econoinvest was a den of gangsters,' said Chávez. Its executives were jailed, but Sansó remained untouched. A bigger scandal erupted soon after when it emerged PDVSA gave half a billion dollars from its employees' pension fund to a former company advisor, Francisco Illarramendi, who ran a fraudulent investment operation from the United States. Venezuelan authorities buried the issue, leaving Sansó and Ramírez untouched. One opposition commentator, noting that both men's spouses and relatives occupied senior legal and administrative posts in PDVSA, called it the dance of the vampires.

Sansó pleaded ignorance about the scandals – 'I only know what I read in the papers' – but made what sounded like a roundabout apologia for government officials who did steal. 'One of Chávez's biggest mistakes was not understanding incentives. He'll want to pay a top guy $15,000 instead of $200,000. Which means you get someone who is either corrupt or inept. Or both.' He pondered the distinction. 'The second category is hurting us more than the first.'

Sansó did not volunteer himself for the first and was emphatic about not belonging to the second. Single-handedly, he said, he had cajoled big corporations into making billion-dollar commitments in the Faja. He had divided up the oil-rich wilderness into blocks and invited rival bids for licenses to drill. Executives from the United States, Brazil, China, Spain, Britain, Russia – all over – took turns tramping into his lair. 'I set up screens to make a sort of maze in our offices. We funnelled the delegations around to give the impression there were rival bidders for each block. There weren't. I completely manipulated them. It was incredible.' Sansó jumped up to show different-coloured blocks on a wall map. 'They paid $2 million each just to meet me. Who else could have done that? This will not sound modest, but I have created more value for Venezuela than anyone else in fifty years.'

Sansó was preoccupied. Even if he survived his newspaper-inspired trouble with the palace and kept his place in the golden circle, he felt vulnerable. Enemies within and outside the government were circling. He said he had 'made provision' for an emergency, implying a foreign bolt-hole, and would flee the moment Chávez fell. 'I would have to get out of here. There is such hatred. They'll come after me. I'm afraid.'

One of the revolution's great ironies was that at the apex of a system of looting and plunder stood arguably its most honest figure, the Monk, Giordani. As planning minister, he constructed the maze of rules and restrictions that let the politically connected make illicit fortunes.

Giordani was ruthless in elbowing aside cabinet rivals, but no one accused him of venality. His flaw was intellectual vanity. Venezuela presented him with a monumental puzzle. It was victim of what economists called a resource curse. An apparent blessing, oil, had stunted agriculture and industry. A Caribbean version of Dutch disease. Partly it was because oil exports made the currency overvalued, so it was cheaper to import everything, and partly it was because oil spawned a culture of bending the rules to make a fast buck rather than sweat with honest toil. More petrodollars equalled more parasites – the paradox of plenty. Giordani's solution, the golden thread connecting a thousand equations, footnotes and calculations, was control. The state would control the economy. Farms, factories, finance, all that was flabby, chaotic, and dysfunctional could be surgically snipped and stitched, smoothed into order and rationality. Private property would be respected, but the private sector would be regulated and transformed, along with the expanding state, by 'endogenous development'. Self-sustaining agro-industrial communities would repopulate the interior, relieve overcrowding in coastal slums and foster revolutionary consciousness. From this chrysalis would emerge a new economy and society. The process would take thirty, maybe fifty years. The comandante, of course, welcomed the prospect of an economy that would respond to command.

The first step was creating special funds. Giordani, working with compliant finance ministers, methodically underestimated the price of oil used in preparing the national budget. Even when oil was headed for over $100 a barrel, they would project just $35. The surplus was channelled to special funds that let the president spend billions outside the official budget and beyond public scrutiny. In the run-up to elections, the palace supplemented this with raids on PDVSA funds – Rafael Ramírez always obliged – and plopped another few billion into the kitty. Giordani batted away questions about auditing, about the underinvestment in transport and energy infrastructure, about integrating the 'missions' into traditional public services. All that could come later. At first few complained because the economy roared, poverty halved, the state payroll doubled and food subsidies reached 40 per cent of the population.

By 2008, however, inflation was running at close to 30 per cent, one of the world's highest rates, and milk, coffee, sugar, black beans and other staples periodically vanished from shop shelves. Nobody went hungry. The poor ate more meat than before; they just had to queue for it in state-run shop or forage on the black market. Economists said the economy was overheating and the currency was overvalued. Giordani smiled. *Tranquilo.* We have a plan. The government spun an ever-widening web of controls, covering the economy. Farmers and factory owners complained raw materials had vanished and state-regulated prices for finished goods were too low. Production slumped. The government filled the gap by importing huge quantities of everything – containers stacked up at ports like vast ziggurats – and taking over farms and factories.

Giordani's mightiest weapon was currency controls: setting a fixed exchange rate for the bolivar to the dollar. The system obliged PDVSA to sell petrodollars (those that remained after it funnelled billions to the government) to the Central Bank, which passed them to an agency called the Commission for the Administration of Currency Exchange, CADIVI. This agency sold the dollars at the official rate to Venezuelan individuals and companies who wished to trade their bolivares for foreign currency. The catch, the epic, gargantuan, problematic catch, was that CADIVI did not sell enough dollars. This meant those first in the queue got their dollars. Those at the back – a factory owner wishing to import rivets, say, or a father wanting to take his family to Disney World – were stuck with bolivares useless outside Venezuela. No foreign bank would change them.

Thus the system bred two exchange rates. Those first in line got the privileged, official rate that artificially overvalued the local currency. A hundred bolivares got you $40. Those at the back of the line had to use the black-market rate, which yielded only $16. Giordani liked the system because it trapped money in the economy and let him tweak and polish his plans to reengineer society. Chávez relished it as a powerful, additional mechanism to reward allies and punish foes.

Foreigners watching the revolution from afar never grasped the existential significance of CADIVI. Hundreds of billions of dollars of a historic oil boom roared through its corridors, giving the power of Croesus to those who controlled the sluice. Insiders created multiple arcane ways – fixed-rate bonds, zero-coupon bonds, treasury bonds, PDVSA bonds – to channel the river. A murmur in the right ear at the right time could make a dozen fortunes, the money blinking from computer to computer, dispersing into offshore accounts, vanishing. The system mocked socialist rhetoric.

Black holes punctured the state's budget. Giordani dismantled an inherited macroeconomic stabilisation fund, which made public reports, and funnelled billions into black boxes, the biggest of which was called Fonden. By 2011 the government was estimated to be spending more than half its revenue outside the central budget. Giordani's office, under pressure from an opposition legislator, outlined how it had spent $40 billion of Fonden money in previous years. But the fund had received $69 billion, leaving a $29 billion hole. PDVSA was just as opaque. It bought back $2.7 billion in foreign debt so it could sidestep an obligation to disclose financial statements to the U.S. Securities and Exchange Commission. A similar veil covered other state agencies such as BANDES, a development bank that answered directly to the palace. The government routinely contracted cronies for public works, without bidding, citing 'emergencies'. It all added up to a mountain of money. Much vanished into overseas accounts: Global Financial Integrity, a global watchdog group, estimated $17 billion on average each year. The big winners were the likes of the PDVSA investment manager suspected of receiving $36 million in bribes to approve illicit financial transactions.

When challenged about corruption at his rare press conferences, Giordani would redden and fire a caustic non-reply to the question. But the Monk was not blind. As leader of the utopians, he had wide contacts and knew what was happening. In a fleeting passage of a little-noticed book he published in 2009, he vented despair. 'The boligarchy is nothing more than the singular or collective grouping of those who throughout this process have devoted themselves to amassing immense fortunes in the name of the revolution . . . Many of them flaunt wealth that they did not have before the arrival of the government in December 1998. These people are professional thieves . . . who have disguised themselves (with red shirts) to take advantage of the honey pot of power for their own personal benefit. These people should be denounced, separated from the socialist process led by President Chávez . . . and tried as common criminals.'

It was a poignant plea. And utterly hypocritical. Giordani had not only created the economic distortions that facilitated the looting; he relied on the worst looters. To spin his web, he needed the Finance Ministry, Central Bank and PDVSA. Venezuela slid toward the bottom of the honesty scale measured by Transparency International, an anticorruption watchdog. Successive finance ministers were accused of pocketing immense fortunes. The Central Bank governor was accused of selling insider information and ransacking the reserves. PDVSA was accused of wholesale kleptocracy. The austere, honest Monk twinkled little bells of complaint but did not lead a crusade against corruption, did not resign, did not redesign his policies. That would have imperilled his authority and elaborate utopian constructs. That would have admitted error.

G iovanni Scutaro was a young, flamboyant fashion designer when he was picked by Carlos Andrés Pérez to overhaul his image for the 1988 presidential campaign. Scutaro had studied in Milan and knew how to make any man look good in a suit. His youthful make-over of the ageing Pérez, who had served as president in the 1970s, helped propel him to another term. Four years later the panicked president wore a crumpled suit over pajamas during Chávez's 1992 coup attempt. By 1999 it was Chávez's turn, as president, to commission Scutaro. 'I got a call from Miraflores that he wanted help with his image,' recalled the designer. The comandante was struggling with his wardrobe. Out of uniform he was lost, veering between sleeveless jumpers, checked shirts and *liquiliquis,* a traditional Venezuelan suit with a Mao-style collar. Scutaro, by then Caracas's chicest designer, with his own boutique, accepted the commission. The priority was to reassure foreign capitals during Chávez's trips that he was not a military thug but a civilised civilian. 'I managed the new image, coordinated everything from underwear, shoes, socks, shirts, ties, overcoats. Chávez is quite dark, so I used light-coloured suits to show his face. The president was thin then; it was easy to dress him. He accepted all my ideas. I really enjoyed it.'

A decade later Scutaro was as flamboyant as ever. In 2011 he offset his dyed-blond hair and blue eyes with ripped jeans, a tight, colourful shirt and four black leather wrist straps. He had just won an award in Miami and had hired Miss Universe to model his latest catalogue of dresses. His role in the revolution, however, had evolved.

He no longer dressed the president, who now boasted an extensive wardrobe and wider girth. 'He's much rounder now. His designers have to take account of that.' Instead, Scutaro now dressed the 'boligarchs' and their women. The term fused 'Bolívar' and 'oligarchs' to underline the new elite's political allegiance. Scutaro loathed the government and scorned the revolution but needed the clients. It had made him an ambivalent facilitator of luxury from the 2003 boom onward. 'Is it incongruous to combine high fashion with socialist revolution?' He laughed. 'You have to put inverted commas around those last two words, amigo. What we are is an oil state with a new elite. And believe me, they're having fun. Flights are full, nightclubs are full, restaurants are full.'

The comandante had repeatedly lauded the poor as virtuous and said to be rich was bad, but the boligarchs exulted in consumerism. They bought SUVs, penthouses, gadgets, yachts, more and better SUVS, penthouses, gadgets, yachts. They rented the former Hilton – taken over by the government and renamed the Alba – on Margarita Island for birthdays and weddings. For parties in Caracas they rented Quinta Esmeralda, a faux-rustic banquet resort that charged $300,000 for receptions and was fully booked year-round. Venezuela made outstanding rum, but the elites preferred imported scotch, notably Chivas Regal. The comandante professed himself appalled. 'Is this the whiskey revolution? Or perhaps the Hummer revolution? Venezuela is one of the countries that consumes the most whiskey per capita. That shames me. It is part of the capitalist curse that is consumerism.' It was rumoured that on a trip home to Barinas, Chávez took a baseball bat to a brother's Hummer. But for all his public railing, he continued letting the boligarchs make money – as long as they served him.

Scutaro watched it all with an arched eyebrow. Tycoons and politicians – or their representatives, if they were being discreet – rubbed shoulders in the glass elevator that led to his temple of dresses in Las Mercedes, a glitzy district in eastern Caracas. Silk or satin, cocktail or formal, above or below the knee, they had one request in common. Red. It must be red. The designer would inwardly groan and reply with a smile: I'll see what I can do. 'They explain that they're Chavistas and it's their daughter's birthday. It's a big deal here when a girl turns fifteen. If the father is with the revolution, he doesn't care about the fabric as long as it's in red. Something simple, $3,000. The more elaborate dresses cost up to $25,000.' The exhibitionism was kept within the rarefied circles of other boligarchs and government insiders. The public at large was kept at a distance. There were no fiesta invitations to the media, no photographs in the society pages and, most important, the boligarchs paid with cash rather than with credit cards or checks, which left trails. Scutaro shook his head, half grateful, half repelled. 'I go to weddings now, and I don't know anybody there. When people from the United States and Europe come here and see our weddings, they go, wow, so much money. There is no equilibrium between perceptions from afar and the reality of what is happening inside the country.'

Scutaro said he tried to keep politics out of his business. 'I try not to sectorise myself. I'm here to work. And so are my staff. That said' – he indicated some women arranging fabrics – 'I've got twenty-five seamstresses, and they're all Chavistas. Well, they were. Now they're all complaining about inflation, insecurity and incompetence.' He sighed and gazed around his shop. 'You might think clothes are simple, but we've got a whole little world spinning right around them.'

I t was seldom visible to outsiders, but boligarchs paid for their bau-
bles and bank accounts in chronic anxiety that one day the legal
and moral miasma in which they operated would dissipate, leaving
them exposed. Their security and liberty relied on a covering mist of
other bankers, businessmen, politicians, journalists and judges, all of
it swirling on money and personal relationships open to betrayal and
blunder.

Such groupings were affiliated to different *tribus,* diminutive for
judicial tribunal, an apt shorthand because tribal clashes regularly
erupted. An unpaid bribe or competition over a government contract
could pit one tribe against another, prompting leaks to the media,
police raids and prosecutions. Most scandals swiftly evaporated,
forgotten, after backroom deals. The corrupt concealed anxiet-
ies behind smiles and conviviality. On very rare occasions the mask
slipped.

In November 2007, during a long lunch in a Miami restaurant, it
happened courtesy of the FBI. Alejandro Antonini, a heavyset, jowly
businessman in his mid-forties, had the fried calamari, the *cotoletta
alla parmigiana* and chocolate cake. Moises Maionica, a boyish corporate lawyer with thinning hair, had the veal marsala and key lime
pie. Unknown to Maionica, Antonini was wearing a wire and recording the entire conversation. It was the latest twist in a tangled saga
that had begun the previous year when a customs official at the Buenos Aires airport found $800,000 in undeclared cash in Antonini's
suitcase. He fled to Miami. In Miraflores, consternation. Antonini
had been travelling with PDVSA officials, and it looked to the world
that Chávez had tried to make a secret payment to the election campaign of Cristina Fernández de Kirchner, Argentina's soon-to-be

president. The palace dispatched a team of fixers, including Maionica, to Miami to buy Antonini's silence, unaware he was collaborating with the Feds in a plea deal. They were later arrested for conspiracy and acting as unregistered foreign agents in the United States.

The value of the wire transcripts was not in learning more about the suitcase in Buenos Aires – it was one of multiple, clandestine payments to allies around the region – but in eavesdropping on how the boligarchs and their operatives spoke in private. It was the eve of the December 2007 referendum. After settling into their seats and scanning the menu, the two men got down to business. Maionica said getting hush money to Antonini was proving complicated because PDVSA could not make a wire transfer to him in the United States while he was under such scrutiny. It would have to be cash, and that would take time. He assured Antonini everything would be resolved quietly. 'Look, in Venezuela nobody talks about anything. Nobody, nobody, nobody, nobody, nobody . . . nobody.'

Chávez, said the Caracas emissary, had instructed Henry Rangel Silva, head of the DISIP secret police, to make the payment. 'Rangel has a secret fund.'

Rangel Silva wanted Antonini to sign a receipt for a $2 million payment, said Maionica, as proof the hush money was delivered in full. 'Otherwise somebody will end up thinking the one who took it was Rangel.' The secret police chief, in other words, was so worried about corruption in government ranks that he wanted a receipt to prove he did not skim the payment.

Over calamari, which they shared, Maionica explained that Chávez had originally asked Rafael Ramírez, his oil minister, to resolve the scandal, then grew so frustrated at Ramírez's incompetence he passed responsibility to Rangel Silva. Conversation turned to how colleagues used extortion and intelligence agency contacts to trip up competitors. They painted a dark world of ambition, greed and betrayal. Maionica said prosecutors jostled for cases ripe with corruption opportunities. 'They're all sons of bitches who want to profit at the expense of others, like, "if I get this one, I'll become a millionaire." '

Over key lime pie the Caracas envoy phoned a senior PDVSA executive in Argentina and used a medical code – Antonini was the 'sick cousin' – to confirm the hush money. Antonini checked the time. Maionica remarked it was a beautiful Rolex. 'I've got the exact same one.' A new version of it (the Yacht-Master II, costing $25,000) was already out, he said. 'Have you seen it?'

Antonini nodded and said: 'I have many.'

The transcription was one of two hundred that surfaced in a trial the following year, by which time Maionica, snared by Antonini, also made a plea deal with the FBI. Back in Caracas, nothing. Chávez, on his television show, shrugged off the whole affair. 'We have nothing to cover up, nothing to hide.' And that was that. Officials played dumb. Suitcase? Antonini? There were no investigations, no prosecutions. Ramírez stayed on as oil minister and head of PDVSA. Rangel Silva, the secret police chief, was promoted to head of the armed forces. Waters closed over the case. 'In Venezuela nobody talks about anything. Nobody, nobody, nobody . . .'

The comandante had swept to power declaring war on corruption and maintained his authority through verbal torrents, but when it came to corruption in his own government, he sought refuge in silence. He sealed not just his own lips but those of people who knew too much and threatened to blab. Most boligarchs willingly remained mute since they had no desire to incriminate themselves. However, some, perhaps a dozen, through bad luck or hubris, were deemed risks and thus banished to the basement cells of DISIP's headquarters, a hulking, concrete hilltop ziggurat known as El Helicoide. They were not tortured, merely left to rot in the soundproof fortress. No journalist could slip in here. Their trials were continuously delayed, or held in camera, so they had no public forum.

The one with the most tales to tell was Walid Makled. The chubby, ambitious son of a Syrian immigrant, Makled started out in the mid-1990s as a small-time hustler who did not want to spend his life working in his father's appliance shop in Valencia, a small city west of Caracas. He bought and sold stolen goods, including contraband confiscated by the national guard. Makled, known as the Turk, prospered as his military contacts rose up the ranks. His big break came during the 2002–3 opposition strike, when he supplied trucks to General Luis Acosta Carles – emitter of the belch that supposedly saved the revolution – and helped to break the strike. Makled was rewarded with concessions to run warehouses in Puerto Cabello, the country's biggest port, permission to buy an airline, Aeropostal, and a monopoly to distribute fertiliser. What more could a budding drug lord need?

Colombian cocaine had long trickled through Venezuela en route to Europe and the United States. Under the comandante it became a stream, then a river. It was not his intention, but it flowed from his decisions. In 2005 he expelled the U.S. Drug Enforcement Administration, which had an office in Caracas, citing espionage fears. And in exchange for loyalty he allowed his generals to grow rich, a tradition dating back to Venezuela's first presidents. This did not mean turning a blind eye. On the contrary, Chávez observed and noted. Eduardo Semtei, a former ally and member of the National Electoral Council, watched him use the leverage. 'Chávez knows everything. He gets intelligence reports detailing who is stealing what. That way if someone steps out of line, bang, he has them.' Thus General García Carneiro, who according to Baduel was accused of trying to skim $20 million from a Russian arms deal, was punished for his excessive avarice not by banishment but by being reshuffled to another ministry, then a governorship. Officers in Bolívar state, the savanna wilderness that inspired Arthur Conan Doyle's novel *The Lost World*, taxed artisans' illegal mining of gold and diamonds. Officers in Apure, Táchira and Zulia on the Colombian border smuggled gasoline. (Venezuela's huge subsidy meant there was a 2,000 per cent profit in reselling it across the border.) The most lucrative trade was with Colombia's cocaine-trafficking guerrillas. Within three years of the DEA's expulsion, estimated cocaine imports soared from 66 to almost 290 tonnes. Some was packed into small planes bound for Central America, some into big planes bound for western Africa, some into boats bound for the Caribbean. The generals who controlled it were given a nickname, El Cartel de los Soles, the Cartel of the Suns, because of the sun symbols on their epaulets.

Makled, with his military contacts, transport infrastructure and cocaine-processing chemicals, thrived. He reputedly trafficked ten tonnes per month. In public he styled himself a legitimate entrepreneur and bribed journalists to write about his philanthropy. He also donated fat envelopes and container-loads of mattresses and electrical equipment to military officers. Wealth and flattery turned his head. The Turk became a celebrity, imagined himself untouchable. His high profile sounded alarm bells in the palace situation room. When one of his brothers ran for mayor of Valencia in the 2008 local elections – the same in which Antonio Ledezma snatched Caracas for the opposition – without the comandante's approval, the palace acted. Police stormed the family ranch, and Makled went into hiding.

His mother wailed to the comandante. 'We have always been Chavistas. Help us!' Two years later, in August 2010, the Turk was arrested in Colombia and soon after, in a series of media interviews from his Bogotá cell, began to sing. 'If I'm a drug trafficker, everyone in the Chávez government is a drug trafficker.' He said he had spent $1 million a month paying about forty generals, vice admirals, colonels, majors and other officials to facilitate shipments. Persuasion was not a problem. 'It was more like they recruited me.' The Americans licked their lips at the prospect of the Turk testifying in a U.S. courtroom.

Miraflores moved swiftly to contain the crisis. The Supreme Court processed a government extradition request at warp speed, setting up a tug-of-war with the United States for the Turk. Just months earlier Chávez had called Colombia's president, Juan Manuel Santos, a Yankee poodle, but now he requested a summit, hugged him and called him brother. He ended a trade freeze, which had been hurting Colombia's economy, and promised to flush Colombian guerrillas from Venezuelan soil. Like Captain Renault in *Casablanca,* he was shocked, shocked that some elements of his government had supported the guerrillas! 'They were making plans to set up some bases for Colombian rebels in Venezuela behind all of our backs.' In April 2011, Chávez gave Santos a further gift by deporting a senior FARC suspect. It clinched the prize. Santos delivered Makled to Caracas, not the United States. The chubby drug lord was escorted off the plane in handcuffs and swallowed by dozens of DISIP agents. He vanished, mute, into the bowels of El Helicoide.

A mid the collective hush, the feigned dumbness of those who saw the corruption but held their tongue, a lone voice shouted. 'All we have done is substitute elites,' it raged. 'We didn't transform the state, because it was a gold mine. And he who finds the mine doesn't share.' Luis Tascón, the National Assembly member who had given his name to the notorious blacklist, now emerged as the revolution's conscience. 'We have been transformed by the state. It is a devouring monster . . . Our top people were born in the barrio, got out and didn't go back. And the barrio continues being the same.' In a series of interviews to a journalist, Ramón Hernández, made into a book, he made a plaintive plea to the comandante. 'I know that inside Chávez rejects corruption. But in power he has made no frontal assault on it. I don't know if he is trying to use corruption as the invisible grease to work the state machinery, thinking he can avoid getting dirty, but it soils everyone.'

Tascón was a *gocho,* an Andean, who grew up in a small town that still enjoyed siestas and felt like another world from Caracas. An early passion for hang gliding was overtaken by politics. He became a left-wing radical while studying electrical engineering in Mérida in the 1990s. Luis and his anarchist friends, he later confessed with a smile, protested over everything, even the death of Freddie Mercury. Tascón's big idea was to abolish corruption and bureaucracy with information technology: clean, paperless, electronic government. Tall and headstrong like many Andeans, he bristled at hierarchy but embraced Chávez as the leader to purge Venezuela's decadent political culture.

Tascón was elected to the National Assembly in 2000 and moved to Caracas, a freshman legislator with an easy smile and modest means. He filled his tiny office knee-high with files investigating corruption at state utilities. Some murmured that he was not as clean as he looked, that he dropped an inquiry into the electrical company after it hired his sister. True or not, Tascón never had much power or patronage. When in 2004 he published on his Web site the names of those who had signed a petition against Chávez, his stated motive was to prevent fraud. He basked in the comandante's praise for *la lista Tascón*. However, he did not seem to anticipate how the government would use it to persecute foes and how it would make his name mud. The opposition branded Tascón the revolution's witchfinder general. Cursed and spat on, he affected not to care, but friends noticed he became anxious and started to chain-smoke.

By 2007, Tascón was respected but carried little weight within the revolution. He began to make ripples by echoing grassroots grumbles about corruption and mismanagement in ministries and state governorships. Nothing too specific, nothing that threatened anyone directly. After Chávez lost the constitutional referendum that December, Tascón grew bolder and said the revolution had been infiltrated by 'right-wing elements' who were looting the state disguised as socialists. 'We must change course before it's too late.' Chávez seemed to agree. In February 2008 he called for 'rectification' and 'criticism' of the revolution. Tascón took this as a cue to strike. The next day he publicly accused José David Cabello, the republic's chief tax inspector, of corruption.

It was an audacious lunge. José David was the brother of Diosdado Cabello, he of the God-given hair, Chávez's cabinet fixer. An attack on the brother was an attack on Diosdado. The revolution held its breath. For all of his cronies in powerful posts, Diosdado was despised by grassroots activists. They considered him the dark lord, an embodiment of the venality hollowing the system, and yearned for his fall. Now Tascón, little Tascón who had no money, no party faction, no powerful patron, had clambered to the ledge and given the giant a push. On his own he could never topple Diosdado. The question was how Chávez would respond. All eyes turned to the palace. This was the moment. A slight nod, a barely perceptible inclination of the head, would tip Diosdado over the edge. Police would raid José David's office, a prosecutor would say evidence implicated Diosdado, the National Assembly would denounce the brothers as capitalist infiltrators, and state media would cheer their comeuppance. Other boligarchs would tremble, and Tascón would be a hero.

Instead, days later at the inaugural congress of the comandante's new socialist party, Chávez unleashed dogs on Tascón. He was denounced as a traitor, a double agent and a peon of empire. He was expelled from the party. Diosdado claimed Tascón, the computer nerd, had on a recent visit to Microsoft been injected with a CIA chip by Bill Gates. Nobody laughed because Chávez was clearly siding with Diosdado. His loyalty and usefulness to the comandante had trumped everything. The comandante rammed home his decision by phoning *The Razorblade,* his favourite talk show, to denounce Tascón as a counterrevolutionary. 'For a long time now Tascón has been behaving strangely,' said Chávez. 'Once I called Tascón and said, look, where is the evidence for this and this and this. Bring it to me. Well, I'm still waiting.'

Ministers joined the attack, calling him a traitor and a spy. Colleagues at the National Assembly who used to play football with him avoided him. Isolated, barred from the palace, Tascón went on television to appeal to the comandante. 'President, you are being deceived. Look around. The corrupt are surrounding you; they are poisoning the revolutionary process. I need to speak t' you directly. Please, give me thirty minutes face-to-face to explain :o show you the files detailing the greed of your entourage. That is all I ask, thirty minutes.' Tascón never got his thirty minutes. Ousted from the party, still despised by the opposition, he was the loneliest man in Venezuela. Hope drained from his smile, and the ashtrays in his little apartment on Libertador Avenue overflowed. He confessed he had a recurring nightmare about free fall: slipping out of his hang glider and grabbing empty air. Tascón was diagnosed with colon cancer and died in August 2010, two weeks shy of his forty-second birthday.

Only in death was he rehabilitated. 'Honour and glory to the departed revolutionary, Luis Tascón's struggle will be forever,' said Diosdado. Chávez too lamented his passing. 'The painful death of a genuine revolutionary man named Luis Tascón touched me deep inside. Beyond our differences, I will always remember this great comrade with the deepest affection and acknowledge his integrity and strength.'

8

THE STORYTELLER

I n the winter of 2009 and the spring of 2010, Venezuela suffered a severe drought. The tropical downpours that nourished the Amazon and sent flash floods pouring through the streets of Caracas abruptly stopped. For months not a drop fell. The time of rain and the time of sun, as the Indians termed the seasons, were out of sync. Rivers dried up, the llanos grasslands turned to dust and fires broke out on the Ávila, the flames licking up tinderbox slopes and casting an orange glow over the city. A unique meteorological phenomenon that had produced spectacular lightning storms over Lake Maracaibo for centuries ceased. Meteorologists said the drought was caused by El Niño, the tropical climate pattern that changes surface temperatures and creates unusual weather patterns. The water level of the Guri Reservoir, one of the world's biggest dams and source of most of Venezuela's electricity, dropped to critical levels. Blackouts rolled across the country, halting elevators and metros, stilling fans and air-conditioning, draping towns and cities in darkness. The government tried to ration electricity to certain hours in the day but bungled the implementation. Power came and went without warning, maddening everyone. To top it all, many engineers said the electricity crisis's underlying cause was lack of maintenance of Guri and the national grid: of three dozen projects launched since 2002, only two had been completed. The rest were either abandoned or advancing at a snail's pace. Protests erupted. Demonstrators dumped surge-damaged blenders, stereos and televisions outside state utility offices. Others burned electricity bills in the streets.

'Hello!' boomed a familiar voice. 'When you hear the pluck of a harp on the radio, maybe Chávez is coming. It's sudden. At any time, maybe midnight, maybe early morning.' It was late Monday evening, 8 February 2010. The previous day Chávez had hosted his weekly television show from Plaza Bolívar, a typical marathon broadcast distinguished by the expropriation of jewellery shops lining the historic square. Now the comandante was back, without warning, on the airwaves. 'You know,' he continued, the tone chatty, 'sometimes I'm awake at three in the morning, working, revising papers, and there are people at that hour listening to the radio, listening to music, driving on the highway. Well, it suddenly occurred to us we could do radio broadcasts at whatever hour . . . and so this is the new programme: *Suddenly with Chávez*. Guerrilla radio!' He chuckled. 'We have many things to report.'

He started by reading extracts from pro-government newspapers that called campus and street protests by university students an attempt to subvert and overthrow the state. Chávez praised the patriotism and passion of counterdemonstrations by pro-government students. 'Wherever the bourgeoisie attacks, we must respond with a force multiplied by a thousand.' He moved on to happy news: a recently expropriated French-owned supermarket chain was about to reopen under state control with a new name, Bicentenario, marking two hundred years of independence. 'We are going to launch tremendous bargains. A 14 per cent discount on goods that are already price regulated, and 18 per cent off those that are not regulated.' Socialism, said the comandante, was rolling back capitalism's avarice. Which brought him to the broadcast's main theme. Turning solemn, Chávez declared a state of emergency to deal with the electricity crisis. 'I call on the whole country: "Switch off the lights." We are facing the worst drought Venezuela has had in almost a hundred years . . . The Guri is falling thirteen centimeters daily.' Miraflores would set an example by cutting its own power usage. The drought, he said, pausing for emphasis, could not be blamed on nature. Nor fickle fate. On the contrary. 'All of this is the result of the destructive system of capitalism, which is unleashing horrific phenomena that are lashing the world.' Capitalism did not stop there, he continued, affronted. Having wrecked the climate and hydropower, it then guzzled what was left of electricity. The biggest energy consumers in Caracas were private companies, he thundered. 'This shows the harm of the capitalist model.' There was also, he said darkly, evidence of sabotage of the national grid. But the population could rest easy. He had prepared an emergency decree that would be ready within days. 'Good night to all of you.' The voice faded, the harp music returned, and so ended the inaugural episode of *Suddenly with Chávez*.

This was the comandante's strategy in a nutshell: Whatever the problem, tell a story. Turn a problem into a narrative, make the country an audience and hold its attention. Cuba, he said, had lent cloud-seeding equipment that would make it rain. 'We're bombarding clouds. We have some planes there, and some equipment that Fidel and Raúl sent us.' He suggested he would personally fly the planes.

'Any cloud that comes in my way, I'll hurl a lightning bolt at it. Tonight I'm going out to bombard.'

He turned the electricity crisis into a near-daily performance. The drought continued, but instead of focusing on energy policy blunders, everyone pictured Chávez in airman's goggles blasting pellets at the sky. He made fresh headlines during a televised cabinet meeting by urging the nation to shower in three minutes. 'Some people sing in the shower, in the shower half an hour. No, kids, three minutes is more than enough. I've counted, three minutes, and I don't stink.' He wagged his finger. 'If you are going to lie back in the bath, with the soap, and you turn on the, what's it called, the Jacuzzi . . . Imagine that, what kind of communism is that? We're not in times of Jacuzzi.' Now everyone was talking about how long they spent in the shower and whether Chávez really did scrub in under three minutes.

He took his spiel about capitalism's destructiveness, a favourite leitmotif, to a climate summit in Copenhagen. 'What we are experiencing on this planet is an imperial dictatorship, and from here we continue denouncing it. Down with imperial dictatorship!' The dignitaries applauded and cheered. 'The rich are destroying the planet. Do they think they can go to another when they destroy this one? Do they have plans to go to another planet? So far there is none on the horizon of the galaxy.' No matter that Venezuela lived on selling oil to the Yankees, or that Chávez's subsidies made its gasoline the world's cheapest, he got a standing ovation.

Problems mounted at home. In addition to the blackouts, the economy was shrinking – the giddy boom that had begun in 2003 screeched to a halt in 2009, then reversed – and enduring one of the world's highest inflation rates. Opinion polls said two-thirds of the population thought the country's situation was negative and that just over half had little or no confidence in the president. Protesters had resumed banging pots and pans during his rallies. The Inter-American Commission on Human Rights, a branch of the Organization of American States, published a 319-page report accusing Venezuela's government of repression and intolerance. From his terrace the comandante watched the Ávila burn and burn.

More problems meant more shows. They took multiple forms. In addition to *Suddenly with Chávez* (which did not last long) and *Hello, President,* there were ever-increasing 'chains' that obliged all channels to transmit a particular presidential event – touring a tractor factory, greeting a Russian delegation, handing out medals – live and without warning. The nation would be watching a film, a baseball game or a soap opera when the screen would abruptly change, showing Chávez's beaming face. 'Aha! The chain is activated. Excellent. Good evening, compadres. So, here we all are. How nice it is to be together. Because I have something important to say.' The broadcast would continue until Chávez said enough. By 2010 he had notched up, over a decade, more than 1,923 chains. Each lasted an average of forty minutes, adding up to almost thirteen hundred hours. The equivalent of fifty-three days. He expanded into new formats: a newspaper column called Chávez's Lines, a Web site – 'I'm going to put a lot of information there. It's going to be a bombardment' – then Twitter.

He had originally scorned the microblogging site as a means for spoiled brats to criticise him and 'sow terror', but its exploding popularity – Venezuela had one of Latin America's highest per capita rates of usage – convinced him to join in. 'I'm going to have my online trench from the palace to wage the battle,' he declared. A camel seemed to have a better chance of passing through the eye of a needle than the world's most prolix leader squeezing messages into 140 characters. But he did it, the inaugural tweet arriving in April 2010. 'Hey, how's it going? I appeared as I said I would: at midnight. I'm off to Brazil. And very happy to work for Venezuela. We will be victorious!!'

Within weeks @chavezcandanga had 450,000 followers. 'This telephone is close to melting. Now I am aware of many things going on here,' marveled Chávez, brandishing his BlackBerry. Every hour he received an avalanche of petitions, complaints, praise, abuse and prayers. It became part of presidential choreography. 'Look at this message,' he said during another event, reading from his phone: ' "We are graduates of UNEFA Zulia [a university], 90 per cent of us are unemployed. Please help, Comandante." ' He gazed at the message, looking concerned. 'We are going to deal with this. We can't ignore it. That would be very irresponsible. We have to listen, talk and find solutions. It is sad if people have no one to believe in, no one to write to, nowhere to go to criticise, to complain, to ask for help.' Some people tweeted him hundreds of times, exclamation marks multiplying with their desperation. It was announced a two-hundred-strong team would help manage his Twitter account. At public events, ministers and officials stood by him, pen and notepads in hand, to transcribe details of tweets he selected. 'Look at this message: "My boss is suffering a terrible lung disease," ' he read, sounding upset. 'Do you realise? These things stay with you. Sometimes I can't sleep because I think "Oh my God!" and I start to reply and I call the ministers: "Help me here. Locate this person." '

It was all part of a strategy that the Information Ministry had outlined in 2007. 'We have to elaborate a new plan, and the one that we propose is the communicational and informational hegemony of the state.' The nation, in other words, was to have but one storyteller.

———

Newspapers and radio and television stations sailed on ostensible freedom of speech while navigating shoals with sharp rocks. One wrong move and a gash could tear the hull. The most spectacular sinking was RCTV, the country's oldest, most-watched channel and, in the early years, Chávez's most strident media foe. After losing its terrestrial broadcast licence in 2007, it struggled on as a cable channel until January 2010, when the government again pulled the plug. Chávez made a tactical decision to keep one opposition TV voice on air. Look at Globovisión, he said. How can anyone say there is not media plurality? It attacks me every day. It was true. The cable news channel fired daily broadsides against the government, images of crime and decay and dysfunction spliced with apocalyptic music depicting Venezuela as Stalingrad.

Globovisión reached only a minority of viewers, however, so its political impact was limited. The government harassed it in multiple ways. Prosecutors launched half a dozen legal actions against the network for allegedly not paying taxes, 'apologising for crime' (it reported a jail riot), 'altering the public order' (it reported an earthquake), and 'promoting political intolerance' (a chat show guest said Chávez could end up hung upside down like Mussolini). Million-dollar fines drained the channel's resources. Its majority owner, Guillermo Zuloaga, fled into exile after being charged with usury and conspiracy. Chávez then accused Zuloaga of plotting his assassination. 'As I understand it, from very trustworthy information, they say they have $100 million to give to the person who kills me. He is one of the fund-raisers, and he's the owner of a television station that is transmitting right now.' The government shut thirty-four radio stations, citing irregularities, and threatened to close dozens more without specifying which ones, leaving all stations nervous. Criticism all but evaporated from the dial. Opposition newspapers were starved of government advertising and regularly sanctioned for supposed violations.

I t was no coincidence that Chávez, who remembered everything, dominated a nation that remembered nothing. Venezuela had chronic amnesia. Indigenous tribes did not write or build cities, leaving no trace of their existence. Termites devoured parchments, erasing colonial archives. (A prescient courtier ensured Miraflores's original furniture was made of termite-immune woods such as canalete and bitter cedar.) Earthquakes leveled eighteenth- and nineteenth-century architecture, and the twentieth century entombed the remnants beneath tower blocks and slums. Schoolchildren learned to genuflect before the blessed Simón Bolívar but little about the complex forces that made their nation. Immigrants – millions of Italians, Spaniards and Portuguese came before and after World War II – looked only to the future. Venezuela's history was vague, a blank slate. Chávez had plenty of chalk to fill it. Growing up in Sabaneta and Barinas, he had absorbed myths and folk songs such as 'Florentino and the Devil', about a *llanero* who fights with Lucifer, and a corrido about the cavalry by Venezuela's great poet, Andrés Eloy Blanco, dedicated to Chávez's great-grandfather Maisanta. It lasted about fifty stanzas, and Chávez memorised every word. His skill at reciting made him popular at children's parties, a theatrical gift nurtured in the army, where he staged plays, emceed ceremonies, gave speeches and lectured at the academy. In power he sharpened his oratory into a precise instrument. It was not the forensic mastery of Cicero, or the stirring beauty of Churchill, but the informal language of the street elevated to something sublime.

It was always difficult to convey his storytelling to foreigners. He used idioms and expressions so particular to Venezuela that Mexicans and Chileans struggled to understand them. And often the stories had no news value in the narrow sense – nothing dramatic, nothing important revealed – so they were omitted from news reports. But these yarns wrapped around his followers like a cashmere scarf, bonding them closer to Chávez. He understood the power of repetition. Repeating not just words and phrases but entire stories, tweaking a detail here, elaborating a character there. A favourite topic was the 2002 coup, revisited again and again, hammered and shaped into a miracle of resurrection.

'How can I forget the feelings of those hours?' he would begin, reminding listeners how he was trapped in his office, with treasonous generals threatening to bombard the palace. 'Suddenly the door opens, and my mother was there. She was there listening behind the door. I imagine she had her ear glued to the wall, her ears became a wall, that woman became a wall, and suddenly she enters . . . It was a moment of death, not a physical death, but a death of the soul, a death of spirit. I was thinking, is this the end? I remember then that my mother enters the presidential office with the same force of the Arauca River when it enters the Orinoco. And that woman gave a speech, that peasant, because my mother is a peasant, a teacher of the fields, forged in poverty, in battle, and I remember my mother looking at me and telling me: "You will never leave, because your people love you." '

In cold print and translated into English, it sounded corny, but carried on the cadence of a tenor voice with impeccable timing, it was moving. In such ways the comandante filled the void left by the cowed, retreating private media, weaving the issues of the day – drought, power cuts, inflation – into a seamless narrative that looped around events in his own life and Venezuela's history, an endless, twisting flow of words. The effect was mesmerising.

Even Chávez's memory, on occasion, faltered, requiring help from someone who knew the revolution's lore as well as or even better than he did. A memory bank that archived the songs, poems and myths of the llanos, the writings of Simón Bolívar, the tangled history of the republic's caudillos and presidents.

Rafael Castellanos. Oracle of the revolution. It took him a while to answer the door. The hallway was compressed into a narrow passage by erupting, waist-high piles of books. They occupied each side of the hall five or six books deep and stretched down the hall in great, jagged blocks that rose to chest level. Some spilled across the passageway, bridgeheads to the other side, and others were beginning to cross on top of them. You didn't walk down the hall so much as angle your body and seek bits of floor on which to do a slow-motion hopscotch.

He had a white mustache, a bald head and brown gimlet eyes behind rimless glasses that gave an owlish look. He appeared to be in his seventies but navigated the obstacle course with spryness. The entire house was a warren of books squeezed onto kitchen shelves, books stacked into living room towers, books arranged into bedroom pyramids, books colonising the bathroom, books heaped on tables, beneath tables, on stairs, behind doors, in front of windows. About eight thousand, reckoned Castellanos.

Caracas's bookworms knew and adored 'Don Rafael' as the

owner of La Gran Pulpería del Libro Venezolano, the Great Venezuelan Bookshop, a cavernous establishment in Sabana Grande that
squeezed more than two million books, pamphlets and documents
into ancient shelves with creaking wooden ladders. It was Caracas's
answer to the Library of Alexandria and just as much of a fire hazard.
It was less known that Don Rafael was the doyen of a group of histo-
rians and scholars who discreetly served as the comandante's intellectual backup. A collective, parallel brain that read, processed and
organised the material that nourished his speeches. It was March
2011.

The terrace overlooked a walled garden with an overgrown lawn.
Two dogs from a neighbor's garden peered through a fence. Half a
dozen parrots in a cage emitted periodic, piercing squawks that Don
Rafael appeared not to notice. Nor did his marmalade tabby, Prín
cipe, who dozed on a chair. With no space left in the house, Don
Rafael, now retired from the bookshop, worked from a large table
with a telephone, a small pile of books, pens, notepads and little
wooden boxes with postcard-sized sheets of paper. He worked from
8:00 a.m. till midnight, taking off two hours every afternoon for a
brisk stroll – 'doctor's orders'.

A historian, writer and literary critic, he was hired in the 1970s to
run Miraflores's archives and became enchanted by the palace ambi-
ence. 'It was named Miraflores because it used to look out onto a
flower market. When you're inside the walls, you get an instinct for
the meaning of executive power. It's difficult to explain. It seeps from
the masonry. You feel it in the air; there's a weight, like an intuition, a
spirit, almost supernatural. They say there are ghosts.' The hooves of
a general's horse. A woman in white. A typewriter's clacking. The
moans of a man knifed in the belly – supposedly Juancho Gómez,
brother of the dictator Juan Vicente Gómez, stabbed to death in his

bed in 1923. 'Some said he was killed by the president's mistress, others that it was a homosexual thing.' Don Rafael worked on and off in the archives until the mid-1990s and got to know and respect several presidents but quietly pined for one to fuse his passion for history, especially Bolívar, and left-wing principles. Then, in 1998, one came.

'It was a sublime moment, like a fairy tale,' he recalled, eyes shining. 'Before the palace was hermetic. It had no contact with the masses. During the dictatorship, people were afraid of Miraflores; they whispered the name. After the dictators there was less fear, but people were still intimidated; they barely knew where it was. It was only a name. To have an audience with a palace functionary, even a lowly one, was a privilege. But Chávez changed all that. He connected the multitudes to the building.' By then, Don Rafael had retired from the palace, but he cheered the comandante. He sent him a biography he had written about Bolívar's deputy, Antonio José de Sucre. 'A year later I received a beautiful letter thanking me and giving an analysis of the book.' The bookseller found a new role as Chávez's personal reader. 'The president, you see, is a great analyst but no longer has time to read. So a group of us do it for him.'

The system was directed by a small, elfish general called Jacinto Pérez Arcay. An academy instructor, he had transferred fervent Catholicism into a worship of Bolívar that included blood sacrifice, resisting imperialism, unifying Latin America and bringing 'balance to the universe'. His lectures dazzled Chávez when he was a cadet in the 1970s. Upon entering Miraflores decades later, Chávez brought the general out of retirement and installed him in an office with a dozen researchers to fashion a new official history and update the cult of Bolívar. Part of his duties was to brief the comandante about historic events and anniversaries that could be woven into official discourse.

When a detail or nuance proved too arcane for palace researchers, or Google, the general would phone Don Rafael and set him to work mining his home or bookshop for certain texts that he would condense into the postcard-sized sheets. 'Sometimes the general will phone me when Chávez is on TV and say, Quick, you know that book, what page is such and such a topic on? I'll tell him, and a few minutes later Chávez refers to it. It's total disorder here, but I know where everything is.' Don Rafael was not just a living encyclopedia but a social glue who hosted generals, ministers and scholars on the terrace. 'Oh, the conversations we have here, marvellous! If my neighbours knew who was meeting here, dear lord!' He winked. 'Around here they're all *escuálidos*.' Squalid ones. Using the comandante's favourite insult.

After twelve years of revolution the bookseller remained a true believer. 'Utopia is realisable,' he said. 'I am sensing a great intellectual awakening. The multitudes are listening to the president. Our youth are thinking, talking, questioning. The Bolivarian process has no comparison with any other revolution. It's a new ideology.' Don Rafael felt privileged to be helping to make history in his autumn years, but really he was helping to rewrite it, feeding chalk to the comandante as he filled the blank slate.

Chávez cast Bolívar as a prototype socialist with a sacred mission to transform Venezuela, a mission he himself would complete. Bolívar and Karl Marx, he said, were complementary architects for Venezuela. (Other times he added Jesus, making a triptych.) It was twaddle. Marx had scorned the Liberator, rightly or wrongly, as a vainglorious reactionary dictator – 'a most cowardly, mean and wretched scoundrel.' The real Bolívar was complex and contradictory. 'A liberator who scorned liberalism, a soldier who disparaged militarism, a republican who admired monarchy . . . [T]he life and work of Bolívar remain full of questions and controversies,' wrote his biographer John Lynch.

Chávez and his scholars were even bolder in rearranging the twentieth century. Traditionally, Venezuelans were taught that the uprising against Marcos Pérez Jiménez in 1958 ended the reign of dictators (so rushed was his flight to exile he left $2 million in a suitcase on the runway) and ushered in multiparty democracy. Chávez needed to reverse this sequence of virtue; otherwise how could he be the nation's saviour? Thus he half rehabilitated a U.S.-backed brute who murdered and jailed thousands, repeatedly praising his public works, his discipline, his patriotism. 'I think General Pérez Jiménez was the best president Venezuela had in a long time,' he declared. 'He was much better than Rómulo Betancourt [an elected president], much better than all of those others. They hated him because he was a soldier.' The democracy that followed the dictator was cast as the true villain: an electoral charade to dupe the people while oligarchs looted the country.

Chávez's family history was reordered to fit the new official truth. His father had been a proud member of COPEI, one of the 'putrid' ruling parties, and despite his modest teacher's salary all six of his children went on to college education and decent careers. The state provided subsidised housing (Chávez lived in one with his grandmother) and free, rickety education and health care, making Venezuela South America's richest country until populism and corruption rotted the system in the 1980s. All this became heresy. The comandante, the nation was told a thousand times, was born in extreme poverty, a mud hut, and grew up in a venal, vicious system. 'It punished the poor. Spat on the poor.' Thus his 1992 coup against Carlos

Andrés Pérez was not a military conspiracy but the cry of an oppressed people. School textbooks were amended so the coup became 'a rebellion that changed the destiny of the republic'.

The nation's amnesia made it easy to mould history, but there was no doubting that Don Rafael sincerely believed the new, official version was the correct one. In the twilight of his life he was convinced he was seeing, and helping to create, something wonderful. 'Our constitution is a document for the world. What the president is doing is transcendental. He is changing our habits. Before this was a country that didn't read. Now if the president recommends *Les misérables,* it sells out. The president is electric, a natural pedagogue. In addition to history, he uses music, the international language, to awaken a nationalist spirit. People sit through three, four hours of his speeches just waiting for him to sing something he remembers from childhood.' He paused. 'Utopia is realisable.'

Hard-core Chavistas did love to hear the president sing, but by 2009 ratings for *Hello, President* had tumbled to single digits. Don Rafael seemed unaware or simply chose not to see. He received his news from state TV, two pro-government newspapers and like-minded friends. He waved away talk of economic decay and violent crime as opposition propaganda. 'Go to New York and see how bad things are there.'

B y 2010 it was easy to forget that the revolution's 'democratisation of mass media' had initially been refreshing. For decades privately owned TV stations had shown a Venezuela of luxury, pale skin and cosmetically enhanced beauty, a vapid, complacent construct. How jolting, then, to see a brown face reading the news or a documentary about salsa groups in the slums. The government modernised the creaky state television channel, VTV, and created new ones, Ávila TV, ANTV, Tves, Vive, Telesur. It revamped the state news agency and launched two daily newspapers and hundreds of 'community' television and radio stations.

The jewel in the crown was to be Telesur, a pan-regional network conceived as a voice for all Latin America and an alternative to CNN en Español. Its architect was Aram Aharonian, a journalist and intellectual who had fled right-wing repression in his native Uruguay. 'The idea was to see ourselves as we truly were,' he said. Stocky, with grey hair pulled into a ponytail, he had the air of a razor-sharp hippie professor. 'We didn't see ourselves through our own eyes. We were presented through a colonial mentality as blond and tall and European, and some of us are, but we're also short, dark, Zambo, Indian. We needed to shake off our inferiority complex and tell our own stories.' For a while after its launch in 2005 it did. It had a headquarters in Caracas and bureaus across the continent and seemed poised to become Latin America's version of Al Jazeera, which had shaken up the Arab world with homegrown, fearless reporting.

Then, from around 2007, Telesur mutated into a mouthpiece for Chávez. It was part of the strategy of 'communicational and informational hegemony' enunciated by Andrés Izarra, the information minister. 'He installed himself in Telesur and took the reins,' said Aharonian. 'For him it wasn't about promoting a Latin American identity and doing something different with television, but serving Chávez's domestic agenda and being a political instrument. That meant propaganda as rolling news. The same garbage as the enemy but from the other side. Bye-bye, credibility, they killed it. Izarra didn't debate. He kicked me out in December 2008.' The Uruguayan, once a comandante favourite, continued to hover on the revolution's fringes, disillusioned but hopeful the revolution would correct course. But Izarra turned the state's ever-expanding media outlets into a disciplined menagerie of attack dogs who tore into opponents, or parrots on news bulletins and talk shows who squawked the comandante's favourite phrases.

A mid the comandante's supporting chorus, one voice stood out. It was distinct not for what it said, since all said the same, but for the accent. An American accent, with the tensed vowels of New York. It couldn't roll the *r* in *revolución* like natives, but commitment to the cause was total. Her name was Eva Golinger. Chávez christened her 'la novia de Venezuela', Venezuela's sweetheart. Those who hated her, and there were many, amended that to bride of the revolution, to evoke Frankenstein. She was intriguing not just as a westerner in the palace but as someone who applauded Chávez's early stories, the ones about inclusion and social justice in the first years of his presidency, and who continued clapping even as his stories turned dark and bizarre. She became, in her own words, an 'insider outsider'.

She was petite, in her mid-thirties, with brown hair past her shoulders, and wore a wary smile. Her apartment was small, bright, well-ordered and warmed by two cats imported from Brooklyn. There were framed photographs of gritty urban landscapes; a bookcase with tomes on the CIA and U.S. foreign policy; a wine rack; a running machine used while watching the right-wing U.S. channel Fox – 'to keep tabs on the empire' – and an impressive stack of movies. The television glowed, silent. 'I always keep it on. You never know when Chávez is going to appear.'

She sat at a small table overlooking a busy street and over careful sips of water told her story. She was born on a U.S. Air Force base and imbibed progressive causes from a young age. Her father was a psychiatrist who had served as an officer in Vietnam, and her mother brought her on women's rights marches. She attended Sarah Lawrence College and in the early 1990s moved to Mérida to explore family roots. Venezuela was in ferment. Chávez was in jail, an enigma, and Mérida's students regularly marched against government austerity (among them Luis Tascón, though she did not meet him then). Golinger taught English, sang in a jazz band and learned Spanish. 'It was an adventure, and I fell in love with the country.' She returned to New York in 1998, the year Chávez was elected, with the band's guitarist as her husband. She obtained a law degree specialising in human rights. 'Music and justice, my two passions.' The 2002 coup horrified her. Suspicious of Washington's role, she used the Freedom of Information Act to obtain U.S. State Department documents that showed the Bush administration knew in advance about the coup. She passed them on to pro-Chávez groups and continued digging, the research gradually taking over her apartment and life.

In early 2004, as Chávez geared up for the recall referendum, Golinger found evidence the United States was funding anti-Chávez groups. She packed the documents into a bulging suitcase and flew to Venezuela to inform the comandante. At first palace aides rebuffed her, thinking she was mad or a spy, but Golinger prevailed and was ushered onto Chávez's plane on his way to a *Hello, President* broadcast. 'They served us breakfast, but we were so busy talking I don't think we touched anything except the coffee. There was an instant connection. The first time you meet him is pretty overwhelming. There is a magnetism, a powerful presence. Yet also a gentleness and vulnerability.' The comandante invited her onto the show to share the revelations, making her a star of the revolution.

Golinger moved to Caracas and began writing books about U.S.

perfidy against the comandante. 'The president can be naive,' she noted. 'He is surrounded by people who want to abuse his power. He has been betrayed again and again. His enemies have created myths and smears. That is where I come in. I hunt down the lies and set the record straight.' He was under attack, she continued, because the United States wanted the oil and to silence an ideological challenger. Thus it fomented a media campaign to demonise him. 'This is a new type of war, and I'm proud to be a soldier on the right side.' She was a regular guest on *The Razorblade*, where she accused opposition figures of being U.S. collaborators. She named names, waved documents.

Outside the revolution she was despised. Insults were hissed on the street. Within the revolution some, such as Lina Ron, the militia leader, called her a CIA plant. *Miguel's Truths*, the muckraking weekly newspaper, hinted she was a Mata Hari. 'Watch out, President!' Golinger said with a sigh. 'What can you do? Some in our ranks don't like me. In fact some hate me. But I just get on with my job, which is defending the revolution and the president.' If that imparted some glory, she implied, so be it. 'There is going to be a movie about me,' she said, smiling. 'The screenplay is already done. It's going to be a thriller.'

Two years later Golinger was editor of the international edition of *Correo del Orinoco*, a state newspaper (one of Don Rafael's chief news sources) and de facto international mouthpiece. Her crowning moment was addressing Chávez, ministers, governors, generals and ambassadors at a special event under the National Assembly's golden dome. 'Here is the light that has opened the path to a better world,' she told them, wearing a red dress and neck ribbon. 'Here is the nucleus of the battle for global social justice . . . The future of humanity is here; that is what I profoundly believe.' Then she cut to the chase. Her latest research, she said, showed that the opposition media – she singled out Globovisión and fourteen radio stations – were in cahoots with the U.S. empire. The audience gasped in indignation. Golinger continued. It was part of a Pentagon plot to smear the comandante in a possible prelude to invasion. Chávez nodded gravely. Generals scribbled down the traitors' names. Golinger urged the assembly to pass a law blocking foreign funding of NGOs and political parties. 'Fatherland, socialism or death!' she cried. 'Long live Venezuela! Long live Comandante Presidente Chávez!' A standing ovation filled the hall.

At Chávez's urging, the assembly rushed through what was dubbed the Golinger law. It was a pretext to bankrupt human rights watchdogs, prison welfare groups and other thorns in the government's side. Most were shoestring operations that monitored issues like oil pollution, police shootings, jail conditions, education indicators. They relied on grants from foreign institutions, such as Germany's Konrad Adenauer Stiftung foundation, to buy computers and pay rent. The law dried up their funding and devastated civil society. Golinger, speaking a few months after it passed, called it a triumph. 'Finally! I'm delighted. This should have been done a long time ago. The infiltration is continuous, and this gives us a tool to stop it.'

'The changes under way are incredible,' she said. 'Venezuela is truly a beacon for the world.' She was not blind to problems, she said. 'The administrative incompetence can be maddening. And the corruption is enormous, I see it.' So why not, from her editor's perch, investigate and denounce it? Her eyes widened. 'No, no, I can't do that. Powerful people are involved. It would be dangerous. I look away and focus on all the positive things happening.' For a supposed champion of truth, it was a damning admission.

A few months later at the palace, where Chávez was giving a rare briefing to foreign correspondents, he wore a tracksuit and held a baseball. 'Who here plays baseball?' he asked. It was a rhetorical question to soften us up, but Golinger shot her hand up. 'Me, me! I play.' He smiled back. 'Ah, Eva.' She nearly burst with joy.

KINGDOM

★

It is a general rule that, in an ill-constructed machine, the engine must be enormously powerful to produce the slightest result. Experience has taught me that much must be demanded of men in order that they may accomplish little.

— SIMÓN BOLÍVAR

9

DECAY

It was always a relief to get out of Caracas and see the rest of the country. When the plane sped down the runway and began to lift, there would be a feeling of lightness more psychological than aerodynamic. The capital was stultifying. Partly it was the endless traffic jams, the jostling, crowded pavements, the fear of crime, and partly it was Chávez. The near-daily public appearances produced a collective draining, a breathlessness. He sucked up all the oxygen. El Silencio, the ring of ministries and offices around the palace, lived off his fumes, and the rest of the city lived off El Silencio, seeking jobs, subsidies, contracts, promises. The air in the city felt thin. A trip to the provinces was a way to decompress, like loosening a tie and feeling a deep, cool breeze.

First, however, you had to get to the airport. On a good day it took forty-five minutes to escape downtown and take the tunnels beneath the Ávila leading down to the Caribbean. On a bad day – an accident or a protest blocking a motorway, a rockfall, a police stop

– it could take more than three hours. Arriving, you remained tense. Armed gangs were known to ambush people in the parking lot stealing vehicles and luggage. Once inside the terminal, you kept your head down and avoided the gazes of national guardsmen, youths in khaki uniforms, who pulled passengers aside for interrogations about drugs that sometimes led to requests for bribes, usually delivered with mock empathy. 'Ay, señor, what a shame, we have to give this suitcase a special search, which means you'll miss your flight . . .' Meanwhile, baggage handlers, trolley pushers and taxi drivers roved the terminal, hissing black-market rates for dollars, euros and pounds. 'Money, money, money change.' Even in the bathrooms there was a scam: empty soap dispensers obliged you to tip cleaners who hovered by washbasins offering green liquid from grubby plastic bottles cut in half. At the check-in desk you prayed for confirmation the plane had arrived.

Once you were buckled into your seat, the engine whirring to life, the jet accelerating down the runway, nose tilting up, the city below shrinking, vanishing, then you could relax. In the provinces Chávez still seeped from television and radio, he still squinted from murals and T-shirts, but he was distant, separated by mountains, valleys, plains and forests. Venezuela was bigger than Texas. The farther you went from the palace, the less suspicious people tended to be. Chavistas still wore red and recited the same slogans but were more open, more relaxed. It became easier to gaze beyond state television's refracted images and see the revolution not as spectacle, not as a one-man show, but as a complex process that affected human lives. Simultaneously, it became harder to remain detached, to merely observe. The temptation grew to take sides.

'Welcome, Mr. Rory! Welcome to La Vecindad! Here, climb in.

And hold on.' Oscar Olachea revved the motorbike, and I gripped the rails of a two-wheeled cart attached to the back like a chariot. I was visiting a Chavista agricultural cooperative in the plains of Barinas for a story on land reform. We bounced along a dirt path, and over the engine's whine Oscar, a cheerful bustle of energy in torn denim and muddy rubber boots, explained how he and fourteen other labourers were turning this marshy corner of the llanos – a patchwork of corn and yucca fields with ninety-one cows, sixty chickens and six pigs – into a thriving farm. 'We're building something. This is going to be our home.'

I spent three days there. Conditions were primitive. Most of the men wore rags and went barefoot despite mosquitoes and snakes. They slept in hammocks in a roughly hewn wooden bungalow. There was no toilet, shower or electricity, so they answered nature's call in the fields, washed from a barrel of soapy water and cooked over an open fire. Rice and beans for lunch, rice and beans for supper. There was no tractor or mechanised agricultural equipment, so clearing brush, chopping wood, harvesting crops and milking cows were done by hand. It could have been the nineteenth century.

All important decisions required consensus. 'Everybody here is equal, and thanks to that we feel richer as human beings. We have no bosses,' said Olachea. 'We share and care for each other. What is that if not socialism?' The government had donated the land and lent start-up money and equipment and seeds. They worked without complaint, kept costs low, awarding themselves a pauper's daily wage of just $3.20, in the belief they were building a future. Nailed to a wall was the co-op's sole adornment: a poster of Chávez in his presidential sash. At night, a half-moon overhead, they sat around a fire in the yard discussing farm business. Then Adelso Lauro, a part-time soldier, would sing serenades about love, courtship and beautiful women. A colleague drummed an upturned bucket; another plucked a *cuatro,* a type of guitar. 'This is part of something bigger,' said Oscar, poking the fire with a stick. 'We're building up the country. We're fixing it.'

At such moments the shrill politicking of Caracas seemed a world away, and the revolution was about not Chávez, or the intrigues of El Silencio, but ordinary people making the best of limited options. If wanting them to succeed was taking sides, so be it. The question was, would they – the millions of peasants, factory workers, professionals and students swept up in Chávez's experiment – succeed? Would the system help or hinder them?

Bounded to the north by the Orinoco, to the east by Guyana, and to the south by Brazil, Bolívar state occupies a quarter of Venezuela. The largest of Venezuela's twenty-three states and potentially its richest, it is mostly uninhabited wilderness except at the confluence of the Orinoco and Caroní rivers. Here sprawls Ciudad Guayana, the country's industrial heartland, a hub of coal mines, iron smelters, steel mills, aluminium plants, motorways and tankers that shipped enormous cargoes via the Orinoco to the Atlantic. This was the same realm that had driven conquistadores mad with rage and sunstroke while seeking El Dorado, but in the 1960s Venezuela's fledgling democracy began to harness its greatest natural riches: iron, bauxite, coal and surging rivers topographically ideal for hydroelectricity. Planners from Harvard and the Massachusetts Institute of Technology designed Ciudad Guayana as an Eden of modernist architecture and industry with power as limitless as the rivers' churn. By the mid-1990s a million migrants had settled in its elongated, purpose-built city. Everything revolved around Corporación Venezo-lana de Guayana (CVG), a state-owned conglomerate that ran the factories and mines. It suffered from corruption, mismanagement and sporadic labour disputes but made a profit and was hailed as proof the nation could shake off its oil-induced sloth and actually make products for export.

Upon taking office, Chávez visited the zone and declared it the cradle of Venezuela's greatness to come. Ciudad Guayana would expand, multiply production and become a global industrial giant, he said. It would wean Venezuela's economy off its addiction to oil. 'Here is our future.' After the government radicalised in 2005, when he declared himself socialist and started expanding the state's role in the economy, Chávez said the factories and mines would also help wean Venezuela off capitalism by transferring control to the workers. 'We are in a fertile moment to plant everything anew, old dreams, old ideas, old concepts, and convert them into new ideas, new dreams, new paths. We are in a marvellous moment of the rebirth of hope.'

'Welcome to Ciudad Guayana! Welcome to Bolívar! It's so won-derful you could come all this way to see us.' Francisco Rangel Gómez beamed. He was a former army general and cabinet minister sent by Chávez to rule this distant fiefdom. Rangel Gómez did not dress the part of a revolutionary. Tall and powerfully built, he had the designer spectacles, striped blue shirt and air of a successful CEO. Nor did he exude the clenched suspicion of the palace. He greeted us, a group of foreign correspondents, as honoured guests.

Rangel Gómez was the baron of Bolívar state. In terms of palace fauna, he was not a utopian or a disciple but a fixer, an ambitious pragmatist whose value was not ideological fervor – he didn't have any – but in making this a fiefdom in the service of the comandante. Chávez appointed him head of CVG in 2000, and Rangel Gómez went on to become state governor. To visitors he wished to impress, he showed a corporate-style public relations video with upbeat music that spliced impressive statistics on water connections, school building and poverty reduction with scenes of tourists on riverboats, smiling schoolchildren, police in shiny patrol cars and men in hard hats operating computerised machinery. Answering questions, the governor said the news was all good. Production up, investment up, employment up, crime down, pollution being tackled. The answers were detailed and delivered with confidence. It was like listening to Bill Gates.

Guides in red T-shirts took us to a pediatric clinic, a factory that cut granite and a botanical garden, all impeccable. Over lunch the next day, at a beautiful spot overlooking the Caroní River, some of the chaperones relaxed. 'I used to be a journalist too,' confided one, an affable middle-aged woman. 'But the newspaper went bust, and, well, there's really no other employer here except the state.' She indicated her red garb. The tone was vaguely apologetic.

The drought had ended a year earlier, in mid-2010, and the reservoir was full at the Guri Dam. Water thundered from the sluices in great, foaming arcs. The comandante had declared the electricity crisis over, but blackouts continued to roil the country, prompting suspicion – denied by the government – that several if not most of the dam's fourteen turbines were sputtering for want of maintenance.

'Not at all,' said our guide, Carlos Sequea, a personable young man in the inevitable red T-shirt. 'They are all working perfectly.'

A rectangular slab of black granite in the middle of wasteland caught our attention. It was a sundial dating from the 1970s, when this field of weeds had been a visitor park with flower beds. Now it was abandoned. The dial was thirty minutes fast. 'Since the president changed the clocks, it's been out of sync,' explained Carlos. He shrugged. 'There's no way to fix it.'

Later, as the sun was beginning to set, we made a detour to Cambalache, a sprawling waste dump outside Ciudad Guayana. Mounds of garbage stretched as far as the eye could see. Every so often municipal dump trucks emblazoned with the words 'Socialist Beautification Plan' tipped new garbage onto the site. Smoke from small fires cast the scene in haze. Hundreds of vultures swooped and pecked at the refuse. Competing with them, picking through cans, cartons, clothing and metal, were human scavengers. Adults and children blackened from the smoke worked in teams methodically sorting what had value from what did not. This was their home. Mangy dogs snuffled alongside them. Flies buzzed everywhere. 'I've lost weight working here,' said Carolina Moreno, a wrinkled pixie who looked older than her thirty-seven years. 'I can't stand to eat with the smell,' she explained. She had improvised a tent out of fabric, which flapped in the breeze, and furnished it with a salvaged plastic chair. Bags of tin cans and scrap metal ringed her little office. 'Been here five years. I'd like to leave but have nowhere to go.' Here she earned $45 a week bagging bits of aluminium. Moreno tapped her baseball cap, which was emblazoned PSUV, the comandante's party. 'I've voted for him up to now but don't know if I will again.' She started coughing, a hoarse hacking sound, and sheepishly waved us away. This hellish scene was not Chávez's creation. The scavenging predated him, and the revolution had brought some improvements to this community of the damned: a dozen cinder-block houses, a literacy program, visits from a Cuban doctor. But most still lived in tents, still suffered rashes, tuberculosis and other diseases, and still had nowhere else to go.

A t Venalum, the country's biggest aluminium maker and exhibition of 'worker control'. Years earlier the government had told its humblest machinists and technicians that they now ran the company. 'Capitalism had its chance. Now let the workers take charge, let socialism flourish,' the comandante had exulted.

Workers in red T-shirts milled around a reception area dominated by a faded billboard of Chávez with his famous quotation: 'We are in a fertile moment to plant everything anew.' At the director's office, where another seven portraits of the comandante hung on the walls, each with its own slogan: 'Advancing together!' 'The future belongs to us!' 'Productivity with social commitment!' 'Let tenderness reign.'

The director was a tall, bearded man named Rada Gamluch. An engineer by training, he had been in the comandante's movement since the early days. During the 2002 coup he had reputedly led a convoy to an opposition television station and made a slitting motion across his throat to journalists. When sworn in as Venalum's president, he had worn militia-style fatigues. But the Gamluch who greeted us wore a spotless cream guayabera shirt, pens poking from a chest pocket. His manner was smooth and professional.

The previous government, said Gamluch, had been on the verge of privatising Venalum in 1998. Chávez had arrived just in time. 'Thank God the revolution averted that. We were able to recuperate the plant for the state. For the people.' There followed, he said, a golden decade of increasing production to over 400,000 tonnes per year. 'We exported everywhere. The workers were proud and grateful to the *comandante presidente*.' But from 2009, he said, the voice dropping, it all went wrong. 'The world economic crisis hit us.' He corrected himself. 'The capitalist crisis hit us.' The West's economic mismanagement meant demand for aluminium collapsed, and with it prices. 'Then, in 2010, prices rose, and we were poised to recover but . . . we were hit by the electricity crisis.' Gamluch crossed and uncrossed his legs. This was delicate terrain. 'Venalum is a big consumer of energy, and, well, some difficult choices had to be made. Venalum had to be' – he groped for a euphemism – 'had to be factored into those choices.' The word he was trying to not use was 'sacrifice'. Venalum, along with the rest of Ciudad Guayana's industries, had been sacrificed.

As the drought worsened in the spring of 2010, Chávez faced three options: reduce the subsidy that gave Venezuelans extremely cheap electricity to compel his citizens, per capita the continent's biggest energy guzzlers, to reduce consumption; ration electricity through scheduled blackouts in Caracas and other cities; or pull the plug on Ciudad Guayana. The first two would hurt his popularity; the third would devastate the industrial heartland. Chávez didn't hesitate. Functionaries from the palace flew to Ciudad Guayana to yank cables from half its machines. Shutting down smelters and furnaces takes time and care to protect complex equipment, but such was functionaries' haste that entire plants were ruined. This was the story from Gamluch, speaking in circumlocutions to avoid criticising Chávez (two portraits gazed from his desk).

Politically, the strategy had largely succeeded. By 2011, Caracas, the comandante's electoral priority, was privileged with regular electricity. Provincial cities and towns received the remainder, which still meant sporadic blackouts but not, the palace calculated, to the point of provoking collective revolt. Chávez's ratings, which had dipped in 2009 and 2010, began to recover in 2011. Ciudad Guayana had paid the price of having too few voters to threaten the government.

Production at Venalum, on which 150 smaller companies depended, had almost halved, and much of that output, because of the damaged machines, was of low quality and unexportable. It needed years of painstaking work and specialised equipment – which the company could no longer afford – to repair the damage. Venalum owed, and couldn't pay, $25 million to suppliers and multiple times that to the tax authorities and state utilities. The company was broke. So were most of its customers – other state firms in Ciudad Guayana. Gamluch's balcony overlooked factories, warehouses, cranes and conveyor belts. It all looked motionless and rusty, like a landscape painting from an earlier era. The only movement came from the Orinoco, its brown waters surging past the silence. 'No one denies there is a crisis,' said the director. Venalum was still breathing, just, thanks to a $300 million transfer from the government. 'To get back on our feet, we need another $400 million.' For an additional emergency injection of funds it had mortgaged future production – should it recover – to China.

As company president it was Gamluch's job to put a brave face on the fiasco. The good news, he said, was Venalum had signed production deals with Cuba and Nicaragua, two of the comandante's regional allies. They were among the poorest countries in the hemisphere; how they could help Venalum seemed unclear, and Gamluch did not elaborate. The even better news, he said, was that the firm had not fired a single worker. All six thousand staff were still on the payroll. Instead of creating jobs and decent public services for the scavengers of Cambalache, in other words, Venezuela's oil boom was keeping decaying industries on life support. 'Thanks to the support of the Bolivarian process and its social commitment, we have been able to protect the workers from hardship,' said Gamluch. 'This shows the revolution's compassion and solidarity.'

A tour of the plant was dispiriting: ghostly factories that echoed if you shouted, assembly lines with cobwebs, a yard of dusty buses missing wheels and windows.

Six trade union leaders tramped into the room and squeezed into chairs around the table. Chunky men with brown skin, chipped nails, work boots, jeans and leather jackets. Between them they represented thousands of miners, machinists, truckers and technicians in six state companies in Ciudad Guayana. Their spokesman was the one who looked like a grandfather, Rubén González. He had a white mustache and a big, bulbous nose. He had spent most of his life working at the state iron ore company, Ferrominera Orinoco, and was proud of it. He was a member of the PSUV and called himself a revolutionary. 'Fighting for workers' rights is the noblest cause,' he said in a husky voice. He had supported Chávez's establishment of the National Union of Workers, a pro-government federation, and cheered in 2007 when Chávez promised better pay, conditions and worker control, declaring, 'I stake my future with the working class.' González smiled at the memory of that speech. 'We got generous collective contracts, more than we asked for. The glass wasn't just full; it was overflowing. Of course we celebrated. And then, well, then it all began to get sticky.'

His colleagues chimed in with denunciations. Political managers from Caracas with no background in industry. Ideological schools set up in factories. Investment abandoned, maintenance skimped, machinery cannibalised. A catalogue of grievances detailing blunders, looting and broken promises. Venalum, they said, had for a time stopped exporting to the United States to vainly seek 'ideologically friendlier' markets in Africa and South America. After months of stockpiling, aluminium managers returned to U.S. buyers, but by then the market had crashed, losing the company millions. To curry favour with Miraflores, another company imported trucks from Belarus, Chávez's European ally, but the cabins were too high for the region's twisting paths, terrifying drivers. The trucks were abandoned. Managers at another factory halted production and sold the company's entire stock before disappearing with the cash. On and on went the denunciations, one anecdote bleaker than the last. Worst of all, said the union men, was that for the previous five years bosses had refused to renew collective agreements, meaning workers lost their rights and half their wages to inflation.

'So,' said González, raising a hand, interrupting the flow of recrimination, 'we went on strike.' At this his comrades went silent because they knew what had happened after he led a stoppage in 2009. He was arrested, charged and jailed for unlawful assembly, incitement and violating a government security zone. He spent seventeen months behind bars. He was now on parole with the threat of a seven-year sentence hanging over him. One of the others had also been jailed. All said they were under surveillance by SEBIN, the successor agency to DISIP. 'We have been punished for representing workers' interests,' said González. 'They are criminalising protest. It's a continuous process of persecution to intimidate us from demanding our rights.'

The comandante had made a genuine effort to transform Ciudad Guayana. He sent Marxist academics to organise worker councils and teach revolutionary theory in 2004. The workers understood solidarity as better pay and conditions, not seizing the means of production, so the initiatives became mired in marathon meetings and squabbles. To break the logjam, the comandante sent political fixers, pragmatists rather than ideologues, who substituted 'worker control' for 'co-management', a euphemism for top-down hierarchy. Few knew anything about industry or running a business. And they were saddled with excessively generous terms that the comandante in a flush of enthusiasm had awarded to the workers. Under pressure to control soaring costs, the fixers cut investment and maintenance, slowly crippling the plants. Few had opportunity to learn from mistakes because they were swiftly rotated and given additional jobs that kept them in Caracas. The ceaseless, merciless struggle for advancement and survival in El Silencio, in which ministers and courtiers vied for Chávez's fleeting attention, created a parasitic ecosystem that atrophied the roots of distant realms such as Ciudad Guayana.

Without oversight, pilfering exploded into a grabbing frenzy. Supervisors sold entire depots in private deals. One director was accused of redirecting twelve trucks with 366 tonnes of steel bars to the black market. Drivers removed GPS devices from trucks so they could make clandestine deliveries. Companies spawned rival mafias whose ambushes and shoot-outs gave Ciudad Guayana the air of Dodge City. Factory after factory ran out of money. The revolution's great hope for the future staggered and tottered. The palace pumped in billions to avert collapse but, alarmed by the vortex of cash, reneged on promises over pay and conditions. The unions insisted the promises be kept, and thus went from palace allies to palace foes.

The comandante admitted problems but shunned blame. He accused striking workers of sabotage and said they did not appreciate his generosity. 'They must be conscious of the reality.'

Ciudad Guayana's decay was replicated across the economy. Venezuela had too much money to collapse, but it peeled, chipped and flaked into moneyed dysfunction. It was the fate of a system led by a masterful politician who happened to be a disastrous manager.

Chávez used a land law and a billion dollars to seize and distribute a million hectares of privately owned land to thousands of new cooperatives. Their members whooped in delight and rode around on subsidised tractors. But there were no financial controls, and many co-ops disappeared with the money. Others flailed for want of experience, training and infrastructure. They lacked spare parts, warehouses, fridges, trucks, roads, buyers. Ninety per cent collapsed. The comandante spent another billion and decreed tighter monitoring and training. Officials went too far and choked replacement co-ops with bureaucracy. (My friends at La Vecindad, I was happy to discover, proved an exception. The co-op did not thrive but at least survived.) The comandante ordered more equipment and credits and seized another million hectares to try again. This frightened private farmers, who feared expropriations, so they stopped investing and sold off their equipment and herds. Co-ops could not fill the gap, because regulated prices for food starved them of profits. Scarcity spread, and shop shelves went bare. Rather than raise prices, which would have hurt his popularity, the comandante imported ever greater quantities of food. When co-ops protested, saying they could not compete, ministers played dumb. What imports? So much was imported the ports were overwhelmed and 300,000 tonnes rotted in containers. Prices jumped again, so the army arrested butchers suspected of selling over the regulated price. Squads of ruling party officials raided shops suspected of 'hoarding'. Rather than risk arrest, supermarket managers kept stocks bare. The comandante insisted the country had achieved 'food sovereignty'. He hosted episodes of *Hello, President* with cattle grazing behind him, in government food shops surrounded by tins of beans and packets of flour, and in government-run restaurants. He would order the camera to do a close-up of an arepa – preferably a *reina pepiada* filled with avocado, chicken and mayonnaise. 'Hmmmm, look at that, smells delicious . . . While some try to starve the people, I guarantee that while Hugo Chávez is president of Venezuela, while this revolution stays alive, every day the Venezuelan people will eat and live better.' In some ways he was right: statistics showed the poor were eating more chicken and beef. Thanks, of course, to oil-funded imports. Venezuela's agriculture withered.

The oil industry itself atrophied. PDVSA became a bloated hydra so overloaded with social and political tasks it neglected its core business of drilling and refining. Starved of investment and expertise, production slumped. Foreign oil companies made down payments for drilling rights but delayed spending the billions needed to develop the Faja wilderness. They did not trust PDVSA as a partner and feared Chávez could decide one morning to expropriate their investments. They played for time, feigning activity. Thus the comandante and chief executives from Chevron, Eni and other corporations played out charades of grand announcements, signing ceremonies and ribbon cuttings for projects that shimmered like mirages. Vertiginous world prices for oil, however, meant even a dysfunctional PDVSA of rising costs and dwindling production earned enough revenue to buy Venezuelans' complaisance. It did so through subsidies. It subsidised food, subsidised electricity, subsidised mobile phones, subsidised cars, subsidised houses, subsidised almost everything. Not everyone benefited – you needed contacts, patience and luck to get some of the juicier subsidies – but the fact the state offered such things cheaper than private businesses made Chávez lord of patronage and magnanimity. He filled the country's cracks with sweet, sticky honey.

A huge gasoline subsidy meant that by 2011 you could fill an SUV's tank for less than a dollar. Motorists tipped gas attendants more than they paid for the gas. The result was congestion, air pollution and a fiscal loss to the state estimated at up to $21 billion each year. Enough to multiply the education budget, double pensions, give cash transfers to poor families or rescue Ciudad Guayana's industries. The comandante railed against his own policy as 'immoral' since it benefited the car-owning rich more than the poor, but he followed his populist instinct to leave it in place. Venezuelans considered cheap gasoline a birthright. What mattered to the average Venezuelan was not that PDVSA was in ruins, or that the policy was insane, but that gasoline was virtually free.

Infrastructure crumbled. The Caracas metro, the shiny pride of South America in the 1980s, became a stifling, pushing, crowded wait for broken trains. Passengers were banned from photographing the mayhem – it would 'cause public alarm' – and striking workers were threatened with jail. To avert rebellion, the authorities slashed prices and filled tunnels with soothing instrumental music and birdsong. Roads and motorways crumbled so often newspapers published maps of the latest holes, 'super-holes' and 'mega-holes'. A traveller on the eve of a long drive was subject to embraces and candlelit prayers as if about to trek across medieval Europe. The government termed sporadic road repairs 'asphalt fiestas' and invited the public to marvel at imported Chinese steamrollers as if they were exotic animals in the Colosseum. 'Just four days left to see this state-of-the-art machinery imported by the Bolivarian Republic of Venezuela,' said a front-page story in *Diario Vea,* a government newspaper. To astonishment and delight the state did build an excellent cable car to a Caracas slum and completed a handful of other projects. But they were exceptions. Rotating ministers and managers, favouring subsidies over investment, eliding auditing and accountability: it was like paving projects with chewing gum.

Some never got started. With much fanfare Chávez announced Venezuela would build thermonuclear plants with Russian help. 'The world needs to know this, and nothing is going to stop us. We're free, we're sovereign, we're independent,' he said in 2010. For strictly peaceful energy generation, he added, and underlined the point by inviting survivors from Hiroshima and Nagasaki to Venezuela. Foreign media took it seriously, producing froth in Washington. Chávez with nukes! In reality, Venezuela's scientific establishment was hollowed, the once prestigious Institute for Scientific Research a husk. Physicists were emigrating, and the country's only reactor, a small research facility, had closed from neglect. After a tsunami wrecked Japan's Fukushima nuclear plant in March 2011, Chávez closed the curtain on his atomic theatre, solemnly halting development for safety reasons and urging other countries to follow his lead in protecting humanity. 'It is something extremely risky and dangerous for the whole world.'

Similar inefficiencies marched like a colony of termites into public services, infesting and gnawing the revolution's social 'missions'. Until then, many of the economic fiascoes had felt like abstractions to those cushioned by state subsidies. But cracks appeared in the network of clinics, schools and training schemes that had saved the comandante in the 2004 referendum and inspired praise and envy abroad. The most important mission, Barrio Adentro, had sixty-seven hundred clinics and twenty thousand Cubans and offered basic medical treatment to fifteen million people. It meant that the likes of Marisol Torres, a grandmother high in the Petare slum of eastern Caracas, could hobble a few blocks for treatment rather than take a hair-raising motorbike taxi ride to a hospital in the valley. 'It's free, and the doctors take good care of me. What's not to like?' she said, beaming. That was in 2007. Within a few years several thousand clinics were abandoned, and the remainder creaked. Many of the Cuban doctors were sent to Bolivia to replicate the system for Chávez's ally President Evo Morales. Others defected to Colombia and the United States, claiming they had worked as virtual slaves. Chávez declared an 'emergency' and tried to relaunch the programme with little success. It was overstretched and undermonitored. Rather than consolidate the small clinics, the government, with an eye to the next election, launched an additional programme called Barrio Adentro II, with bigger clinics, then Barrio Adentro III and Barrio Adentro IV.

The scheme limped on, but more and more patients were referred to the parallel, traditional public health system. And here was a disaster because hospitals, a legacy of previous governments, had been starved of funds in order to cosset the clinics, which were flagships of revolution. So Marisol Torres found herself riding a motorbike past boarded-up clinics to the dilapidated hulk that was Domingo Luciani, Petare's biggest hospital. Outside, traders sold bandages, sanitary towels, toilet rolls and sheets. Inside was perpetual gloom – the lights were broken – cracked tiles, overflowing bins, out-of-order elevators, defunct machines, expired medicine and despairing staff who claimed to be among the world's worst paid. Many supplemented their wages by selling snacks, DVDs, toothpaste, chewing gum, penicillin and syringes to patients and relatives.

Senior government officials shunned the public system and discreetly sought treatment at private hospitals – elitist heresy.

There was, at times, comedy in the ineptness. How could you not laugh when piles of rubble were painted yellow to spruce up Caracas before a summit? Or when camera angles framed Chávez so the bridge behind him looked finished? Or when the ubiquitous, perennial 'Out of Order' signs on escalators and elevators were replaced with 'Maintenance Under Way', then 'Socialist Modernisation'?

Like wounded beasts, revolutions in decline often lapse into violence, so it was merciful that Venezuela's settled for absurdity. But at what point did a nation's slide into black comedy stop being funny? Every blunder, every wasted dollar, extracted a human price. That the consequences were dispersed and quietly absorbed into millions of lives did not make the waste less tragic.

I t was probably the most exciting moment in Jonathan Rosenhead's long, distinguished career. The professor emeritus of operational research at the London School of Economics was invited to Hugo Chávez's suite at the Savoy hotel, a temple of opulence in central London, to explain his management theories to the president. It was May 2006. Earlier that day Chávez had given a four-hour talk at Camden town hall to British supporters, broadcast back to Venezuela as a sort of *Hello, President,* and now he was at his hotel gesturing to Rosenhead and a colleague to take a seat. 'He was very sensitive,' the professor recalled. 'He knew exactly what we were feeling. He wasn't the bombastic type at all.' For the next hour the two academics, controlling their nerves at meeting this famous, mercurial leader, outlined the principles of operational research, a branch of management science that uses mathematical modeling and statistical analysis to guide decisions. Chávez was attentive and asked intelligent questions. 'I was very impressed by how he grasped the concepts,' said Rosenhead.

Operational research had proved useful in World War II by helping British mathematicians calculate the optimal way to sink submarines, drop bombs and lay mines. After the war it had been broadened and applied to commerce, industry and government but by the 1960s was out of fashion. Business executives and civil servants said it didn't work. Rosenhead, however, stuck with the discipline, developing theories, publishing papers and lecturing at the University of Sussex. Among his students was a young Venezuelan called Jorge Giordani. 'I didn't think much of him at the time; he was just another Latin.' Over the next three decades Rosenhead became an expert in his arcane field, making recommendations about channeling a messy world into optimal decisions. 'Rather than trying to consolidate stable equilibrium, the organisation should aim to position itself in a region of bounded instability, to seek the edge of chaos,' he wrote. 'The organisation should welcome disorder as a partner, use instability positively. In this way new possible futures for the organisation will emerge, arising out of the (controlled) ferment of ideas which it should try to provoke.'

Rosenhead was respected in academic circles but largely ignored by the outside world. Then, in 1999, he received a call from his former student. Giordani had not forgotten his old professor's lectures and now as planning minister in Chávez's new government invited him to help palace utopians transform Venezuela. It was the beginning of a close collaboration that led to Rosenhead's 2006 meeting with Chávez at the Savoy. He visited Caracas every year to work as a consultant from Giordani's ministry.

Rosenhead came in May 2011 to advise on the electricity crisis. He stayed at the five-star Gran Meliá. The streetlights in front of the hotel were not working, casting the last stretch of walk in darkness. The government used the hotel, along with the Alba, formerly the Hilton until it was nationalised, to host important visitors. Cuban, Russian and Iranian voices wafted around the gilded lobby. Rosenhead, tall and lean with a bald pate and thin grey beard, physically resembled Giordani. Over a rum he explained his role in the revolution.

'I came here in 1999 to advise on something very abstract, I don't remember what, but they ended up throwing me at the Vargas disaster [the Ávila mudslides]. I was flown over the site and came up with proposals to rebuild the state.' Political wrangling stymied his recommendations. 'None of it was acted upon, it was all ignored.' Nevertheless, he came every succeeding year to work with Giordani, sometimes lodging at the Monk's house and enjoying long, animated discussions over supper. 'He's very cultured and sophisticated with a great sense of humour.'

Prompted by Giordani, Chávez endorsed Rosenhead's ideas. One of his books, *Rational Analysis for a Problematic World Revisited*, a forgotten text in Britain, was translated into Spanish by a state publishing house. 'It sold out,' said Rosenhead, smiling. Enthused by Rosenhead's theories on joint problem sharing, Chávez took ministers on a nationwide tour to meet mayors and governors.

Rosenhead did not speak Spanish and worked through bilingual officials from the Planning Ministry. Over the years he wrote dozens of reports on multiple topics – energy, industry, transport, finance, housing. Once, he said, he was given two days to write six reports on six different subjects. He dutifully churned them all out and submitted them. And then . . . nothing. He asked his minders about the fate of the reports. They shrugged. He asked about the president's plan to integrate decision making across state agencies. Blank looks. He asked about his transport recommendations. Silence. He asked for responses to his studies on infrastructure and finance. There weren't any. When Rosenhead challenged Giordani over the information vacuum, his friend smiled enigmatically and said such was a consultant's fate. 'No feedback, none at all,' said Rosenhead. 'Quite extraordinary. This is the only place where this happens.' The professor said he had heard rumours the country's infrastructure was in trouble. 'I get the impression Chávez has applied the concepts of operational research in ways I would not.' He paused and sipped his rum. 'Maybe if it was a more organised country, operational research would work here.'

10

THE GREAT
ILLUMINATING JOURNEY

The neighbourhood of El Cementerio sits on a hill and comprises two streets of bleached single-storey houses whose facades are peeling and peppered with little holes, as if woodworms had acquired a taste for concrete. One of the streets is lined with carcasses of old cars mounted on bricks, childish messages daubed in the dust of their windscreens. Its worn appearance is deceptive, for the neighbourhood is young. Just thirty years earlier it was woodland. After migrants from the countryside settled here, it became known to the people of La Victoria, the town at the bottom of the hill, as part of 'up there', the hillside barrios paved and slabbed by arrivals with little money. There is nothing to distinguish it from other barrios save a graveyard whose name no one seems to know, so the neighborhood is simply called El Cementerio. The Cemetery.

On a July night in 2010, while the comandante was breaking off relations with Colombia over another diplomatic spat, Richard Nuñez assembled his lieutenants to make sense of a different crisis.

Earlier that afternoon a young neighbour on a bus returning from school had flicked a piece of popcorn at an older boy from another barrio. The boy slapped the child and according to some versions confiscated the popcorn. The child went home to El Cementerio crying, prompting his mother and aunts to stomp down the hill to García de Sena Street and confront the older boy, jabbing and shouting. His relatives jabbed and shouted back, making an angry scrum. Later that evening, as a setting sun glinted off its tin roofs, shots were fired into El Cementerio. Nobody was hit, but the barrio had the feeling it portended further hostilities. Nuñez tried not to eye the gun poking from folded jeans on the top of the cupboard. '*Tranquilo*. Nobody do anything.'

Richard was seven when Chávez came to power and now, just over a decade later, still looked a boy. Big brown eyes in a round brown face, slender build, none of the tattoos, jewellery or taut facial muscles of hunter and hunted so common to gang members. But he was leader of El Cementerio's gang, a rabble of about two dozen youths who guarded its realm like a mini-republic. It was already at war with the Fifth of July gang, from another barrio, over a motorbike stolen two years earlier. The woodworm holes – made by bullets – marked ongoing hostilities. The shots at sunset seemed to come from the popcorn protagonist's barrio, suggesting its gang, Los Pelucos, was opening a new front. Or were the shots just a letting off of steam? El Cementerio's warriors were divided. Some wanted to hunker down as if under siege and hope the crisis would blow over; others wanted to attack Los Pelucos. Richard's quiet voice prevailed. 'We won't hide, and we won't go ambushing. We'll be on our guard, go about our business and see what happens.' He would lead by example by riding his motorbike into town the next day.

Growing up, Richard did well at school and was good at fixing machines. His ambition was to be a mechanic, maybe run his own workshop. How he instead found himself a reluctant street general making decisions about life and death is the story of El Cementerio, of its gang's rise and fall and resurrection amid senseless slaughter, and Hugo Chávez's quixotic, doomed effort to create a society 'of morals and enlightenment'. Let us rewind to set the scene. In the 1950s, La Victoria, a short drive west of Caracas, was a village of two thousand people ringed by sugarcane plantations. When Chávez came to power half a century later, it was home to fifty thousand people, most descendants of rural migrants, marooned without jobs and proper housing in a culture of machismo, switchblades and alcohol.

In El Cementerio everybody knew each other and many were related. Most men were gone – absconded, dead, jailed – leaving matriarchs to raise broods alone. Wars broke out between gangs for trivial reasons, but the undercurrent was competition to sell cannabis to outsiders. Wedged in by bigger rivals, El Cementerio responded with tough leaders, none more so than Darwin Ospino, a.k.a. Pata Piche, or Rotten Foot. The nickname was ironic. Fastidious about deodorant and aftershave, Ospino was the neighborhood's closest thing to a metrosexual. His fame, however, rested on killing. His first time was at a party. A rival gang turned up, jeering and hustling, and Ospino dropped one of them with a 765 pistol. The police didn't arrest him, didn't even look for him, not even after Ospino found a taste and talent for killing, taking out rivals on the street, dragging them from homes, from bars. He shot a woman's husband, then widowed her again after she remarried.

All this happened while Chávez was focused on a new constitution and wresting control of the state oil company. The criminal justice system – police, laboratories, courts, jails, parole officers – was not a priority. The president set a new tone by saying it was justified to steal if you were hungry. At the same time he rotated interior ministers so fast ministry officials were left confused and unsupervised. By the time Ospino quit the El Cementerio gang in 2003, exhausted from stress, he had killed twenty-six people. Victims' relatives were too afraid to identify him and the police too distracted to chase. Ospino got a job as bodyguard for Jesse Chacón, a close Chávez ally who served, for a while, as interior minister. Few would dare attack a minister with such a fearsome character by his side, went the logic, and with no charges against Ospino there was no legal impediment to hiring him. (Laid off in 2009 when a banking scandal toppled Chacón, Ospino told me he cherished his years working for the government. 'It was awesome. I learned a lot.')

In 2004, El Cementerio chose a new leader, José Daniel Nuñez, Richard's older brother. There were more guns, blood and money on the streets, and the neighbourhood felt under threat. Violence rose because the stakes rose. In addition to cannabis, gangs were now dealing the far more lucrative cocaine. Chávez had expelled U.S. counternarcotics officials, accusing them of espionage, and in exchange for loyalty turned a blind eye to army generals' deals with cocaine-trafficking Colombian guerrillas. Venezuela was a transit route for the United States and Europe, but increasing quantities spilled into the domestic market, giving gangs means to buy weapons, corrupt police and get high.

José Daniel, who physically resembles Richard, was by common consent exceptionally bright and, depending on how you look at it, incredibly lucky or unlucky. Shot fourteen times during an ambush, he survived and hobbled out of the hospital, one-eyed, and hunted down his assailants. 'One at a time,' said Richard, awed. Caught and jailed, in prison he was stabbed thirteen times and again survived, fuelling rumours he made a pact with the devil for immortality. Belief in Santeria, a voodoo-tinged African-Caribbean import, was widespread, especially among gangsters who prayed to *santos malandros,* holy thugs, for success and survival. Who else, after all, could they turn to? Many of El Cementerio's mothers dealt drugs, as did the head of the neighbourhood association, who had a sideline renting pistols. The state was largely absent save for police, and they were brutal and corrupt, selling bullets, extorting shop owners, moonlighting as kidnappers, auctioning prisoners for execution. Police killed between five hundred and a thousand people per year, mostly young men in slums, and were very seldom charged. Officers accidentally shot dead the Nuñez boys' grandmother while chasing a suspect through their home.

Which returns us to July 2010 and the popcorn-triggered tension. With Ospino retired and José Daniel in jail, how to respond to the Pelucos' nocturnal shooting into the neighborhood was Richard's call. His decision to act normally – he did not want to cower or declare war – was brave but misjudged. When he rode his motorbike into town the next day, they were waiting for him. The street was packed with traffic, and he had just passed the police station when bullets struck, hitting him in the belly and arm and hurling him to the ground. He had not been shot before. The pain was instant, excruciating. He crawled for cover, bullets hissing, embedding in asphalt. Traffic continued to rumble past, oblivious. It did not seem real. A lull, seconds feeling like minutes, then more shots. Someone shouting. 'Go, go, go!' A motorbike engine roared and faded. The attackers did not have the nerve to finish the job. There would be other opportunities. The popcorn war was just beginning.

Four months later, in November 2010, Richard was recovered from his wounds. Seven members of his gang were dead, including one shot thirty times in the face. Richard did not follow the news much but was vaguely aware of some grand event at the National Assembly in Caracas. (Chávez had convoked allies, including Eva Golinger, to rebut criticism from the U.S. Congress, calling it an imperialist plot to destabilise his government and 'bloody the streets of Venezuela'.) 'This existence, always afraid, looking around the corner, over your shoulder . . . it's not good.' Worrying about ambushes, wondering what day would be your last, calculating odds, it all became complicated, one decision after another. Leave the gun at home or stick it under his shirt? Risk taking a girl to the cinema or watch a DVD at home? Keep tabs on that unfamiliar Chevrolet or let it go? Richard felt his jaw begin to tighten like those of the gangsters he saw in clenched mug shots. He worshipped his jailed brother but possibly lacked the ruthless streak. His mother, Yelitza, a stout, powerfully built matriarch, seemed unsure he was up to it. 'He is softer, more gentle than José Daniel.' It was not clear she meant it as a compliment.

Whatever his personality, Richard's fate was being determined by circumstance. Against the odds, he had stayed at school and was shortly due to graduate, but he felt duty-bound to defend El Cementerio's reputation, clout and income. 'I've been in shoot-outs but haven't killed anyone.' He rubbed the bullet scar on his belly. 'I won't kill. That's not me.' A pause. 'But I can't let enemies come in and take what they want. I can't.' Richard's fantasy was that the father he barely knew would drop by one afternoon and take him to a movie. Afterward, blinking in the foyer lights, they would finish their Cokes. 'Papá can't visit. They'd think he was bringing me ammunition or something and kill him.' Asked about the comandante, he shrugged. He didn't care much for politics but would catch fragments of the comandante's speeches. 'I like them. He's trying to make things better.' Would he vote for Chávez? A bashful smile. 'Sure, if I live long enough.'

The gang's struggle, and Richard's reluctant generalship, showed in microcosm how Venezuela's social contract shredded under Chávez. Forces were unleashed that gave Richard, and countless more like him, little choice but to trade childhood for a gun. What made it surreal was that one of the revolution's main aims was to breathe life into Simón Bolívar's famous exhortation for ethics and enlightenment. 'Morals and illumination are our first necessities.' The Liberator's appeal floundered amid the chaos and bloodshed of the independence war, but the comandante launched it anew, claiming solidarity would blossom now that the people, vested in his rule, had regained dignity and power. The Liberator's sacred work would be completed with socialist and communal values replacing capitalist individualism. The comandante called it the Great National Moral and Illuminating Journey. 'Education, morals and enlightenment in all spheres, everywhere, at all times.' He had spoken of this upon taking power, and by 2007 he had formalised it into an official campaign, inaugurating moral and enlightenment training brigades and creating a presidential council to guide schools and universities toward the new consciousness.

The campaign did improve lives and elevate learning through literacy programmes, which reached rheumy-eyed grandmothers in the slums, and expanded education, which let poor students stay in school and move on to free tuition at Bolivarian universities. The comandante, a talented didact, urged followers to read history, philosophy and poetry, brandishing his latest favourite tome as an example. 'I was up all night devouring this. Stupendous.' Housewives and taxi drivers found themselves debating colonial history, social consciousness and the global economy in communal councils and evening classes. Teenagers who normally would have dropped out enrolled in colleges to study architecture, engineering and literature. A new state-run film studio, Villa del Cine, contributed by producing social documentaries and costume dramas about Venezuelan history. State television talk shows discussed gender equality, the rights of indigenous people and the role of trade unions. All this unfolded, noted the comandante's supporters, while the West hiked education fees and wallowed in shallow materialism.

Yet in the end the Great National Period of Ethics and Enlightenment – another name for the project – proved a tragic failure. The individual intellects and spirits it lit did not fuse into a collective radiance. They flickered in isolation, marooned candles amid a dark, rising tide of anomie. The problem was not ideological zealotry. For all the Cuban echoes and Orwellian touches, Venezuela never seriously attempted totalitarian brainwashing. Nor was the problem administrative incompetence of the sort that ruined agriculture and industry. The Bolivarian universities creaked and groaned with unqualified professors and overcrowded classes but were better than nothing. The problem was as unexpected as it was brutal: violent crime. The rate of muggings, kidnappings and murders exploded, spreading fear like shrapnel. The state lost the ability to keep citizens safe, to protect them from each other.

It was baffling. The maximum leader who liked to micromanage everything lost control of society's most fundamental requirement, security, wringing his hands while criminals shot, stabbed and strangled with impunity. It was not supposed to be like this. Poverty was falling and new social missions were bringing services to neglected barrios to ameliorate, as the government put it, decades of 'savage capitalism'. Chávez's opponents were also stumped. They called him a dictator, but real dictators – Trujillo, Pérez Jiménez, Fidel, Kim Jong Il – kept streets safe for ordinary people. The great journey shuddered to a halt because towns and cities were quarantined by fear.

The revolution inherited grave social problems and made them worse. In 1998, the year before Chávez took office, there were forty-five hundred murders, a grim per capita rate on par with much of Latin America. A decade later it had tripled to more than seventeen thousand per year, making Venezuela more dangerous than Iraq, and Caracas one of the deadliest cities on earth. Eight times more murderous, it was calculated, than Bogotá, Colombia's capital. With less than 1 per cent of cases ever solved, it was, all things considered, a good place to commit murder. Kidnappings, previously a rarity, became an industry with an estimated seven thousand abductions per year. To allay their terror, the rich and the middle class invested in bodyguards and armoured cars, or emigrated, but most of the killing and dying was done by gangs – by some estimates, there were more than eighteen thousand – in slums fighting for drugs, turf, women and prestige.

The mayhem undermined official rhetoric about moral renewal and the poor being repositories of virtue and authentic national spirit. The government tried blaming the violence on U.S.-backed Colombian mercenaries out to destabilise the revolution, then on capitalism's legacy of individualism. It deployed the national guard to bolster police, but the violence swirled around the bewildered soldiers, just as it did the police, and they returned to barracks. Street policing was the most visible part of the criminal justice system's failure. Police, along with prosecutors, judges, bailiffs, jail guards and parole officers, were underpaid and overstretched. Chávez's lack of interest left them in a limbo of dysfunction where caprice, delays and bribes became normal.

As corpses stacked up, the comandante stopped the Interior Ministry's musical chairs and left one minister, Tarek El Aissami, in place. He tried to rebuild the police force and regain control by rounding up thousands of criminal suspects, including Richard's brother, José Daniel. Gridlocked courts kept them without trial in stifled, rapidly overcrowding jails while younger gang members took over the streets. A terrified society called them *malandros,* supposedly feral thugs, and watched them flit across television screens and newspapers as cadavers or hooded suspects paraded by police. Less than human, they were anonymous ciphers who did not speak, leaving their motivations, their world, incomprehensible. A government minister played down murder rates by saying many victims were *malandros* and so didn't really count. By 2010 the Great National Moral and Illuminating Journey sounded hollow when everyone knew someone who had been wounded, killed or kidnapped.

Society drifted into metaphorical and literal darkness. By dusk, streets emptied, shops shut and people triple-bolted doors. The rich refitted their vehicles with Kevlar and bullet-resistant glass. Poorer motorists tinted their windows to render themselves invisible so potential attackers would not know if it was a grandmother or a burly man at the wheel. You could crawl through rush-hour traffic, thousands of vehicles bumper to bumper, and barely see a human face: everyone was hidden inside bubbles of black glass, an eerie, alienating experience. Power blackouts extinguished streetlights and turned nights a deep, inky black. Poverty was no defence against kidnappers who settled for modest ransoms. A single mother in Barinas had to sell her fridge to free her three-year-old daughter. People were snatched from malls, campuses, nightclubs.

A gang abducted the Chilean consul from outside a hotel, beat him and shot him in the buttocks, just for his car and phone. Airport taxi drivers pulled guns on passengers and drove off with their luggage, the Associated Press bureau chief, returning with his family from vacation, among the victims. The women's baseball world championship was suspended after a stray bullet hit a Hong Kong player. A mother in Petare wailed that she had lost three sons in two years. Solidarity tours from the revolution's foreign sympathisers evaporated. With police overwhelmed, lynch mobs doused criminal suspects with gasoline and burned them alive. A neighborhood in Catia, one witness told the newspaper *El Universal,* became exasperated with a criminal nicknamed El Evangélico. 'They ran him down until he got tired, then they killed him. Everybody was fed up with the police doing nothing. Sometimes they'd arrest him, take his cash, then release him a few hours later so he could rob us again.'

Normally, all this would devastate a president's support, especially if he was left-wing and could be painted as 'soft on crime'. Chávez, to his credit, did not lunge for the death penalty and violent crackdowns, perennially popular but ineffective remedies in Latin America and the Caribbean. And still he managed to escape political damage. It was astonishing. His ratings held up while voters were held up, tied up, cut up, broken into, held down, gunned down and buried. Chávez achieved this feat by doing something against his nature: he shut up. On crime, which polls said concerned voters more than any other issue, his lips were sealed. Caracas could endure a particularly grisly weekend, more than sixty dead, convoys of funeral corteges, and he had nothing to say. Thugs could abduct ranchers in Táchira, shoot police in Zulia and rape in Amazonas without presidential comment. Grieving mothers with banners and whistles could block motorways in Valencia demanding justice for slain children, and from Miraflores silence. The comandante simply refused to own the problem. In muteness he sought and found refuge. Opponents tried in vain to cast him as Nero fiddling while Rome burned, but most Venezuelans blamed gangs and local authorities. The comandante was absolved.

The government's media dominance helped to play down the crisis. No matter that high-ranking officials travelled with multiple guards – several were involved in shoot-outs with would-be muggers – they smothered news, withheld statistics, massaged numbers. A newspaper was banned from showing violent images (it upset children), a television station was fined for covering a jail riot (it alarmed the public) and radio stations were warned against reporting ransom payments (it encouraged kidnapping). Ambulances waited for crime-beat reporters to leave their posts at Caracas's main morgue before delivering corpses. All the while state media trumpeted the latest advances in the Great National Moral and Illuminating Journey – new school computers, a ban on violent video games, a publication of Bolívar's quotations – as proof of deepening 'humanisation'.

Nowhere was the gap between rhetoric and reality wider or crueler than in jails. 'It is said that no one truly knows a nation until one has been inside its jails,' Nelson Mandela once wrote. 'A nation should not be judged by how it treats its highest citizens, but its lowest ones.' Judged on words, the comandante, who like Mandela went from prisoner to president and knew squalid conditions firsthand, was a champion of reform. Upon taking power in 1999, he announced a 'dignity plan' to clean up jails that he called 'among the worst and most savage in the world'. Every subsequent year he solemnly repeated the importance of humanising facilities that were renamed 'centres for the holistic attention to people deprived of their liberties'. Plans were announced, strategies devised, commissions created, initiatives hailed. 'We must substitute this punitive system for a humanist system,' the comandante said in 2011. 'Prisons must be centres of formation of the New Man.' By then jails had gone from being merely appalling to stinking, fetid, overcrowded, disease-ridden abominations where a decade's worth of five thousand inmates had been stabbed, bludgeoned, burned, strangled and shot to death. Many died in gladiator-type contests known as the Colosseum – fights to the death observed by guards, documented by local media and denounced by human rights organisations. The prison population tripled to almost fifty thousand inmates, all packed into facilities designed for twelve thousand. Almost three-quarters were held for years without trial.

Chávez built no gulags or torture chambers and was doubtless sincere in wanting an enlightened penal system. The officials he appointed were largely well-meaning. Yet barbarity resulted. The banal truth was he cared, but not enough. His focus was always the next election, and there were no votes in rehabilitating jails, so it slipped down the agenda. In a state that revolved around one man – ministers and institutions were stripped of initiative – his sporadic attention proved fatal. A particularly bloody riot would briefly focus his gaze. How did this happen? Fire minister whatshisname! Put so-and-so in there to sort it out. Here, that's $120 million for a new jail. Hop to it! The new minister, replacing senior officials with his own team, would wade into the mess and devise quick fixes to placate the comandante only to find the boss's attention – and budgetary approval – had wandered to other topics. A few months later another riot would erupt, and an indignant comandante would fire the minister for incompetence, starting the cycle again. In twelve years the penal service went through seventeen vice-ministers for corrections and was overhauled eleven times – declared autonomous, folded into a ministry, unfolded, merged, moved, spliced, consolidated, expanded, renamed, co-opted, amalgamated – leaving officials dizzy and despairing. It would have been comical were the consequences not so diabolical.

Y ou think it can't go on like this but it does every week some new mad instructions and if you say anything you're branded a troublemaker and sent to tour the jails on the border and trust me you don't want to tour the jails on the border so you keep your mouth shut and just get on with it but when you hear the stories about what's happening dear God it makes your skin crawl and to think you're part of it is just intolerable, intolerable but at my age I'm not going to get another job am I so I just sit there at my desk with a silent scream all day processing reports and photographs that make me want to throw up my lunch I'm telling you it's bad bad bad.'

The mid-ranking official in the penal service whom we shall call Sarah paused for breath and took a sip of papaya juice. She always spoke in torrents after leaving her office as if the words had dammed up all day and demanded sluicing. It was a tic common to many mid-ranking officials, men and women in their forties and fifties who had never particularly liked the comandante and were now squeezed between Chavista superiors and young graduates from the Bolivarian universities. They loathed being part of the system but stayed for the salaries and perks. By her second papaya juice Sarah would slow down.

'The office is ridiculous, far too many people, all these kids with diplomas, and half can't write or spell; they just sit there all day waiting for something to happen and wondering when they'll get their free holiday to Cuba. I went, enjoyed it, but didn't think much of the place. At my grade a Mercedes takes you to the airport. The directors get an SUV with bodyguards. Enjoy it while you can, that's what I tell them, because none last long. If they're incompetent, they get fired, eventually, and if they're good, they get poached for other jobs. Ysmael Serrano, one of our best directors, a lawyer, serious, engaged, understood the problems; he's just getting to grips with things when the president scoops him up to head the presidential Twitter account. Twitter! And we're dumped with a successor who has to learn everything from scratch.' A television on the wall of the café showed the president at that moment in ebullient form addressing an auditorium of workers in red T-shirts. A young girl with cerebral palsy was carried to the stage. 'We are going to deliver justice so that nobody suffers,' he said, hugging the child. 'This is a revolution for everybody, above all the weakest and most vulnerable.' The audience applauded. Sarah barely registered it. A television in her office was tuned in to state channels all day, beaming one presidential event after another, and she had learned to zone out.

'The worst of it,' she continued, 'is that we have built new jails but they're barely used. The *pranes* [the name for prison gang leaders] won't let us transfer their members. We can't force them. They control the inside. They've got grenades, machine guns, telescopic sights, computers, mobile phones, money, contacts. No director wants to mess with that. At this point the government cares only about appearances. We invite TV crews when we're inaugurating a soap factory or orchestra or something; the rest of the time it's about keeping bad numbers down. You know the latest trick? Strangling. A strangled inmate can be registered as suicide. In some jails there's a tacit encouragement to do business this way. It takes pressure off us and gives the *pranes* a free hand. There was one this morning in Los Teques, another a few days ago in Barinas, José Obeimar Roa Cárdenas. A thief who offended one of the gangs, don't ask me how, so they throttled him and dumped the body in the yard. José Obeimar Roa Cárdenas, twenty-six years old, write that down because you'll never hear his name again. He's not even a murder statistic.' Sarah turned defensive. 'I want to speak out. I've kept records at home, pictures, horrible stuff, it's all in files. But how can I use it? If I do, I'll be fired, lose my pension and be prosecuted. I've got the muzzle.' She inflated her cheeks and pretended to chew. *El bozal de arepa.* The arepa muzzle. An expression signifying loyalty, in the form of *omertà,* to those who pay your livelihood. It shamed her, but Sarah, like so many others in the revolution, kept chewing.

As the Great National Moral and Illuminating Journey went off the rails, supporters defended the comandante by saying he meant well, that his heart was in the right place. The disasters were certainly not intentional. Chávez did not want violent crime, or mayhem in prisons, and tried in a distracted, ham-fisted way to control it. He gained no political benefit from the suffering. That much of it stemmed from his hypercentralised, improvised style of rule did not negate the mantra, repeated as a defensive shield, that he meant well. But even if that was true, so what? Good intentions in the palace did not allay fear or salve grief. To blithely say it was the thought that counted, that the revolution was genuinely seeking a better way, as some apologists did, was to abnegate responsibility. Venezuela was a country of twenty-eight million people, not a laboratory of mice.

It was clear, in any case, that the comandante was capable of malice. These were the occasions he shed the rhetorical cloak of ethics and radiance and gave honest expression to ugly intent. His purpose would bare itself with a defiant flourish heedless of damage to his reputation. It happened when he was angry or felt threatened, and the purpose was always the same: project power. There was an exhilaration to such moments, a liberation from casting off euphemism and allowing words – words so often mummified in official jargon and chicanery – to convey rather than conceal what he wanted to say: I am in charge, do as I say, or else. The only thing that varied, on such occasions, was the nature of the threat. Or else what? To wayward allies that could mean public humiliation or losing a seat at the banquet. To opponents it could mean property expropriated, commercial licenses withdrawn, or intercepted phone conversations broadcast on state television. Or jail. Compared with the comandante's tyrant friends (Assad, Saddam, Gadhafi, Mugabe, Lukashenko), this was mild stuff.

Justice, a favourite word, a climactic rallying cry delivered with a punch in the air, proved his undoing. Venezuelan justice, that is to say its legal system, sold its soul long before Chávez. Judges, prosecutors and lawyers – with some noble exceptions – shared a carousel of bribes, jobs and influence with politicians and businessmen. When Chávez came to power, he vowed to clean up the system. Whatever his original intentions, after the shock of the 2002 coup and general strike the priority was not judicial honesty but loyalty to the government. He purged thousands of judges and replaced them with obedient successors. New Supreme Court judges set the tone by being filmed in their robes chanting pro-Chávez slogans. After 2004 most judges did his bidding: twisting the constitution this way and that, harassing private businesses, jailing political opponents (three dozen at most, usually for short periods). The judicial takeover was not subtle, but the comandante took care to greet partisan judgments as if delivered from an impartial Olympus. The revolution, he would say piously, was founded on the rule of law.

December 10, 2009. María Lourdes Afiuni, head of the Thirty-first Control Court of Caracas, studied the defendant. He was paler and older than the glossy, posed photographs published in newspapers, less sheen and swagger, but then two years and ten months in the basement cell of the Directorate of Intelligence and Prevention Services did things to a man. Before his arrest he was Eligio Cedeño, superstar. The boy wonder from the slums who saw all the angles on financial trades and owned his own bank, and an estimated $200 million fortune, by the time he was forty. Then, in 2007, the comet crashed. He was charged with evading currency controls and became Eligio Cedeño, cautionary tale. Exactly what he did to infuriate the comandante remained unclear – some said he had funded opposition politicians, others that there was a scandal involving a Chávez relative – but either way his case was toxic, and it was assumed Cedeño would spend decades inside. Prosecutors dragged their feet so that after almost three years he was still awaiting trial. Under Venezuelan law any prisoner held that long without trial was entitled to be released. Now Cedeño was sitting in Afiuni's courtroom for another hearing, gazing back at her, bearing a whole world of trouble.

Like the comandante, the judge was a single parent who adored her job, drank too much coffee, ate whatever was put in front of her and smoked on the sly. She never learned to cook, didn't care for it, preferring to wallow in law books and, when not working, spend time with her teenage daughter. The father was long gone. Afiuni was overweight and skimped on makeup but partly yielded to Venezuela's feminine ideal with blond highlights. A low-profile, mid-ranking jurist, she steered clear of politics and rattled through her caseloads of muggers, kidnappers and wife beaters with brisk, tough rulings. And then along came Eligio Cedeño, the hot potato that three other judges had already passed on. The point of the hearing was to pave the way for a trial, but prosecutors, as was their custom, failed to show. They assumed Afiuni would set a date for a new hearing and send the banker back to his cell. Instead, nerves jangling, she released him on bail. 'What do I do with him?' asked a puzzled bailiff. 'He's not going back,' she replied. The tycoon was free. He walked out of the court, past prosecutors in the hallway gabbing on mobile phones, hopped on a motorbike taxi and vanished into midday traffic.

Back at the courthouse, pandemonium. Prosecutors, waking up to what happened, shrieked at police to snap handcuffs on Afiuni, assuming she had been bribed. Other officers started combing the city for Cedeño. He went into hiding and surfaced two weeks later in the United States seeking political asylum. There were two possibilities. The banker had bought the judge in a prearranged plot. Or she had taken the penal code seriously and concluded it was unjust to keep holding him without trial. Whatever the truth, it swiftly vanished under the lava of rage that erupted from the palace. Rather than summon the attorney general and Supreme Court for private instruction, Chávez went on television to let everyone know what should happen. Seated in the palace in front of a Bolívar portrait and wearing a military-style blue jacket over a red T-shirt, sartorial code emphasising comandante over president, he made it clear Venezuela was looking at its sole source of authority.

'María Lourdes Afiuni made a deal,' he said, his finger stabbing at the camera. 'This bandit of a judge, a bandit, didn't say anything to any prosecutor. She sent for the prisoner, put him in the courtroom and then took him out through the back door. He escaped . . . This is worse than a murder! That judge has to pay for what she has done.' In earlier times she would have been put before a firing squad, he said. 'We have to give this judge and the people who did this the maximum sentence, thirty years in prison in the name of the dignity of this country!' He told the Supreme Court to immediately prosecute Afiuni and directed the National Assembly to pass a law deterring judges from such outrages in the future. In Kafka's dystopias, faceless bureaucracies were the instruments of persecution. For appearance' sake, Chávez usually hid behind judicial lackeys when he wanted someone arrested, ruined or exiled, but not this time.

And so María Lourdes Afiuni went to jail. Technically, of course, it was a center for the holistic attention to people deprived of their liberties, but everyone called it Los Teques women's jail. Perched on a wooded hilltop west of Caracas, it sat across the valley from the military prison which since April that year had hosted Raúl Baduel, another prisoner who had underestimated presidential vengeance. The women's facility was bursting – its population had tripled in four years – and Afiuni had convicted dozens of her fellow prisoners, some of whom vowed to drink her blood.

January 2011. Nelson Afiuni packed the last of the Tupperware into two large bags on the backseat. 'You'd think my sister might have learned to cook by now.' He shrugged and smiled. 'Nope. Heat stuff in the microwave, that's it. This should last a week.' It was a balmy Sunday morning, visiting day, and the last stretch of road to the jail was lined with pine trees and hanging plants, making the city below feel very distant. After thirteen months' incarceration Afiuni was a reluctant celebrity. Human rights activists made a rumpus over the case, ensuring she had a secluded cell away from would-be blood drinkers.

Hundreds of prisoners' relatives laden with food, medicine and contraband (chiefly cannabis, cocaine, mobile phones) queued at the entrance. It was the same curiously lax approach as at Baduel's jail, which allowed the comandante's most famous prisoners to gab to foreign media. Serious tyranny would surely instil greater diligence in its sentinels.

In Venezuela prisoners wear their own clothes, and on visiting day the women – visitors and inmates – go for glamour. Tight jeans, tight T-shirts, heels, lipstick, bangles, belly piercings. Or, if you are María Afiuni, baggy jeans, shapeless sweater, sneakers, no makeup. She was perched on her bunk toying with a BlackBerry. Prisoners were not supposed to have phones, least of all smartphones that allowed them to communicate with the outside world via Twitter. Afiuni's daily tweets had attracted tens of thousands of online followers, including the justice minister. Every so often a comment would annoy him enough that guards would search the cell and confiscate the phone, whereupon friends would smuggle in a replacement and she would resume tweeting. 'Gone through nine of these so far,' she said, stashing the phone under her bunk. The comandante had stripped her of liberty and sabotaged any chance of a fair trial but let her denounce him daily from her cell with an illicit phone. It made no sense. Afiuni nodded. 'Yep.'

The cell was small and bright, with a kettle, microwave, television, DVD player and stick under the door to keep out rodents. There were candles, a statue of the Virgin Mary, and a portrait of the archangel Michael slaying a dragon whose features bore a distinct resemblance to Hugo Chávez. 'A gift from a friend.' Rather than learn to cook – 'sorry, but I'm useless, a disaster' – she passed the time with jigsaw puzzles, movies, a stack of books and her phone. Though for her own safety she seldom went outside, conditions in the jail had shocked her. Prisoners preyed on each other for money and sex. Everything – medicine, food, mattresses, chairs, water – had to be bought or rented. Afiuni had been attacked but declined to go into details. 'I knew conditions were tough but didn't realise just how degraded. If I was back on the bench, I'd find it difficult to send any-one to jail unless the system was changed.' If she was back on the bench. The chances of that, she knew, were zero while the coman-dante was in the palace. He had invested his authority in branding Afiuni an enemy of the people and could hardly let her wear a judge's robe again.

There had been something about Chávez's anger, its caution-to-the-wind vehemence, that some interpreted as meaning he knew – knew for a fact – that Afiuni had been bought. It was plausible. So many judges tailored rulings to the highest bidder that the justice system felt like an auction. Cedeño could have offered millions. Did he? Afiuni did not take offence at the question. 'No, he didn't. I didn't volunteer for this case. And neither I nor my family ever had any con-tact with Cedeño. There was no bribe.' The voice was husky, the gaze even. Prosecutors charged Afiuni with corruption and abuse of power but after apparently finding no evidence of illicit payment accused her of 'spiritual corruption'. Her guilt or innocence would probably never be reliably established. The justice system was rotten and the case too politicised. She still had no trial date.

Afiuni sighed. She expected trouble from the Cedeño case but did not anticipate it defining her life. 'I knew it was sensitive, knew they'd be angry. I just didn't think they'd go so far as to jail me.' Voices and salsa music drifted in from the sun-drenched yard outside, where other prisoners hosted their guests, all on rented seats. The atmosphere was festive, but the judge did not dare mix with the others. Along with decapitation, she had been threatened with burning and rape. 'Chávez's instruction was that I was not to feel sunlight on my face. Well, you can see how pale I am.'

She lit another cigarette. 'I've too much time for these now. Don't tell my mom or daughter how many I get through.' Pasty, drawn and saggy, Afiuni did not look well. Within months she would be operated on for problems with her uterus, then treated for cancer. The only positive side to incarceration, she said, was seeing the justice system from the sharp end. Her neighbours included a kidnapper ('she was in love with her boyfriend, and he was in a kidnap gang, you know how it goes'), a woman who killed an abusive husband, and a corrupt ministry official who was teased by all for being possibly the only one of her kind to be caught and jailed for such a thing. Afiuni had befriended them and helped with their cases, prompting a stream of petitions from prisoners in other wings.

When she discussed her own case, her voice hardened. Career over, health failing, daughter growing up without her, fate in the hands of a capricious ruler, it all hurt. 'I'm here as the president's prisoner. I'm an example to other judges of what happens if you step out of line.' The torment was not knowing how long she would have this role, one she played, from Chávez's view, very effectively. Venezuela's judges were so terrified that they did not dare join the international outcry at their colleague's arrest, nor visit her. For the first time Afiuni, who as a girl watched television courtroom dramas and idealised judges, sounded bitter. These were friends, peers, people she had mentored, looked up to, lunched with, congratulated on their birthdays. And they all turned their backs. 'Occasionally, I get a message that so-and-so sends commiserations but they're afraid to speak out. That makes them cowards and accomplices.' She was about to say more, expound on the betrayal, then shook her head. It was too raw. Later, visiting time over, Afiuni folded the chairs, hugged her brother and closed the door of her cell. The pasta, he said to the disappearing figure, was in the square Tupperware.

A fiuni's case marked a point where even the comandante's most exalted intellectual champion would not follow. For a decade Noam Chomsky, the feted scourge of capitalism, had lauded the revolution as a beacon and counterweight to U.S. imperialism. The passion was reciprocated. Chávez had turned one of Chomsky's books, *Hegemony or Survival: America's Quest for Global Dominance,* into a bestseller after brandishing it during a UN speech in 2006. Three years later he hosted the professor with pomp and bear hugs in Caracas. The man voted the world's top public intellectual by *Prospect* magazine said Venezuela was taking steps toward a better world. The comandante mischievously suggested Washington could repair diplomatic ties by making him ambassador to Caracas.

But by 2010, Chomsky, from his home near the Massachusetts Institute of Technology, where he taught linguistics, had become uneasy. As a self-described libertarian socialist, he was suspicious of state authority, and the comandante was amassing ever more of it. Some other academics in the United States, Europe and Latin America who had previously defended the comandante were feeling the same way. They confided misgivings in private but not in public, fearing accusations of betrayal from one side, naïveté from the other. So they remained silent. Chomsky had winced when Chávez centralised more powers and used enabling laws, but it was the Afiuni case that tipped him over the edge. Human rights activists at Harvard's Carr Center relayed details of her plight. Alarmed by her cancer, authorities in February 2011 softened her confinement to house arrest but proceeded with the case. Chomsky wrote a private letter to Chávez requesting clemency. When there was no reply, he wrote an open letter in July 2011 lamenting 'cruelty' and 'degrading treatment' that had violated the Bolivarian revolution's principles. 'In times of worldwide cries for freedom, the detention of María Lourdes Afiuni stands out as a glaring exception that should be remedied quickly, for the sake of justice and human rights generally and for affirming an honourable role for Venezuela in these struggles.'

It was a stinging rebuke from Chávez's cerebral champion, and worse was to come. In a telephone interview after the letter, Chomsky, the croaky voice weighing each word, circumlocuted his way into calling the comandante an authoritarian caudillo. 'Well, it's obviously improper for the executive to intervene and impose a jail sentence without a trial. I'm sceptical that [Afiuni] could receive a fair trial. It's striking that, as far as I understand, other judges have not come out in support of her . . . That suggests an atmosphere of intimidation.' The professor praised Venezuela for standing up to U.S. bullying and championing regional integration and voiced continued hope that revolution was a step toward a better world. He was not going to explicitly denounce his ardent friend. But he returned, crablike, to the comandante's waywardness. 'Anywhere in Latin America there is a potential threat of the pathology of caudillismo, and it has to be guarded against. Whether it's over too far in that direction in Venezuela I'm not sure, but I think perhaps it is. Concentration of executive power, unless it's very temporary and for specific circumstances, such as fighting World War II, is an assault on democracy. You can debate whether [Venezuela's] circumstances require it: internal circumstances and the external threat of attack, that's a legitimate debate. But my own judgment in that debate is that it does not.' It was not pithy or direct and would not fit on a tombstone, but in his roundabout, halting way the revolution's greatest defender had declared an epitaph for the Great National Moral and Illuminating Journey.

11

PROTEST

Luis Blanco spent his life guarding money and power without ever having any of his own. He was a security guard at an apartment block in Altamira, one of Caracas's nicer areas, and inhabited a cramped cubicle by an electronic gate that he opened and shut with a white button on his desk. His job was to monitor visitors, take packages and jot down in a folder the comings and goings of vehicles, one shinier and bigger than the other. Luis took pride in his work, keeping impeccable notes, and always wore crisp white shirts. Tall, slender, with silver hair parted at the side, he had a distinguished countenance that could have belonged to a patrician banker. When he was outside the cubicle, visitors at times mistook him for a resident and addressed him with the formal 'usted'. At this Luis would smile, and the illusion would dissolve because wide gaps separated his teeth. The visitors, embarrassed, would belatedly notice the worn shoes and the building's name on his shirt and automatically, with a seamless mental click, address him with the familiar 'tú'. Luis, still smiling, would reply, addressing them as 'usted'.

The cubicle was his realm, and he made the best of it, scrubbing the seat-less toilet in a microscopic bathroom whose door never closed properly, storing Tupperware meals of rice and beans out of sight, stacking packages in neat piles, letters in alphabetical order. Some nights he would lay a thin mattress on the floor and curl in a fetal position, barely fitting in the space, to steal a few hours' sleep. His one vice was alcohol. A few times a year he would drink too much and weave out to halt a resident, exclaim on the beauty of the day and heartily wish him or her all the health in the world. But mostly he stayed in his hut, a spectral presence opening and closing the gate to cars with tinted windows.

Many residents, however, did not trust him. It was not personal; they barely spoke to or knew him. It was, from their viewpoint, simply common sense. As a *vigilante,* the local name for a security guard, Luis was by definition poor, underpaid and in a position to sell information to thieves and kidnappers. Such cases were widespread. Keep your distance, neighbors advised. Don't tell him anything.

Luis was born in 1956, two years before Pérez Jiménez fled the palace and Venezuela won democracy, to a lower-middle-class family in El Valle, a poor hillside neighborhood. After his father absconded, the family struggled, but Luis, starting as a messenger, worked his way up to being a junior clerk in a bank. After the bank tripped along with Venezuela's economy in the 1980s, Luis's fortunes declined, and he worked in restaurant kitchens. In 1998, the year Chávez was elected, he got the security guard job in the apartment block and stayed. As it happened, Chávez's election opponent Irene Sáez, a politician and former Miss Universe, lived in the building. Though younger than Luis, she jokingly referred to him as her son.

Luis was not offended, smiled his crooked smile, but voted for Chávez. Because finally here was hope. A leader who understood the struggles and humiliations of the barrios.

Luis installed a tiny television in the cubicle and watched, mesmerised, the revolution take form. The 1999 constitution, the 2004 recall referendum, the social missions, the episodes of *Hello, President,* the comandante's 2006 reelection, the 2009 referendum abolishing term limits. He cheered it all and revered 'mi comandante'. His commitment to the revolution survived evidence of corruption – government officials bought apartments with cash and moved into the building, army officers 'borrowed' Ferraris from a dealership to race up and down the avenue in front of his cubicle – and cruel, personal blows. In July 2010 his police officer son was beaten, throttled and killed by escaping prisoners who had help, it seemed, from other officers. Three months later thieves shot Luis's twenty-year-old grandson for his motorbike. Untreated for seventeen hours (local clinics weren't working), he went into a coma and died. Luis's heart cracked, and the smile was never quite the same; there was hesitation, a forcedness. But if something died in him, it was not faith in the revolution, which only grew stronger. And here was the nub. Because of Chávez, Luis felt empowered. At work he was nobody, one of a million anonymous, barely acknowledged security guards. But back in El Valle he was part of the revolution, an active and respected member of the communal council. A man whose opinion mattered, who was politely but firmly buttonholed in the street by neighbors and asked to consider this, resolve that. He would scribble the petitions in a notebook and smile. Of course! He would raise it at council. They would shake his hand, suddenly hopeful. Thank you, Luis!

Early attempts at people power such as the Bolivarian Circles and electoral battalions, platoons and squadrons had faded after Chávez lost interest, but from 2005 he had invested laws and billions of dollars in the communal councils, calling them the revolution's most important motor, a 'new geometry of power' to deepen social-ism and advance development, leading to a communal state. Each was to be formed by a citizens' assembly of two hundred to four hundred families that shared a common history and geography. The assembly would identify work committees for the council dedicated to particu-lar issues – housing, water, electricity, food, sports, media relations – and elect delegates from each committee to the council's executive. In addition, it would elect administrators, treasurers and comptrol-lers. Councils had power to audit public administration, from hospi-tals to ministries, making the state truly accountable. Resources were redirected from mayors and state governors – legacies of discredited representative democracy – to these 'explosions of popular will'. By 2010 there were around thirty-one thousand councils nationwide.

February 2011. The inauguration ceremony of Luis's new neigh-borhood council. Steep slopes, potholes, slab concrete, grilled win-dows and satellite dishes abounded. A man on a motorbike roared by doing wheelies. Others huddled in doorways sipping beer. It was 11:00 a.m. Luis was anxious to make a good impression. 'We are all patriots here.' He pointed out a house at the end of the street. 'The government built that. A fine job.' It had been a long struggle to reach this day, he confided. Previous councils faltered, he said, with-out elaborating, but stalwarts had regrouped for this new attempt. 'Compatriots, comrades, there you are!' A dozen or so women in red T-shirts assembled chairs on a basketball court and passed around papaya juice. Luis, lean and strong for his years, hauled tables to the court. Alí Primera, a left-wing activist and troubadour who died in the 1980s, sang from speakers.

No, no, no, enough praying
many things are needed
to achieve peace . . .
Nothing can be achieved
if there is no revolution . . .
no, no, no, enough praying.

It felt festive, but the women were agitated. The mayor's office had failed to deliver an awning, so the ceremony would boil in midday sun. 'I'm completely committed to this process, given everything to it, and they can't even lend us a fucking tent for a few hours.' Worse, only half of the committee had shown up. Grumbles tumbled out. 'Previous councils collapsed after members disappeared with the money,' María Hernández, a young mother, said with a sigh. 'That happens a lot.' As a result, the state bank that distributed funds had become very cautious and bureaucratic, demanding endless paperwork that drained time and energy, said another woman. 'People get fed up, drift away. Carneiro really screwed this up.' Luis returned to the conversation. 'It's difficult persuading people to get involved in politics,' he said, a touch defensive, 'but here we are today, making a fresh start.' The women nodded, not wishing to dispute this. 'You know,' continued Luis, seeking a brighter topic, 'Carneiro helped get all this started.' General Jorge Luis García Carneiro. El Valle was proud of this local hero who was head of the army, then defence minister, then minister for social development and popular participation, in which role he sponsored the councils. Yet Raúl Baduel, in his prison interview, said Chávez moved García Carneiro from defence to punish him for allegedly seeking a $20 million bribe in a Russian arms deal. It was an unsubstantiated claim that prosecutors did not pursue. García Carneiro's new fiefdom, the governorship of Vargas state, was a cesspit of corruption and misrule that has left many survivors from the 1999 mudslides still homeless.

Two hours late the inauguration ceremony got under way. Half the committee was still missing, and those who did turn up wilted in the furnacelike heat. The guest of honour was Jesús Farías, a National Assembly member and son of a well-known Communist Party figure. Farías, who studied economics in Germany, was tall and pale-skinned and wore a baseball cap and an expensive, hiker-style red shirt with breathable fabric. The rhetoric soared over the sweating congregation on the chipped, weedy basketball court. 'We are branches on a tree with a mighty trunk. We are advancing, consolidating. Because now' – a pause, so everyone redoubled efforts to squint through the glare – 'now the people are in power. The people are power!' Farías waited for the applause to subside. 'Let us pray for our children, our revolution and Comandante Chávez. Let us swear an oath: fatherland, socialism or death! Remember, you are our hope!'

Everyone stood and cheered, and for a moment the disappointments, the heat and the cracked surroundings were forgotten. The words lingered in the air. We are the power. The hope. Council members queued to receive beige certificates. Luis, a popular figure, was singled out for praise. 'With Luis we are going to build the country Bolívar dreamed of.' He stared at his shoes, blushing with pride. Farías signalled an aide to fetch something from his car. A surprise gift for the new council. Members murmured in anticipation and resumed their seats. All eyes on a black bag as it was passed to Farías. He cleared his throat.

'In the name of the revolution I give you this basketball.'

How to define the silence that followed? Everybody stared at the orange sphere. Farías gazed back. Droplets of sweat pooled under his chin. Luis rose to his feet and clapped. The rest joined in, reluctant, ragged applause, still in their seats. The guest of honour smiled – or was it a wince? – and headed to his car. The ceremony was over.

A cross Venezuela many councils breathed life into grassroots government: planting trees in plazas, distributing subsidised food, fixing houses and roads, liaising with government agencies. Useful, practical empowerment. Chávez called them the revolution's most important motor.

On paper the idea was promising. Popular will and energy would complement and eventually replace traditional local government to realise a direct democracy dreamed of since Rousseau. Unlike other initiatives that fell by the wayside, the comandante persisted with the councils after their launch in 2005, calling them the 'socialist restructuring of the geopolitics of the nation'. He drew elaborate flowcharts depicting society and state with multiple arrows, representing power, converging on a pyramid that represented the councils. Chávez would, of course, keep control by tying council purse strings to the palace. And by weakening mayors and governors, the councils could in fact bolster central executive authority. Nevertheless, it was a bold experiment in devolution.

After a fitful start – the 2006 presidential election, 2007 referendum and 2008 regional elections distracted the palace – the councils multiplied and by 2009 were officially a great success. State television showed a nationwide blossoming in a weekly programme called *Constructing Republic* that opened with an upbeat jingle and scudding fluffy clouds in a blue sky before reporting on councils taking charge, tackling problems and asserting the new geometry of power.

F ebruary 2010. After the main news of the day – the comandante expropriating jewellery shops at Caracas's Plaza Bolívar – it was time for *Constructing Republic*. The jingle and opening credits faded to reveal soaring mango trees, dappled sunlight and a courtyard with about two dozen men and women seated in a circle. Casually but neatly dressed in jeans and polo shirts, dark brown skin, on the hefty side and squeezed into the plastic chairs. Typical Venezuelans from the coast, in other words, and not the type you usually saw on private television channels that recoiled from crooked teeth and imperfect bodies, especially dark ones, and filled programmes with pale, cosmetically enhanced beauties.

'Strengthening Popular Power in Morón,' said the legend at the bottom of the screen. Morón was an impoverished crossroads of shantytowns and truck stops near the country's biggest port, Puerto Cabello. An ugly dump that travellers sped through en route to somewhere better. Runaway slaves found sanctuary here in the seventeenth century, and it was as if the state never forgave the place. It had fallen through the cracks of successive national, regional and local governments. Right into the 1990s there were families living barefoot without electricity or running water. An oil refinery and petrochemical plant brought pollution but few jobs for locals; workers lived in compounds and came into town for alcohol and sex. Morón's nickname was Mojón, meaning turd.

And now here it was on state television showing a swept courtyard, verdant garden and civic determination. It was straight to business. 'Welcome,' said the moderator, Josefa Riera, a grandmotherly black woman with spectacles perched on the end of her nose. 'We are here at a gathering of communal councils to discuss their achievements, projects, visions and missions and their objectives to develop their communities. We give the word first to Eligio Monsalve from Las Colinas.' The microphone was passed around so everybody got to talk. At the end everybody agreed the solution to development was greater consciousness. And coordination. Consciousness and coordination. The words were written and underlined. The moderator thanked everybody for their contributions, they all clapped and the credits rolled.

It was not, it must be said, exciting television. Nobody argued or challenged a point or told a story, and the cameras never left the courtyard, so Morón itself remained invisible. But so what? A revolution cannot always march and sing. To transform the material world, it must stop and sit and haggle over a million little things. With Chávez there was so much thunder – soon after this programme he was at a summit denouncing British occupation of the Falkland/ Malvinas Islands – that it could have been refreshing to listen to ordinary people discuss, without drums and cymbals, an experiment in direct democracy.

In the 2006 presidential election Morón voted overwhelmingly for the comandante. He erected billboards saying 'Gracias, Morón, 81.46%' and renamed the motorway after Cimarrón Andresote, leader of a slave revolt and symbol of resistance. The first councils, formed here the same year, invoked the seven gifts of the Holy Spirit, a scripture reference, for the good to come: continuous consultation with the community, mobile committee meetings, monitoring of public services, crime prevention, agricultural development, working with state ventures, especially the port, Puerto Cabello, and Pequiven, a petrochemical plant, to create jobs and infrastructure.

By the time of the February 2010 broadcast the town was restless. Seven gifts. What about just one or two? Patience, pleaded the councils, we are working hard. Their members were drained by feuding over the mayor, Matson Caldera. In theory, councils were separate from municipal authority, but Caldera, a member of the comandante's socialist party, had a caudillo's cunning. He paid lip service to the councils' revolutionary transcendence and autonomy but muscled in, planting supporters and relatives in council posts, swallowing their funding and expanding a web of nepotism and patronage that muzzled dissent with jobs and money. The mayor's image and name were plastered and invoked all over town, a micro personality cult.

The comandante had warned against meddling by mayors and governors, but palace officials were too distracted by rotating ministers and organisational changes to enforce it. In any case, the comandante contradicted his anti-meddling warning by ordering councils to campaign for mayors and governors in local elections. Fighting elections and referenda sapped Morón's council members. Already overloaded with meetings, they lacked time for their regular jobs and families. Attendance dwindled. Those who remained felt depleted. Suspicions grew that some members were making secret deals with private businesses. Others were accused of pocketing funds, including some of those featured in the televised mango tree assembly. They all denied wrongdoing, and none were charged. In February 2011, a year after the broadcast (and the same month El Valle received its basketball), Morón's enraged council members stormed the town hall and accused the mayor of smears and corruption. He rejected the accusations and branded them terrorists. The police and courts were too clogged with murders and kidnappings to investigate, so the feuding lingered, unresolved, destroying trust.

Morón's infighting left the town leaderless amid mounting economic and social problems: overcrowded schools, dilapidated clinics, a crumbling motorway, an unfinished, abandoned railway, weeklong power blackouts, monthlong water shortages. Some farmers were ruined because a little bridge, their sole route to market, collapsed and was not rebuilt, others because the government flooded markets with cheap, imported food in the hope of capping inflation. The petrochemical plant, Pequiven, could not offer jobs and grants, because it was buckling from blackouts, strikes and management upheaval (the comandante fired its president supposedly because he raised prices, 'a capitalist act'). Puerto Cabello, the country's biggest port, could not help, because it was tangled in its own problems: a scandal over containers of rotting food and fallout from the arrest of Walid Makled, the drug lord who had run much of the port.

The government tried to wish away the brewing tempest with a pretence of progress. Billboards showed the comandante in a white lab coat or builder's hat smiling and saluting over slogans. 'Technological development!' 'Made in socialism!' The colours quickly bleached in the tropical sun. Local radio, now mostly in state hands, did its bit with cheerful jingles and stories. 'Don't miss the exhibit of Chinese bulldozers,' enthused one news broadcaster. 'They are on display for two days before starting work on the motorway, fortifying the revolution.' Massaged statistics that classified the hordes of impoverished street vendors as gainfully employed were hailed as triumphs.

Morón's patience snapped. Where traditional authorities had failed, now so too were communal councils. State propaganda made the disappointment only more bitter. Neighbourhoods started daubing grievances on banners and marching out of their slums, chanting and waving fists. Morón's demands were not political. They did not seek insurrection, only water, electricity, jobs, roads. They ratcheted up the stakes by blocking roads.

A human rights advocacy group, PROVEA, counted 1,763 demonstrations nationwide in 2008, jumping to 3,297 in 2009, hovering at 3,114 in 2010, and approaching 4,000 in 2011. The situation room beneath the comandante's office, his eyes ears, and tactical command center, monitored about ten protests daily. For protest leaders the objective was simple: create enough havoc – *bululú* in local slang – so palace watchdogs felt compelled to act, to dispatch negotiators, fire a governor, throw money at a mayor, redirect a motorway, whatever it took to defuse the demonstration. Competition drove escalation because so many towns' hopes had turned to ash. The situation room did not tackle every eruption, only the most disruptive, so as protests multiplied, they competed for attention. Whoever caused the most aggravation won.

In this contest Morón had a competitive advantage. Two motorways fused in the town, a femoral artery linking western, eastern and central Venezuela. Cut it and the economy hemorrhaged. So communities took turns marching down to the highway to block traffic. It was easy. A few dozen people, some placards, tires, lighter fluid, and, presto, government attention. Sometimes they did not even bother burning tires. It was enough to link arms across the four-lane highway. A monstrous traffic jam would form trapping thousands of trucks, buses and cars in a honking, impotent, sweltering fury.

The meagre road infrastructure meant there was no alternative route, no escape. Side roads led to nowhere via marshes and rocky wildernesses. Turning to the radio for information was futile since the dial was dominated by state and pro-government 'community' channels that either ignored the mayhem ('after the break, details of the Alba summit') or gave curt, useless reports accusing protest leaders of sabotage. In such circumstances Twitter became the best and sometimes only source of information, simultaneously acting like a nerve impulse to the palace, jolting the situation room into action.

Protests did not always work. Sometimes police broke up the barricades, or officials sent protesters home with false promises. But the tactic was successful enough to be imitated. Unpaid wages, unpaved roads, leaking roofs, stale school meals – to the motorway! Petrochemical workers formed their blockade beneath a billboard illustrated with a photograph from the comandante's last visit to the plant. 'Advancing with Pequiven!'

One blockade in September 2011 – parts of Morón had been without electricity for weeks – continued into the night, unleashing criminal gangs against stricken motorists. After robbing wallets, phones and jewellery, they started looting trucks en route from the port. The protesters – men, women, and children – joined in like an ant army, prying open containers, smashing windows and heaving away televisions, tinned tuna, cooking oil, furniture. The air turned festive. 'Merry Christmas!' Two barefoot men slung a squealing pig between them and roared off on a motorbike. The free-for-all lasted until dawn.

A lmost anywhere else authorities would have broken up blockades that were illegal and caused havoc, but in the comandante's realm they were largely tolerated. The police and the national guard were seldom deployed, and the few protesters who were detained were swiftly released. It was odd. Why would an otherwise authoritarian regime use a slipper when a bit of jackboot would, for once, have been widely considered legitimate? Partly because tear-gassing demonstrators would have violated the comandante's image as the great benefactor. He dated his movement to the 1989 Caracas riots against economic austerity and did not want people saying the pendulum had swung.

The main reason, however, was that the protests did not directly threaten him. It was the strangest thing. A resentful, frustrated populace staging thousands of little insurrections – and the palace, calm. Rulers from Nebuchadnezzar to Mubarak feared such unrest because they knew a brook trickling down a mountain could meet other brooks, gather volume and become a mighty river roaring toward the throne. Such a surge helped sweep away the comandante in the 2002 coup, but now, almost a decade later, he did not panic. The protests were a dispiriting panorama, true, but divide and rule kept them ephemeral, glistening flashes.

Protesters, after all, were not starving waifs. On the contrary, many were chubby and, according to statistics, consuming more protein and sugar than ever before. Average real incomes had soared from 2003 to 2008, dipped during the recession and then recovered from 2011. Gasoline was free, and government shops, for those with patience to queue, still supplied heavily subsidised groceries. Crime, crumbling public services, and the paucity of decent jobs stoked frustration but not collective action. Oil revenues and loans from China generated enough cash to buy off protests. Even when strikes spread to nurses, teachers, students, farmers, pharmacists, civil servants, bus drivers, subway workers, doctors and police, there were enough petro-dollars to stuff in their pockets and send them, grumbling that it was not enough, back to work. As long as protests remained atomised, the palace was safe.

S tate television seldom mentioned the unrest – making occasional exceptions to brand some leaders as coup plotters – so there was little media echo. It was as if the body politic had measles, irritating, fleeting blotches, but that the comandante himself was vaccinated. After all he was the great sponsor of people power, pay raises and public works, spending hours with maps and diagrams explaining the details. If subsequently the promises failed to materialise, that was the fault of ministers, managers and communal council leaders, fools and knaves who betrayed the comandante. This magical thinking became encapsulated in a slogan that appeared and multiplied throughout 2011. 'Viva Chávez, abajo el gobierno.' Long live Chávez, down with the government.

Some only professed to believe it. They still wore red and shouted revolutionary slogans but hinted at heresy. Aporrea, a pro-government Web site and sounding board, glinted with exasperation. 'Comrade President, you must tone down the populist discourse a bit and rapidly tackle corruption in the communal councils, Fundacomunal [a funding agency] and the Ministry of Communes. The decision is in your hands. The disappointment in the communities is enormous, and every day we are losing people. We cannot create socialism while such incompetence and corruption exists.' Others, in whispers, dropped the charade.

Let us call one of them Rodolfo, an unshaven, exhausted, laid-off oil worker from Maracaibo camping with colleagues outside the National Assembly in Caracas. They had been there for three weeks seeking jobs. In private Rodolfo called the president an architect of fiasco, a charlatan. He scoffed at the banners tied to railings that proclaimed his group 'revolucionarios' and 'ultra-Chavistas'. Theatrical props, he said. When a television camera appeared, Rodolfo broke into a loud, urgent voice to say the comandante was being deceived. Once Chávez knew the truth, he would surely reinstate the comrades. 'The comandante will save us.' To directly accuse Chávez meant expulsion from the 'process', losing benefits and rights, or hope of benefits and rights, so the sceptical, the disillusioned and the outright nonbelievers forked their tongues. They would preface every criticism with 'Yo soy Chavista.' I'm Chavista. It was calculation, not cowardice. In the absence of a credible, united opposition, there was no alternative to Chávez. Revolution was the only game worth playing.

The multiplying protests of 2011 did not threaten the palace. Divide and rule neutralised their potency. But by exposing the failure of many communal councils, they cost the comandante something precious. This should have been his glory year, an apogee of laurels and vindication, because economic crisis exposed deep discontent in the West. Alienated voters occupied Wall Street, rioted in Athens and London, marched through Madrid and Paris. They called themselves the 99 per cent and demanded curbs on the ultra-rich 1 per cent, who, they said, had usurped capitalism and liberal democracy.

Imagine the comandante's excitement. He had long warned capitalism was in crisis and liberal democracy a con by greedy elites. Look to Venezuela, he cried, look how we are forging real democracy, new geometry. A radical experiment with lots of money guided by an elected, charismatic rebel, why not? It could have become a beacon and drawn attention, envious comparisons, praise. If this fantasy played out in the comandante's head, imagine the crushing disappointment when the real world proved indifferent. Crime, economic atrophy and the multiple protests rendered the Chávez model toxic. No acclaim rang in his ears, no wisdom seekers queued outside the palace. In this moment of intense global yearning for another way, he was shunned even by those who had cheered him in earlier times. They flew over Venezuela ignoring the figure on the balcony of Miraflores waving like a shipwrecked sailor. Down here. Look down here. Newly elected left-wing presidents such as Ollanta Humala in Peru, Mauricio Funes in El Salvador, and José Mujica in Uruguay, obvious potential allies, steered clear as if he had the pox and instead invoked Brazil's former president Luiz Inácio Lula da Silva and his apparently magic formula of easing poverty through government programs, a market economy, and traditional representative democracy. Foreign leaders still visited Caracas for summits and oil deals, and many still had personal affection for the comandante, but none sought to emulate him. 'The Chávez of 2006 is nothing compared with the Chávez of 2011. He made a series of errors,' Yehude Simon, Peru's former prime minister, told journalists.

Such criticism remained unheard in the palace. Even as many communal councils faltered, and with them the conceit that Chávez was delivering power to the people, nobody spoke out. The generals, of course, were handpicked loyalists and for good measure allowed to stuff their pockets. The opportunists bobbed along, playing dumb. But what of the third faction, the coalition of progressives, feminists, labour leaders and indigenous rights activists? They had come of age politically in the 1980s and fused into a movement in the 1990s. When Chávez emerged from jail in 1994, he had fame from his coup attempt but no money, no organisation, no political experience. He swept to the palace four years later largely because he was adopted by this coalition. It comprised thousands of dynamic individuals with passionate democratic convictions. What happened to them?

A single smashing of revolutionary ideals would have been traumatic and triggered an exodus, but incremental chiselling permitted exculpations. If the comandante overruled party grass roots to impose candidates, well, there was strategic need. If he ignored evidence of corruption, well, the timing was delicate. Chip, chip, chip at principles until all that was left was Chávez. By 2011 a few progressives had trickled away, but the rest bowed their heads and stayed. You found them behind ministry desks, at party offices and in state-backed organisations, some still with the bandannas, T-shirts and slogans of their activist days. Mother Earth. Power to the people. Disarm patriarchy. Workers of the world, unite. Human rights correct human wrongs. These were the mid-rankers who administered funding requests for Luis Blanco's communal council, moved Morón up and down the list of priorities, studied oil pollution in the Faja.

Back in their activist days, they were united in vocal passion. Now in power, they shared stifled silences. Environmentalists said nothing about pipelines through wildlife reserves or the gasoline subsidy. Feminists bit their lips when Chávez belittled female opponents with sexist remarks (he said he would not sleep with Condoleezza Rice even if it was for the fatherland) and leered at the camera to tell his then wife, 'Prepare yourself, Marisabel, you're going to get yours tonight.' Trade unionists held their tongues when collective contracts expired and strikes were criminalised. Radicals lost their voice when Chávez, during thaws with Colombia, took responsibility for extraditing suspected guerrillas without due process.

If power corrupts and absolute power corrupts absolutely, what of those who did not wield power but merely hovered around it, inhaled it – were they contaminated? The coalition of progressives, after all, had possessed an integrity alien to the kleptocratic generals and boligarchs. Some stayed simply to keep their jobs. The salaries and perks were not extravagant, merely comfortable, and that was enough to breed inertia. A job supplies identity, routine and security. Yank it away and the void beckons. That is why so many bureaucracies, movements and empires survive so long. The comandante understood this and so multiplied ministries, agencies, missions, councils, cooperatives. As economic waves swamped the private sector, those inside the ship of state clutched their sinecures all the more tightly. Some retained shreds of idealism and would pluck excerpts from the comandante's speeches. 'See! He still backs labour rights.' Others surrendered to cynicism. 'It's all bullshit. They ignore all my recommendations, but there's nowhere else to go.' This was from an engineer, Isabel, who did environmental impact reports for the state oil company. She would vent her fury to me while pedalling in a gym, her fury growing as she accelerated and reddened. When she described the pro-government marches she was forced to attend, the pedals would become a blur. '¡Malditos! ¡Desgraciados!' Servants of true tyranny could at least tell themselves they had no choice, they were following orders. Chávez's bloodless rule denied the excuse of physical fear. Disobedience meant maybe losing their jobs, not their heads. A plastic sword, and still they kneeled.

12

THE ILLUSIONIST

In the spring of 2011 the comandante's superhuman energy faltered. He lost his appetite, tired easily and complained of aches. His knee throbbed so much he had trouble walking and had to use a crutch. He waved it at cameras, made a joke, then vanished from public view. May gave way to June, a time of intense heat and sudden, violent downpours that burst gutters and flooded streets. Chávez was nowhere to be seen. Presenters on state media, bereft of cues from the palace, hesitated. How to opine on a topic without knowing the comandante's view?

A rumour that he was seriously ill wafted across Caracas like a zephyr, a whisper of unknown provenance. Most people scoffed. The man was indestructible. A human tornado. And still only fifty-six years old, three decades younger than the eternal Fidel. When Chávez still did not surface the rumour gusted stronger. Ministers called it a lie, a vile fabrication. Then, in early June, the government announced he had a pelvic abscess and would be operated on in

Havana. One word galed across Venezuela. Cancer. The government flailed its arms, tried to beat back the notion. 'The only thing that has metastasized is the cancer of the right-wing media,' said the vice foreign minister, Temir Porras. Eva Golinger, the comandante's American champion, scorned the 'wild myths' and 'frenzied orgy of fictitious stories' about cancer.

And then, on a humid evening on the last day of June, Chávez surfaced in a grainy broadcast from Havana. Looking ashen and subdued, speaking from a script – who could remember him ever using a script? – he said Cuban doctors had diagnosed 'cancerous cells' and removed a tumour from his pelvic area. He asked for God's help. 'This [is] the new battle that life has placed before us. I neglected my health and I was reluctant to have medical checkups. It was a fundamental mistake for a revolutionary.' He cleared his throat, looked up at the camera, resumed reading. This moment, he said, reminded him of the dark hours of the 2002 coup. 'Then, also, I sent to my beloved Venezuelan people that message, written from the Turiamo naval base, where I was held prisoner, an overthrown and imprisoned president. It was a cry of pain, from the bottom of another abyss that I felt swallowed me in its thrall and sunk me.' He said he was starting a long road of treatment. For the first time anyone could remember, the comandante looked frightened.

A clap of thunder rolled across Venezuela. Disbelief and shock on both sides. A trick, he's faking, said opponents, but their eyes shone with excitement. It's not what it seems; there's a plan, a strategy, cried allies. The idea that there was no Plan B, that disease had outflanked the situation room, and that initiative lay not with the comandante but with his malady left both sides bewildered. Now what do we do?

Days later, with the country wondering if he would ever come back, a plane landed at Caracas airport and to everyone's astonishment the president emerged, smiling. He hugged ministers, sang a song and raised a fist in triumph. 'It is the beginning of my return!' Later that day he appeared on the palace balcony to address euphoric supporters below. 'We will win this battle for life.' He had begun treatment and would fully recover, he said. Venezuela digested this claim uncertainly. Weeks passed, clammy with rumour. Salvador Navarette, a Venezuelan doctor who had previously treated the president and his family, told a journalist, Victor Flores, that the cancer was terminal and that Chávez would die within two years. The article triggered uproar. Men from the intelligence agency Sebin swooped on Navarette's clinic in Caracas. He fled to Spain. The government said the doctor was a traitor and a liar. It held a press conference with three other doctors, wearing white coats, to reassure the nation. No, they could not specify the type of cancer, nor its location, those were state secrets. But the prognosis was excellent. The comandante would be fine. The comandante would live.

It seemed an age since a human river had swept the country's youngest-ever president into Miraflores in 1999. It was easy to forget that as a candidate he had once said if elected, he would serve only one term. With each victory the horizon extended. I will stay until 2012, he bellowed to rallies. Then it became 2021, then 2030, then 2050. It was a return to the caudillo tradition after an interregnum of liberal democracy, the so-called Fourth Republic, which for all its warts had established peaceful alternations of power. Chávez cast himself as an artist with a brush, beholding the revolution's unfinished canvas. His multiple personas – painter, singer, poet, horseman, warrior, father, teacher, thinker, leader – projected the idea he was indispensable, a philosopher king. 'Nietzsche says the most beautiful thing about man is that he isn't an end but a bridge between the animal and the "superman", the "ultra-man",' he once said. 'I'm quoting Nietzsche and also expressing my agreement with those maxims of philosophy and life: to transform the world.'

Courtiers greeted such musings with reverence but it was easy to conclude Chávez had spent too long under a blazing sun on the palace terrace. The British writer Christopher Hitchens published an account of a conversation with Chávez in which the president doubted the existence of al-Qaida and the NASA moon landings, saying Yankee television trickery could fake anything. The impression he was out of touch deepened when Arabs rose up in the spring of 2011. Instead of hailing popular revolts against oppression and stagnation, or even claiming to have inspired them, Chávez accused the rebels of being Western-backed terrorists and defended cronies like Gadhafi and Assad. Before, because he lambasted the US and Israel, Arabs chanted his name with joy. No longer.

So accustomed to seeing his opinions reflected in state media, his personal projector, the president brooked no contradiction even from physical surroundings. He would invite foreign journalists to the palace to extol the revolution's latest advances, heedless that the building itself betrayed him: a peeling, cracking facade, broken window frames, missing roof tiles, garden balconies reeking of urine. Other Latin American presidential palaces were impeccable, even those of much poorer countries, but Miraflores suffered the same neglect and shoddy work that plagued the nation's infrastructure. A minister confided that rain leaked into the comandante's private lift. Palace employees privately grumbled about unpaid overtime and slashed benefits. And yet Chávez would bask in camera lights and describe shiny developments and strategic victories.

A true dictator always risks sliding into a fantasy realm, his wishful thinking echoed by sycophants. When reality intrudes – a mob at the gates, insurrection – it is usually too late. Chávez was no dictator. He remained a hybrid, an elected autocrat, and this saved him. Elections tethered him to reality, yanked him from the precipice. In the urgency of campaign the muddled philosopher found focus, became a shrewd cruncher of reports and polls: Ratings holding up in Vargas, good. But dipping in Lara. Why? What's going on? He would demand statistics and back copies of local newspapers, summon mayors. Woe to them if they dissembled because his political antennae hummed with instinct and experience. When a new social mission advertised information help lines in the local press, Chávez personally phoned each one to check they were working; they were not, and he roasted the officials responsible. He governed with caprice, but when it came to courting votes he was realistic, unsentimental and utterly professional.

By autumn 2011 the palace looked ahead to the October 2012 presidential election with alarm. Chávez was gravely debilitated. Soon after his ebullient homecoming he had rushed back to Havana for more surgery, followed by chemotherapy. He insisted he was recovering but refused to release medical records, creating a nation of amateur oncologists, all speculating whether the malignant cells in his abdomen had been tamed or w re dividing and growing uncontrollably, murdering their host. In ie unaccustomed silence, with no presidential tirades or ballads or schemes filling the airwaves, it was harder to disguise that the revolution was failing, its great projects stalled, factories rusting, fields withering. Venezuela exported the only thing it could, oil, now accounting for 96 per cent of export earnings compared with 80 per cent a decade earlier. The bolivar – which he had renamed the 'strong bolivar' – had lost 90 per cent of its value against other currencies. With the economy dysfunctional and crime rampant doctors, dentists, engineers, accountants, architects, scientists and artists emigrated. Hundreds of thousands left, Venezuela's first diaspora, scattered on a desolate wind.

Time weighed heavily in Miraflores. In previous presidential elections, of 1998, 2000, 2006, Chávez had proclaimed new eras, but the years piled up and now he owned the past, his decisions etched in consequence. And how to invoke the future, his traditional refuge, when the body of reinforced concrete was cracking?

The opposition sensed its moment. Setting aside squabbles, it formed a coalition, the Democratic Unity Roundtable, and held an election to choose a candidate. Three million people voted, a record for a primary. The winner was Henrique Capriles Radonski, an intense, ambitious man with a runner's wiry physique. Just thirty-nine years old, he had served as a legislator and mayor before ousting Diosdado Cabello, the comandante's chief fixer, as governor of Miranda state in 2008. A wealthy bachelor, he dated models and scooted around town on a motorbike. Capriles billed himself as a centrist who would woo disillusioned Chavistas by promising to reboot faltering social programmes. 'I've never lost an election,' he told followers. 'We can do this.'

A decaying revolution, a ravaged body, a vigorous challenger: Chávez was in trouble. Thirteen years earlier, after accompanying the president-elect on the moonlit flight which brought him from Havana to Caracas, and to power, Gabriel García Márquez had made an observation and a prediction. 'I was overwhelmed by the feeling that I had just been travelling and chatting pleasantly with two opposing men. One to whom the caprices of fate had given an opportunity to save his country. The other, an illusionist, who could pass into the history books as just another despot.' Chávez did not succumb to classic despotism. But as Venezuela headed into 2012, an election year, the other half of García Márquez's bleak prophecy unfolded.

I t was 6 January 2012, el Dia de los Reyes (the Day of the Kings), a national holiday to honour the wise men who brought gifts to the baby Jesus. Those who were not at the beach listening to music were at home watching television. Abruptly the airwaves, as one, switched to the sight and sound of worshippers at the shrine of Our Lady of Coromoto, Venezuela's holiest site, in Guanare, in the western plains. It was a *cadena*, a chain broadcast. The comandante had news. He appeared, wearing a dark blue shirt, and entered the basilica surrounded by aides, soldiers and worshippers. He was barely recognisable as the Chávez of old. His face and body were bloated. His hair was thin and barely covered his scalp. He walked gingerly.

Since his diagnosis the country had got used to visual shocks. First he was thin, from the surgery to remove the tumour, then swollen and bald like Humpty Dumpty from the chemotherapy. Some supporters shaved their heads in solidarity. The exact nature of the cancer remained a mystery. Contradictory reports sprouted from diplomatic and medical sources in Caracas, Sao Paolo, Moscow, Miami and Madrid. The real information was in Cuba, which had skilfully managed Fidel Castro's illness and decline. A story spread that Havana sent tissue samples marked 'Chávez' to top laboratories around the world – but that the samples came from different cancer patients, to keep everyone guessing.

The president would disappear for days and weeks, prompting feverish rumours, his enemies gorging on the possibility he was near death, only to surface, Lazarus-like, and punch the air in exultation. He changed the slogan 'Fatherland, socialism or death' to 'We will live and we will win' and expunged all references to *muerte* from official discourse. 'There will be no death here; we must live.' Even so, many supporters braced for the worst and looked with hopelessness at the ministers who might replace him.

And now, with ten months until the election, he was at Venezuela's most sacred Catholic shrine, a basilica consecrated in 1996 by Pope John Paul II, greeting worshippers, embracing priests, placing rosary beads around a statue of the Virgin. The comandante, sweating from the humidity, stood by the altar with a microphone and announced he had come to give thanks. The battle had been hard, an existential test, and now it was over. He was cured. There was not a cancerous cell in his body. It was a miracle.

'I came here to keep a promise I made in Cuba six months ago,' he said, his voice solemn. 'It was a very difficult time. I put my life in the hands of holy God, Christ the redeemer and the Virgin Mary of Coromoto. I asked God and the Virgin to give me life. Because in truth my life is not mine.' He paused, and the congregation waved red banners, willing him to go on. 'It is dedicated to the struggle for the humble, for the poor, for the people. That is my life. And when I, a humble soldier, knelt before God, knelt before Christ and the Virgin and the spirit of the savanna, before the profound faith of this heroic savanna, when I knelt as a humble soldier on this earth, I made that promise.' The great chamber exploded in cheers and applause.

Lest anyone doubted he was back and fully in charge, he beckoned an army general and former intelligence chief, Henry Rangel Silva, a man the United States accused of drug trafficking, and put his arm around him. 'Today I make public his appointment as the new minister of defence of the Republic, here in this sacred temple, before the Virgin of Coromoto.' It was a warning not only to the United States but to the opposition, because Rangel Silva had publicly said the armed forces would accept no change of government. The congregation stood and cheered again. Celestial music played, and the comandante waded into the throng as if it were the old days. It established the election campaign's narrative: Chávez was resurrected.

Two weeks later, standing on the national assembly podium, he provided what many took to be proof: a state of the nation address lasting nine and a half hours. A record. No break, no pause: a display of stamina to quell any lingering doubts. An opposition deputy who challenged him on a point was slapped down with the glee of old. 'An eagle does not hunt flies.' Deputies staggered away from the tempest drained and exhausted; Hurricane Hugo still gusted.

It was all a phantasm. The cancer was breaching his defences. Chávez was dying. Drugs could only do so much. To prolong his life and minimise the pain the comandante needed to rest. He did the opposite. He commanded his body into action, barnstorming the country, leading cavalcades, orating, dancing, singing. He fought the agony, defied the fatigue, turned winces into smiles, limps into struts, marshalled his dwindling reserves into reckless attacks against the body's craving for stillness and rest. Only those closest to him saw the anguish and organisation – the cocktail of steroids, painkillers, choreography and sheer willpower – behind the deception. If cynical, here too was heroism and pathos. For once the slogan 'Fatherland, socialism or death' had meaning. The comandante was accelerating his death, sacrificing his life, as he saw it, for the revolution. He could not avoid physical extinction, but if he won the election his followers would remain in power, controlling the state's immense patronage and authority, as they fought a new election after his death.

The illusion prevailed. Supporters believed he was cured. Chávez seemed so robust a conspiracy theory took hold among some opponents that there was no cancer, that it was staged to wrongfoot them. 'I'm not fooled,' a Venezuelan acquaintance, a copywriter, an educated, sophisticated woman, told me. 'That fucker is just fine.'

Concealing a body's decay was one thing, what of a nation's? The 2010 drought had long ended, but blackouts, the product of mismanagement and underinvestment, only worsened, knocking out traffic lights, plunging baseball games into darkness, destroying electrical equipment and forcing people to sleep outdoors to escape baking homes. The electricity ministry accused its own workers of sabotage on the basis that 'matches were found' near the site of some outages. It also accused a possum of gnawing through a substation's cables. A bridge collapsed in Miranda state, another in Monagas, and engineers warned that others were sagging. Unemployment hovered at 8 per cent, comparable to that of the United States and better than Europe, but a statistical ruse classified the millions of sidewalk vendors and informal sector workers as employed. In the first six months of 2012 slaughter worsened in the jails – more than 300 dead – and on the streets, with an estimated 9,500 murdered.

'Tremendous achievement! Venezuela is Latin America's leading user of Twitter. And in our use of Facebook, we are 20 points above the Latin American average.' So gushed Andrés Izarra, the minister of popular power for communication and information, during a Twitter summit in April to celebrate the second anniversary of the comandante's account, @chavezcandanga. 'Twitter is the microphone of the state. It is cultivating a new form of direct communication with the people.' Ministers, including the justice minister, ostensibly responsible for keeping the streets safe, attended to reinforce the idea this event, the main news on state media, really was news.

It was part of a strategy of distractions, every day a new story. The president said an American mercenary had been arrested on the Colombian border on suspicion of plotting his assassination. Another day it was a U.S. submarine incursion. Then he suggested a spate of cancers afflicting the region's leftist leaders was part of a CIA plot. 'Would it be so strange that they've invented technology to spread cancer and we won't know about it for fifty years?' Intelligence agents questioned the crossword compiler of the newspaper *Últimas Noticias* on suspicion of inciting assassination because answers to clues included 'kill', 'gunfire' and 'Adán', the name of the president's older brother. State television said a team of psychologists and mathematicians detected the codes. The president unveiled a 3-D reconstruction of Simón Bolívar's face. 'Bolívar is the fight that does not end; he is born every day in ourselves,' he intoned. He declared the national pantheon too humble for the Liberator and ordered the construction of a $140 million mausoleum, built with imported tiles and marble.

These tricks earned polite applause and kept eyes on the stage, but were merely the warm-up. The main spectacle was the economy. Moribund dysfunction was transformed – poof! – into glittering whirl and a rain of cash. The comandante had taken care to prepare the stage. Jorge Giordani, the monkish economy minister, directed petrodollars into special funds – the biggest, called Fonden, alone swallowed an estimated $100 billion – over which Chávez had personal control. It helped that the price of a barrel of oil had rebounded from its tumble in 2009 to hover at $100. Even this was not sufficient for the illusion, so the government borrowed billions more from China.

This itself required conjuring because the revolution could hardly acknowledge the ceding of sovereignty, even if it was to China rather than the IMF. Thus the palace put on a little show when a delegation from the China Development Bank came to deliver a thick white book titled *The Strategic Development Plan, 2013–2030*, detailing dozens of bilateral accords from oil to railways, factories, housing and farming. The comandante, wearing military fatigues and shiny black boots with red laces, still bald from chemotherapy, clapped his hands in delight. 'I would like to thank you for this wonderful guide for the next twenty years. Applause!' Ministers applauded. Chávez signed and stamped the book with Venezuela's official seal, cementing, he said, a historic anti-imperialist front.

What the book really sealed was Venezuela's prostration. Beijing had long groaned at Chávez's clumsy references to Mao, the Cultural Revolution and their shared Yankee foe. 'Not a serious person,' Chinese diplomats and executives murmured. But they held their tongues and funnelled loans in exchange for access to the Faja oil reserves. The catch was that Venezuela's state oil and natural gas company, PDVSA, was too debilitated to keep its end of the bargain and build roads, refineries and pipelines in the wilderness. China watched in alarm as its 'development' loans evaporated in the Caribbean haze. The white book handed over at Miraflores was not a tome of solidarity but a list of finger-wagging prescriptions and warnings about the bills faced by future Venezuelan generations.

What mattered, as the election neared, was having the means to confect a boom. Chávez ordered big pay raises for state workers – he was most generous with the army – and a blitz of new payments to pensioners, mothers, children and students. For the first time the money supply exceeded $100 billion. To tamp down inflation, which was the hemisphere's highest, the government fixed the prices of fifteen thousand goods, everything from coffee to toothpaste, based upon 'scientific analysis' of what constituted fair prices. Soldiers and civilians in red T-shirts patrolled warehouses and shops to ensure that businesses complied, even if it drove them into bankruptcy. At the same time, ports worked overtime offloading containers from around the world to keep shelves stocked. It was like shaking a bottle of champagne and holding down the cork. Inflation and devaluation waited down the line, but in the short term the strategy worked. People had money in their pockets.

And many, for the first time in their lives, had hopes of a decent roof over their heads. Venezuelans expected their government to supply cheap housing, but the comandante had built less than his predecessors. Three million people – almost a tenth of the population – lacked adequate accommodation. Thus was hatched the Great Housing Mission, a scheme to build two million houses within five years. 'I will not rest in the quest to solve this drama inherited from the curse of capitalism,' said the comandante. It was impossible to build so many houses so fast, not least because nationalised cement and steel factories were sputtering and private contractors feared building anything that could be expropriated. So the government paid firms from Belarus, Russia, China and Iran inflated prices to throw up apartment blocks, often slapdash, all over the country. They also painted slums – those visible from the motorways – bright red, yellow and blue, Venezuela's national colours.

By mid-2012, the comandante claimed to have reached 96 per cent of the housing target for that period. Every few days he or a minister appeared on television to hand keys to a jubilant citizen. The 96 per cent number was fanciful, but many homes had indeed been built, or at least redecorated, and it was enough to give hope to those on the waiting list. The list was the key. The government bombarded the population with text messages urging it to register for a home. Millions flocked to mobile registration centres where they received receipts with a name, the date, a registration number and a stamp. A well-off person cannot understand what it means to possess such a slip of paper, cannot appreciate the solemnity with which a poor person memorises it, makes copies and guards it as something precious, a potential passport to comfort and dignity. A vote for Chávez would keep it valid. The list did not just give hope – it gave the government a formidable database come election day.

The wizard of Miraflores was not finished. He ramped up another mission, Mi Casa Bien Equipada (My Well-Equipped Home), which distributed 1.3 million subsidised washing machines, dishwashers, stoves and flat-screen televisions from the Chinese company Haier, with Chávez's name and face stencilled on the boxes. How do you explain to someone who has never had to live without a washing machine what it means, after a lifetime of scrubbing, to suddenly have one? 'My, oh my, oh my, oh my! Thank you!' squealed an elderly woman, her expression beatific, during one of the comandante's home appliance ceremonies. A mock kitchen was built in Miraflores so he could display the latest models without moving far from his desk. The comandante had swung the 2004 recall referendum, and subsequent elections, with free health clinics, schools and courses. Many were now closed or fraying, but rather than revive them he calculated that his socialist revolution would win more votes by boosting private consumption.

The comandante notched up forty-seven hours in 'chain' broadcasts, but in the last weeks of the campaign the country's degradation at times punctured the Potemkin facade. The Amuay oil refinery in the Paraguaná peninsula exploded in a giant fireball, killing forty-two people and sending mushroom clouds into the sky.

Survivors blamed a gas leak and lack of maintenance. Workers at the Caruachi hydroelectric plant heckled Chávez during a visit to demand unpaid wages and the restoration of collective bargaining rights. Viewers, surprised by this rare failure of official choreography, heard shouts of '*justicia*', justice, until state television cut the broadcast. The news agency Reuters published an investigation of Fonden's black accounts and tracked some of the missing billions to white elephants – an abandoned newsprint factory, a 'city of aluminium' – and on ill-fated investments in Ecuadorean bonds and Lehman Brothers–issued derivatives. 'That is not Chávez's money. That money belongs to 29 million Venezuelans and as such the information should be available to everyone,' wailed Carlos Ramos, an opposition legislator. A jail riot at Yare prison – the same one where Chávez served time for the 1992 coup attempt, and which he promised to transform – left twenty-five dead. A technician from Corpoelec, the electricity utility, was shot dead in the town of San Mateo, apparently by residents angered by continued blackouts. Living in the shadow of Miraflores, which was ringed by police and soldiers, was no protection from violence. Days before the election José Ramón Montilva, a fifty-six-year-old shop owner who worked a block from the palace, was shot in the neck and throat by a would-be car thief. The police and soldiers declined to treat him, reportedly to avoid bloodstains, leaving relatives to take Montilva to a private clinic where he died. The killer escaped.

On 4 October, three days before the election, Chavez was due to address a huge crowd in downtown Caracas, an ocean of red on Avenida Bolívar. Some were government workers compelled to attend – bussed in and ticked off lists – but most came out of choice.

A bruised sky blotted out the sun. It began to rain. A wild, hammering downpour. A rumour spread that Chávez would cancel. Then, suddenly, there he was amid the throng, grinning, waving, blowing kisses. He raised his arms like a victorious boxer and broke into a jog. By the time he was on the stage he was drenched, a black jacket sticking to his body as if coated in oil. 'Long live youth, long live the rain,' he bellowed. He punched the air and the crowd cheered. He denounced his opponent as the candidate of oligarchy, corruption and austerity. He did not use the name Capriles but '*el majunche*', an insult meaning loser, someone of low quality. The crowd repeated the insult with glee. Chávez continued. 'Who is the candidate of the people? Who is the candidate of youth? Who is the candidate of the fatherland? Who is the candidate of happiness? Who is the candidate of life? Who is the candidate of the future?' The crowd roared. He paused for breath. Rain dripped off his head and shoulders, streaked down his cheeks. He scanned the upturned faces, as if calculating their number, weighing their humanity. 'Let's convert this Bolivarian avalanche into an avalanche of votes . . . with this rain we have been blessed by the hand of God!' The cheers became deafening. Supporters joined him on stage and music blasted, a fast merengue beat with a catchy chorus, 'Chávez, heart of the people'. Fireworks fizzed overhead and red confetti rained on the stage. The president mimicked playing a guitar. Then, the stage slick, the heavens pouring, his body in torment, he danced. He danced and he danced.

Three days later, on 7 October, Chávez triumphed. He won 8.1 million votes versus 6.5 million for Capriles, 55 per cent versus 44. Not the landslide of 2006, when he crushed Manuel Rosales by 26 points, but still emphatic. More than 80 per cent of the electorate voted, a historic turnout. Capriles had whipped up huge crowds as he barnstormed through villages, towns and cities, and won 2 million more votes than Rosales. But the comandante's red machine went into a higher gear and delivered him 800,000 more votes than he had won in 2006. His big fear – abstention – was not realised. Chávez won twenty-one of twenty-three states. Of all the regional results, perhaps the most telling was in Morón, the municipality that regularly blocked motorways to protest crumbling public services: Chávez, 73.4 per cent; Capriles, 25.9 per cent.

Some in the opposition complained that fleets of state vehicles ferried voters to the polls; that Chinese and Cubans swelled the electoral register; that state media smeared Capriles. He was accused of being gay, Jewish and a Nazi. Capriles accepted defeat, congratulated the comandante. 'To know how to win, you have to know how to lose. For me, what the people say is sacred.'

Chávez, as was his custom, took to the palace balcony to greet rapturous supporters below. 'Truthfully, this has been the perfect battle, a democratic battle,' he thundered, brandishing a replica of Bolívar's sword. 'Venezuela will continue along the path of democratic and Bolivarian socialism of the twenty-first century.'

A ruined body, a ruined country, and he won. He masked death and desolation. Chávez's last campaign was his greatest illusion. García Márquez foretold it. But even as the comandante gave his victory speech, the illusion began to fade. The pain had become unbearable. The thousand-watt grin was fleeting. He barely smiled.

Days after the election Chávez replaced his vice president, Elías Jaua. A callow apparatchik, his lack of a personal support base in the movement had guaranteed his loyalty to Chávez but now that was a liability. To give the revolution a chance of outliving him Chávez needed a credible successor. He chose Nicolás Maduro, his veteran foreign minister, as the new vice president. A burly former bus driver who had loyally served his chief, Maduro had support among military and civilian factions and, crucially, the Cubans.

Diosdado Cabello, the cabinet fixer, was now head of the national assembly and a pretender to the throne but bided his time. He accepted Maduro's elevation. Ambitious ministers and provincial governors circled warily. For years advancement had meant sheathing initiative, lest the glint outshine the comandante. Was now a time to shine?

Chávez returned to Cuba for emergency surgery. Christmas came and went and he remained hidden. With the election safely behind them officials admitted the boss was gravely ill. A respiratory infection nearly killed him in January 2013. Doctors performed a tracheotomy, opening his windpipe to facilitate breathing. Chávez was too weak to attend his inauguration but the government held an eerie ceremony in the national assembly to perpetuate the fiction that Havana's mute, invisible patient remained in charge. Loyalists with red T-shirts marched through Caracas to celebrate his new term.

The country mouldered. Uribana prison erupted in a riot which left 61 dead and 120 injured. Robbers beat to death Napoleon Pisani, a seventy-year-old historian, at a museum next to the Liberator's new mausoleum. A leaked report revealed that almost a third of the CICPC, Venezuela's version of the FBI, was itself under investigation for crimes. China became so worried about its loans vanishing into Venezuela's populist swamp it hesitated to lend more. Chicken, flour, milk and sugar became scarce, prompting mayhem at supermarkets when deliveries arrived. Giordani, the economy minister who had strangled domestic production with his controls, blamed the debacle

on people's avarice and 'dollarised nymphomania.' To close a yawn-
ing deficit the government introduced austerity measures and deval-
ued the bolivar by a third – the fifth devaluation in a decade. The
only countries to match its precipitous decline were Iraq, Myanmar,
Congo and Uzbekistan. In ministries officials sighed and exchanged
conspiratorial winks. We turn the wheel and cannot stop it. *Todo
bochinche, agarra lo que puedas.* It's all a mess, grab what you can.

Around midnight on 18 February, fourteen years after the flight
with García Márquez, Chávez took off from Havana for the last
time. The plane climbed, banked and headed south under a Caribbean moon. Fidel Castro bid him farewell in a letter read on Cuban
TV and radio. 'You learned much about life, Hugo, during those difficult days of suffering and sacrifice.' The plane landed at Caracas at
2.30am, a homecoming without warning or fanfare. He was taken to
a specially prepared, heavily guarded military hospital.

No one imagined it would end like this. Helpless, invisible, silent.
Hugo Chávez's life blazed drama, a command performance, and
friend and foe alike always envisaged an operatic finale. He would
rule for decades, transform Venezuela and Latin America, and bid
supporters adios from the palace balcony, an old man, his work complete. Or a parallel fantasy: he would tumble from power, disgraced
and defeated by the wreckage of revolution, ending his days a
hounded pariah.

Instead, just fifty-eight years old, he lay stricken, hooked to tubes,
a hole in his throat, a phantom president. The government insisted
that the comandante remained in charge. 'The patient is in a state of
progressive and favourable recovery of the normal values of his vital
signs,' said a typically opaque communique which left the country

guessing. Satirists mimicked official bulletins. 'The president is stable, some days less stable, some days more stable, and sometimes in a state of excessive stability.'

The charade stopped one baking hot afternoon when Maduro, flanked by other ministers, appeared on television to make an announcement. 'We have just received the most tragic and awful information,' he said. The voice wavered. Tears welled. 'At 4.25pm today, March the 5th, President Hugo Chávez Frías died. It is a moment of deep pain.'

The funeral was vast. Hundreds of thousands queued for days under a broiling sun to bid farewell to the comandante. Dressed in military uniform and red beret, he lay in an open casket at the chapel in the military academy, the same academy where decades earlier he had studied as a cadet, befriended Raúl Baduel, and dreamed of insurrection. Dozens of presidents, prime ministers and princes joined the pilgrims. Chávez's mother, Elena, clutched the coffin, weeping. 'My all has left me. Good bye my giant,' tweeted his daughter Maria Gabriela. Opponents stayed home and kept their voices low, awed by the displays of grief, worried about what might follow.

Maduro announced the body would be embalmed and displayed 'for eternity' in a crystal urn, like Lenin and Ho Chi Minh. But the Russian experts summoned to Caracas scotched the notion. The body was not preserved properly or on time. Chavez was too decayed. So Maduro announced his chief would be buried at the Museum of the Revolution. Formerly a military museum overlooking Miraflores, it was where Chávez had directed his 1992 coup, a bungled operation which nevertheless made him a media star.

A snap presidential election was set for 14 April, pitting the young governor Capriles, once again the opposition's candidate, against Maduro, now the acting president. Capriles criss-crossed the country railing against crime, inflation, shortages, and power cuts. He avoided criticising Chávez directly but assailed Maduro.

The stand-in president lacked charisma but deployed state patronage and Chávez's ghost. By one count he named the chief more than 7000 times during an increasingly baroque campaign. Maduro declared that Chávez had been assassinated, that the cancer had been induced. 'We have no doubt that our fatherland's historic enemies looked for a way to harm our comandante's health. We already have plenty of clues about this.' A scientific committee was set up to investigate. Maduro declared his martyred chief 'the redeemer Christ of the Americas' and called himself his 'apostle' and 'son'. Chávez, he said, had intervened in heaven to produce South America's first pope in the form of Argentina's cardinal, Jorge Mario Bergoglio, who was elected Pope Francis.

Government adverts deified Chávez and attributed quasi-divine powers. 'From his hands sprouts the rain of life.' At rallies Maduro imitated the comandante's martial walk and gestures. He would start singing the anthem and his voice would merge into a recording of Chávez's. He announced that while praying the comandante, reincarnated, visited him. 'All of a sudden, a little bird circled three times around me, stopped on a wooden beam, and began to sing a pretty song. Then I, too, began to whistle.' Maduro whistled like a bird, then continued. 'The little bird looked at me in a strange way. He sang, circled me once and flew away. And I felt his spirit. I felt him giving us a blessing, saying now the battle begins, go to victory.'

It was a new religion, with Maduro as chief priest.

The economy continued to warp, prompting another currency

devaluation, the second in two months, though it was veiled as a new currency auction system. The owner of Globovisión, the last opposition TV channel, succumbed to official fines and harrassment and agreed to sell it to a pro-government buyer.

Maduro could not hold crowds' attention like the master – who could? – but he wore a Venezuelan flag like a cape, evoking a superhero, and revived accusations that Capriles was gay.

O pinion polls predicted a Maduro landslide. Grief over Chávez, combined with the government's cash, media and institutional control, would surely trump voter grievances and safeguard the revolution. But official election results delivered a shock: Chávez's heir won 7,575,506 votes, or 50.78% of the poll, and Capriles 7,302,641, or 48.95%. A wafer-thin win. Hundreds of thousands of previously chavista voters defected or abstained. Maduro, for all his phantasmagoric campaigning, was proving a poor illusionist. At his victory speech ministers looked shaken. The spell was fading.

Capriles claimed fraud and demanded a recount. Maduro agreed, then balked. Furious opposition protestors blocked streets, set fire to government property and clashed with police. Dozens were killed and injured. Maduro called the protestors coup-plotting fascists. 'If they want to overthrow me, come get me. With the people and the armed forces, I am here.' The government threatened to jail Capriles. The government threatened to jail Capriles. It was an inauspicious beginning for chavismo without Chávez.

H ugo Chávez left a mixed legacy. He could boast real accomplishments. He taught barrio dwellers they were the majority and deserved a place at the table, that they were human beings with a right to dignity. He scolded the wealthy, the masters of the valley, for shopping in Miami with petrodollars while ignoring the shacks on the hills. He told them their sense of entitlement was obscene, and he was right. He empowered communities through communal councils, an ambitious and largely well-meant attempt at grassroots democracy. He challenged Eurocentric history and celebrated Latin America's indigenous heritage. He called time on U.S. meddling and emboldened neighbours to pursue their own interests, not Washington's. He took rightful pride in Latin America's coming-of-age.

Yet the abiding legacy was waste. A sublimely gifted politician with empathy for the poor, the power of Croesus and the result, fiasco. While he thundered about bringing equilibrium to the universe and polarised his country, foaming passions into hate, neighbours built more sustainable economies and tackled long-term poverty. Allies like Bolivia, Nicaragua, and Ecuador saluted the comandante but did not emulate his economic model, for that way lay ruin. Brazil seized regional leadership. Venezuela atrophied. Nothing worked, but there was money and spectacle. An empty revolution, then. No paradise, no hell, just limbo, a bleak, misty in-between where ambition and delusion played out its ancient story. The farces and follies did not add up to despotic horror but they bore the melancholy echo of opportunity squandered, of what might have been, and there was the tragedy.

19 April 2013

Bibliography

Castellanos, Rafael Ramón. *Los fantasmas vivientes de Miraflores*. Caracas: Pomaire, 1994.

Coronil, Fernando. *The Magical State: Nature, Money, and Modernity in Venezuela*. Chicago: University of Chicago Press, 1997.

Corrales, Javier, and Michael Penfold. *Dragon in the Tropics: Hugo Chávez and the Political Economy of Revolution in Venezuela*. Washington, D.C.: Brookings Institution Press, 2010.

Ellner, Steve. *Rethinking Venezuelan Politics: Class, Conflict, and the Chávez Phenomenon*. Boulder, Colo.: Lynne Rienner, 2009.

García Márquez, Gabriel. *The General in His Labyrinth*. New York: Everyman's Library, 2004.

Garrido, Alberto. *Revolución bolivariana 2005: Notas*. Caracas: A. Garrido, 2005.

– – –. *Testimonios de la revolución bolivariana*. Caracas: Ediciones del Autor, 2002.

Golinger, Eva. *The Chávez Code: Cracking U.S. Intervention in Venezuela*. Northampton, Mass.: Olive Branch Press, 2006.

Gott, Richard. *Hugo Chávez and the Bolivarian Revolution*. New York: Verso, 2011.

Hernández, Ramón. *Las revelaciones de Luis Tascón*. Caracas: Libros Marcados, 2008.

Humboldt, Alexander von. *Personal Narrative of a Journey to the Equinoctial Regions of the New Continent*. 1814–25. London: Penguin Books, 1995.

Jones, Bart. *Hugo! The Hugo Chávez Story from Mud Hut to Perpetual Revolution*. Hanover, N.H.: Steerforth, 2007.

Karl, Terry Lynn. *The Paradox of Plenty: Oil Booms and Petro-States*. Berkeley: University of California Press, 1997.

Kozloff, Nikolas. *Hugo Chávez: Oil, Politics, and the Challenge to the U.S.* New York: Palgrave Macmillan, 2007.

Krauze, Enrique. *El poder y el delirio*. Barcelona: Tusquets, 2009.

Lucien, Óscar. *Cerco rojo a la libertad de expresión*. Caracas: La Hoja del Norte, 2011.

Lynch, John. *Simón Bolívar: A Life*. New Haven, Conn.: Yale University Press, 2007.

Marcano, Cristina, and Alberto Barrera Tyszka. *Hugo Chávez: The Definitive Biography of Venezuela's Controversial President*. New York: Random House, 2007.

Muñoz, Agustín Blanco. *Habla el comandante Hugo Chávez Frías: Venezuela del 4 de febrero 92 al 6 de diciembre 98*. Caracas: Fundación Cátedra Pío Tamayo, 1998.

Nelson, Brian. *The Silence and the Scorpion: The Coup Against Chávez and the Making of Modern Venezuela*. New York: Nation Books, 2009.

Ponniah, Thomas, and Jonathan Eastwood, eds. *The Revolution in Venezuela: Social and Political Change Under Chávez*. Cambridge, Mass.: Harvard University, David Rockefeller Center for Latin American Studies, 2011.

Tarver, Micheal, and Julia Frederick. *The History of Venezuela*. New York: Palgrave Macmillan, 2008.

Tinker Salas, Miguel. *The Enduring Legacy: Oil, Culture, and Society in Venezuela*. Durham, N.C.: Duke University Press, 2009.

Understanding the Venezuelan Revolution: Hugo Chávez Talks to Marta Harnecker. New York: Monthly Review Press, 2005.

Uzcátegui, Rafael. *Venezuela: Revolution as Spectacle*. Tucson, Ariz.: See Sharp Press, 2011.

Wilpert, Gregory. *Changing Venezuela by Taking Power: The History and Policies of the Chávez Government*. London: Verso, 2006.

Web site

http://caracas.chronicles.com

Index

Abrams, Elliott, 71
Acosta, Yoel, 47
Acosta Carles, Felipe, 94, 141
Acosta Carles, Luis, 94–96,
    142, 173
Aeropostal, 173
Afiuni, María Lourdes, 242–49
Afiuni, Nelson, 244
Aharonian, Aram, 195
Aissami, Tarek El, 234
al-Assad, Bashar, 273
Al Jazeera, 195
Allende Gossens, Salvador, 77
al-Qaida, 71, 273
Altuve, Lídice, 124
Amuay oil refinery, 283–4
Andrés (pseudonym), 97–100
Andresote, Cimarrón, 259
Antonini, Alejandro, 170–72
Aporrea (Web site), 265
Argentina, canal link with, 31
Arias Cárdenas, Francisco, 47–48
Ávila National Park, 41–42
    landslide (2000), 43–46, 131
    recovery efforts in, 46

Baduel, Cruz María, 141, 147
Baduel, Raúl, 82, 140–50, 289
    and attempted coup (1992), 4, 80, 142
    fall from power of, 145–47, 149–50

imprisonment of, 147–50, 244, 245,
    255
My Solution, 147
rise to power of, 142–43
and turning points, 142, 144–45
BANDES (development bank), 165
Barrera Tyszka, Alberto, 60, 70
Berlusconi, Silvio, 21
Betancourt, Rómulo, 193
Blanco, Andrés Eloy, 187
    'The Toothless Ones', 12
Blanco, Luis, 251–56, 268
Bolívar, Simón:
    anniversaries of, 51, 141
    Chávez's esteem for, 3, 15, 88
    Chávez's references to, 12–13, 27,
        191–93
    descendants of, 153
    disillusionment and death of, 20
    mausoleum planned for, 280
    reviving, 40, 60, 89, 143
    at Samán de Güerre, 141
    serial fornication of, 51
    statues and images of, 10–11, 37, 38, 68,
        72, 280, 286
    and wars of independence, 20, 51
    writings and speeches of, 33, 39, 43, 134,
        189, 201, 231
Bolivarian Circles, 74, 253–54
Bolivarian democracy, 112

Bolivarian Intelligence Service (SEBIN), 128, 129, 214
Bolivarian Militia, 152–53
Bolivarian revolution, 15, 17, 26
   'boligarchs' of, 168–69, 170, 171, 172
   changing direction of, 53, 55–56, 69–70, 98, 248–49, 253, 257, 274–5, 288
   Chavistas, 139, 146
   defectors from, 45, 47–48, 53–57, 91–92, 100, 160–62, 166, 184, 207, 265–66
   and operational research, 221–24
   socialist, 143, 207, 288
   as unfinished portrait, 272
Brazil, economy of, 292
Bush, George W., 46, 71, 82, 197

Cabello, Diosdado, 122–23, 126, 177–79, 275, 287
Cabello, José David, 177–78
CADIVI (currency exchange), 164–65
Caldera, Matson, 260
Camacho, Jorge, 34
Camejo Mujica, Gloria, 34
Capriles Radonski, Henrique, 275, 285–86, 291–92
Caracas, 117–18
   class inequality in, 58–59
   earthquakes in, 36–37, 187
   El Cementerio gang, 225–31
   El Silencio, 64, 118, 215
   Fifth of July gang, 226
   gangs in, 225–31, 233
   government bureaucracy in, 118–28, 216, 268–69
   La Casona (presidential residence) in, 32, 37, 50
   La Francia, 14, 16–17
   La Gran Pulpería del Libro Venezolano, 190
   Los Pelucos gang, 226, 229
   Miraflores in, see Miraflores Palace
   Parque Central Towers inferno, 123
   Plaza Bolívar in, 9–17
   urban decay in, 15–16, 17, 187, 203, 218–21
Caracazo riots (1989), 20, 40, 59, 94, 264
Carla (pseudonym), 51–52
Carmona, Pedro, 74, 75, 77–80, 81–82, 142
Carroll, Rory:
   career of, 21–22
   on Hello, President, 108–17

Caruachi hydroelectric plant, 284
Castellanos, Rafael, 78, 189–92, 194, 198
Castro, Cipriano, 36–37
Castro, Fidel, 44, 71, 182, 270, 276
   and April 2002 crisis, 76–77, 98
   and conspiracies, 100, 149
   and Cuban economy, 102
   Cuban G2 in situation room, 98–100, 102
   friendship of Chávez and, 1, 2, 4, 27, 46, 47, 98, 288
   revolutionary slogans of, 143–44
   and Venezuela's oil, 98, 102
   visit of Chávez and, 99–100
Catholic Church, 12
Cedeño, Eligio, 242–43, 246
Chacón, Jesse, 228
Chávez, Isaías 'Látigo', 86–88
Chávez Colmenares, Hugo Rafael (son), 49
Chávez Colmenares, María Gabriela (daughter), 9–10, 11, 12, 49, 289
Chávez Colmenares, Rosa Virginia (daughter), 49
Chávez Frías, Adán (brother), 30, 85, 86, 88, 90, 280
Chávez Frías, Hugo Rafael:
   accomplishments of, 291–2
   and April 2002 crisis, 72–77, 81, 82–83, 98–99, 188, 264
   as artist, 272
   assassination fears of, 100, 130–31, 280, 290
   attempted coup (February 1992), 2, 3, 20–21, 36, 40, 47, 48, 49, 63, 80–81, 90, 91, 112, 122, 142, 144, 167, 193–94, 271, 284, 289
   biographies of, 60
   birth of, 3, 42, 84–85
   and cancer, 270–72, 274–80, 286–88
   and constitutional referendum (2007), 111–12, 139–40, 146–47, 150, 177
   and Cuba, see Castro, Fidel
   death of, 289
   disillusionment with, 45, 47–48, 57–58, 60, 62, 267, 275
   early years of, 3, 63, 84–90, 92, 140, 193
   election (1998), 2, 21, 40, 50, 59, 60, 98, 267, 276, 275
   family of, 32, 37, 49–50
   final public appearances of, 271–72, 276–78, 284–87

and foreign affairs, 273–74
forms of address, 134–35
funeral of, 289
as illusionist, 272, 274, 278, 280, 281, 283, 284, 285–86
impulsiveness of, 133
inauguration (1999), 15
international image of, 46–47
interviews with, 1–5
life story rewritten, 193–94
and media, *see* media
middle class attacked by, 59–61, 93
and the military, 143–44, 149, 150–53
nickname Tribilin, 84
and operational research, 221–24
opponents of, 60–61, 70–71, 74–75, 76, 79, 92, 93, 94, 108–9, 153–54, 271, 274–75, 278, 279, 285, 289, 291
at Our Lady of Coromoto shrine, 276–78
as philosopher king, 273–74
plans for future projects, 14, 55
polarisation as strategy of, 60–61, 81, 92–93
popularity of, 17–18, 26, 40, 48, 54, 101, 108, 235
portraits of, 127–28
power wielded by, 70, 108, 112
public image of, 167–69, 241, 264, 272–73
reelection (2000), 48, 275
reelection (2006), 22, 108–9, 139, 143, 275, 285
reelection (2012), 153, 272, 274, 276, 284–86
return to power, 82
rise to power, 2, 3, 40, 149, 172
and Rosa Inés (grandmother), 85, 86, 87, 92
as storyteller, 4, 12–13, 185, 187–89, 196
supporters of, 53–54, 58, 93, 240–41, 267–68, 272, 273, 287, 291
and term limits, 154–55, 272–73
ubiquitous images of, 17, 23, 38,
and waste, 290, 292
and wife Marisabel, 32, 48–51
and wife Nancy, 49, 141
Chávez Rodríguez, Rosinés (daughter), 49, 136
China Development Bank, 280–81, 287
Chomsky, Noam, 248–50
Cincinnatus, Lucius Quinctius, 146
Cisneros, Gustavo, 75, 95

Ciudad Guayana, 206–15
and failing economy, 210–12
scavenging in, 209, 212
trade union leaders in, 213–15
Venalum in, 210–14
Clausewitz, Carl von, 65, 88
Clinton, Bill, 44, 46, 71
CNN en Español, 195
Colmenares, Nancy, 49, 141
Colombia:
diplomatic relations with, 225, 268
and drugs, 151, 173–75, 228
Columbus, Christopher, 19, 115
Conan Doyle, Arthur, *The Lost World,* 174
Constructing Republic, 257–59
Cortés, Hernán, letter to Chávez from, 34
Crespo, Joaquín, 36
Cuba:
G2 intelligence service, 98–100, 128, 129
and Soviet Union, 98
and Venezuela, 18, 59, 98–100, 102, 143–44, 150, 182, 212
CVG (Corporación Venezolana de Guayana), 207–8

Day of Indigenous Resistance, 62
Democratic Unity Roundtable, 275
Diego de Ordaz, 19
DISIP (Directorate for Intelligence and Prevention Services), 38, 45, 128, 171, 173, 175, 214
Duhalde, Eduardo, 149
'Dutch disease', 160, 163

Econoinvest, 161
El Cartel de los Soles, 174
El Dorado, 19, 206
El Evangélico (criminal), 235
El Helicoide, 173, 175
El Niño, 180
Engels, Friedrich, 116

Faja, oil in, 158, 268, 281
Falkland/Malvinas Islands, 259
Farías, Jacqueline, 133–34
Farías, Jesús, 256–57
FBI, 170–72
Fernández de Kirchner, Cristina, 170
Ferrominera Orinoco, 213
Fifth Republic, 45, 63
Fleischer, Ari, 77

Flore, Victor, 272
Fonden (government fund), 165, 280, 284, 286
Fourth Republic, 45, 63, 272
Funes, Mauricio, 267

Gadhafi, Muammar al-, 273
Gamluch, Rada, 210–12
Gandhi, Mohandas K. (Mahatma), 116
García, Carlos, 53–57, 60
García Carneiro, Jorge Luis, 148–49, 255
García Márquez, Gabriel, 1–5, 26, 39, 80, 117, 142, 275–76, 286, 288
Gates, Bill, 178, 208
Giordani, Jorge 'Monk', 64, 67, 69, 121–22, 124–26, 162–67, 222–23, 280, 287–88
Global Financial Integrity, 166
Globovisión, 70, 186, 199, 291
Golinger, Eva, 196–200, 230, 271
Gómez, Juancho, 190
Goncalves, David (Rey David), 131–32
González, Rubén, 213, 214
Gramsci, Antonio, 98, 116
Great Housing Mission, 282–83
Great National Moral and Illuminating Journey, 231–34, 236, 240, 250
Great National Period of Ethics and Enlightenment, 232
Guaicaipuro (folklore), 61–62, 68
Guevara, Che, 38
Guri Reservoir, 180–81, 182, 208
Guzmán Blanco, Antonio, 11

Haier, appliances imported from, 283
Hannibal, 88
Hello, President:
    author's appearance on, 108–17
    changing content of, 24–25, 197, 216–17, 221–24
    communal councils on, 28–31
    at Plaza Bolívar, 9–17, 181, 258
    ratings of, 194
    shifting locations of, 16–17
Hernández, Carmen Elisa, 73
Hernández, María, 255
Hernández, Ramón, 176
Hitchens, Christopher, 273
Humala, Ollanta, 267
Humboldt, Alexander von, 105, 124
Hussein, Saddam, 47

Ibarra, Helena, 130
Illarramendi, Francisco, 161
Indecu (state regulatory agency), 95
Iraq war, 102, 108, 158
Istúriz, Aristóbolo, 136
Izarra, Andrés, 133, 195–96, 279

January 23 slum, 35
Japan, Fukushima nuclear plant, 2011 tsunami, 219
Jana, Elías, 286
Jesus of Nazareth, 192
Jiménez, Rafael Simón, 84, 86–87, 89–92
John Paul II, pope, 277

Krauze, Enrique, 39

Lameda, Guaicaipuro, 62–70, 80–82
    and April 2002 march, 74–76, 81, 82
    as budget controller, 63–65, 125
    and PDVSA, 65–69, 79, 81
    retirement of, 69
    turning points for, 69–70, 142
Lauro, Adelso, 205–6
Ledezma, Antonio, 153–54, 174
Lope de Aguirre, 19
López, Leopoldo, 153
Lula da Silva, Luiz Inácio, 267
Lynch, John, 193

Maduro, Nicolás, 120–21, 287, 289–91
Magallanes (baseball team), 30, 71
Maionica, Moises, 170–72
Maisanta (Chávez's great-grandfather), 133, 187
Maisanta software, 104
Maisto, John, 47
Makled, Walid 'the Turk', 173–75, 261
Maldonado, Nicia, 109–10
Mandela, Nelson, 236
Mao-tse Tung, 88, 116, 281
Marcano, Cristina, 60, 70
Marksman, Herma, 49, 141
Márquez, Gustavo, 125
Mars, Chávez's comment on, 137–38
Marx, Karl, 38, 39, 116, 192
MAS (Movement for Socialism), 87, 88, 90
media:
    @chavezcandanga, 185, 279
    Al Jazeera, 195
    and April 2002 crisis, 72–77, 82

and attempted coup (1992), 21, 91
author's interview on, 108–17
broadcast from Our Lady of Coromoto
    shrine, 276–78
centralised agency for, 25–26
chains, 184–87, 279, 276, 283, 286
Chávez's Lines (newspaper column), 184
and Chávez's private life, 51
Chávez's skills with, 22–31, 47, 60–61,
    91, 104, 134, 135, 187–88, 270
Chávez's speeches on, 55–56, 73, 184,
    190, 203, 276–78
CNN en Español, 195
Constructing Republic, 257–59
democratisation of, 194–96
government monitoring of, 97, 274
Hello, President, 9–17, 24–25, 28–31,
    184, 194, 216–17, 221–24
and Information Ministry, 185–86,
    195–96
live presidential broadcasts (cadenas), 24,
    133, 276, 283
Miguel's Truths, 129, 198
and ministers' paranoia, 128–30
and national strike (2003), 94–96
and natural disasters, 44, 182–83
opposition in, 61, 70–71, 76, 96, 128,
    186, 199, 272, 291
political campaigns in, 48, 91, 107
privately owned, 70, 75–76, 92, 112,
    186–87
propaganda broadcasts on, 195–96, 236,
    240, 261, 262–63, 265, 274, 280
The Razorblade, 38
RCTV closed, 109, 112, 139, 186
satellite images, 27–28, 29
state television, 17, 23, 25, 195, 257, 265,
    270–71, 274, 280, 282
Suddenly with Chávez, 181–82, 184
Telesur, 195–96
Twitter, 184–85, 239, 245, 263, 279
Villa del Cine, 232
Western propaganda in, 273
Mercury, Freddie, 176
Mi Casa Bien Equipada (My
    Well-Equipped Home), 283
MinCI (Ministry of Communication and
    Information), 25–26, 31, 118
ministers:
    Chavez's control of, 26, 67–69, 109–10,
        120, 121, 126, 127–29, 149, 215, 234

clothing worn by, 134–35
as disciples, 120–21
faces as masks, 135–38
as fixers, 122, 123
flattery used by, 133–35
and government bureaucracy, 119–28,
    238, 268–69
ideas from, 41
meals at palace, 130–31
skills needed by, 132–33
unpredictability used against, 65, 228,
    234
as utopians, 121, 269
Miquilena, Luis, 45, 70
Miraflores Palace, 32–39, 272, 275, 289
    April 2002 march on, 72–77, 99
    archives of, 190–91
    attempted assault on (February 1992),
        2, 3, 36
    balcony, 286
    construction of, 36, 187
    deterioration of, 273, 281
    meals in, 130–31
    official wish taker in, 35
    political battles in, 45
    and power, 78, 190, 191, 268
    presidential quarters in, 33, 50
    president's office in, 36, 283
    provisional government (2002), 77–80
    romantic life in, 51–52
    Sala de la Esperanza (Office of Hope)
        in, 35
    situation room in, 96–97, 98, 99–100, 271
Mixed Company for Socialist Rice, 133
Monsalve, Eligio, 259
Montilva, José Ramón, 284
Morales, Evo, 220
Morena, Carolina, 209
Morón, 268
    community councils in, 258–60, 261
    protests in, 262–64, 286
    TV show about, 258–64
Movement for a Fifth Republic (MVR), 40
Mujica, José, 267
Müller Rojas, Alberto, 92–93
Museum of the Revolution, 289
Mussolini, Benito, 186

Napoleon Bonaparte, 88
National Electoral Council, 101
National Union of Workers, 213

Navarrete, Salvador, 93, 272
Negroponte, John, 71
Neruda, Pablo, 40
Nicaragua, and Venezuela, 212
Nietzsche, Friedrich Wilhelm, 39, 273
Nuñez, José Daniel, 228–29, 230, 234
Nuñez, Richard, 225–31

Olachea, Oscar, 205
OPEC, 47, 158
Orihuela, Nuris, 137
Orinoco River, 18–19, 30–31, 124, 206
Ortega, Carlos, 74, 79
Ospino, Darwin 'Pata Piche'/'Rotten Foot',
    227, 228, 229
Our Lady of Coromoto shrine, 276–78

Panama Canal, 88
Panamco bottling plant, 95
PDVSA (Petróleos de Venezuela SA),
    156–62
  bureaucracy of, 66, 165, 217
  Chinese investment in, 280–81
  corruption in, 161, 164–66, 171–72
  executives of, 65–66, 73, 81, 94,
    156–57, 166
  and foreign oil companies, 158, 159,
    162, 217
  and Lameda, 65–69, 79, 81
  and national economy, 66–67, 159,
    164–66, 281
  nationalisation of, 65, 217
  and national oil policy, 157, 217–18
  and national strike, 94, 96, 158, 160
  oil drilling, 65, 217
  and politics, 67–69, 159
  and presidential actions, 68–69, 73,
    96, 155
  and social missions, 159, 163, 217
Pequiven petrochemical plant, 261
Pérez, Carlos Andrés:
  and attempted coup, 2, 3, 36, 167, 194
  and oil nationalisation, 65
  reelection of (1988), 167
Pérez Arcay, Jacinto, 191–92
Pérez Delgado, Pedro, 3
Pérez Jiménez, Marcos, 35, 40, 193, 252
Perón, Eva and Juan, 50
Peru, military government in, 88
Pinochet, Augusto, 88
Pirela, Nouvy, 34

Pisani, Napoleon, 287
Plaza Bolívar:
  buildings expropriated, 13–14, 15,
    16–17, 26–27, 30, 181, 258
  Hello, President episode filmed at, 9–17,
    181, 258
Plekhanov, George V., The Role of the
    Individual in History, 39
Perras, Temir, 271
Primera, Alí, 254
PROVEA (human rights advocacy group),
    262
PSUV party, 143, 213
Punto Fijo Pact, 40
Putin, Vladimir, 46–47

Radical Cause, 88
Ramírez, Eddy, 73
Ramírez, Rafael, 133, 159, 161, 163, 171–72
Ramos, Carlos, 284
Rangel Gómez, Francisco, 207
Rangel Silva, Henry, 171–72, 277–78
Razorblade, The (TV), 38, 128–29, 178, 198
RCTV, 70, 109, 112, 139, 186
Reagan administration, 71
Reich, Otto, 71
Revolution Will Not Be Televised,
    The (documentary), 83
Rey David (King David), 131–32
Riera, Josefa, 258–59
Rodolfo (pseudonym), 265–66
Rodríguez, Jorge, 13–15, 26–27, 30
Rodríguez Chacín, Ramón, 151
Rodríguez de Chávez, Marisabel (wife),
    32, 48–51
  and divorce, 50–51
  election to Constituent Assembly, 50
Rojas, José, 64
Rojas, Laura Thais, 28–30
Ron, Lina, 152–53, 154, 198
Rondon, Teresita, 100–101, 104
Rosales, Manuel, 108–9, 154, 285–86
Rosenhead, Jonathan, 221–24

Saab, Tarek, 133
Sáez, Irene, 252
Salazar, Raúl, 44
Sansó, Baldo, 156–62
Santeria, 229
Santos, Juan Manuel, 175
Sarah (penal service official), 238–40

Schultz, Lucas Estrella, *The Path of the Warrior,* 39
Scutaro, Giovanni, 167–69
SEBIN (Bolivarian Intelligence Service), 128, 129, 214, 272
Semtei, Eduardo, 173
September 11 attacks, 71, 152
Sequea, Carlos, 208
Serrano, Ysmael, 239
Silva, Mario, 38, 128–29
Simon, Yehude, 267
Soviet Union, collapse of, 98
Strategic Development Plan, The, 281
Sucre, Antonio José de, 191
Suddenly with Chávez, 181–82, 184
Sun Tzu, 65, 88, 146

Tascón, Luis, 103, 176–79, 197
Tascón list, 101–4, 176–77
Telesur, 195–96
Televen, 70, 112
Torres, Marisol, 219–20
Torrijos, Omar, 88
Transparency International, 166
Twitter, 184–85, 239, 245, 263, 279

United States:
    CIA, 280
    Drug Enforcement Agency, 173
    FBI, 170–72
    and Latin America, 88
    Securities and Exchange Commission, 165
    September 11 attacks on, 71, 152
    State Department, 197
    and Venezuela, 71–72, 82–83, 150, 152, 197–98, 277–78, 292
Urdaneta, Jesús, 45, 141
Utopia, 194

Valle Arriba, 35
Velasco, Msgr. Ignacio, 71
Velasco Alvarado, Juan, 88
Venalum, 210–14
Venevisión, 70, 75, 112
Venezolana de Televisión, 25
Venezuela:
    2013 elections, 290
    agricultural cooperatives, 205–6
    April 2002 crisis, 72–77, 81, 82–83, 98–99, 188, 264, 271

attempted coup (February 1992), 2, 3, 20–21, 40, 47, 48, 49, 80–81, 90, 91, 112, 142, 144, 193–94, 271, 284, 289
barrios, 42, 176, 219–20, 225–31
Bolivarian revolution in, *see* Bolivarian revolution
Bolívar state in, 206–9
cacerolazo protests in, 61, 71, 286, 291
Caracazo riots (1989), 20, 40, 59, 94, 264
cattlemen's association, 56
caudillo presidents of, 88, 114, 193, 260, 272
class inequities in, 58–59
climate of, 42, 180, 183, 208
coat of arms, 135–36
communal councils of, 28–30, 111, 253–55, 257, 258–60, 261, 265, 266, 267, 268, 292
constitutional referendum (2007), 111–12, 139–40, 146–47, 150, 177
constitution of, 40–41, 55, 79, 109, 110, 111, 143, 194, 242, 274–75
corruption in, 160–66, 170–76, 177, 178, 217–18, 268, 277, 287
criminal justice system of, 227–28, 233–35, 236–40, 241–48
and Cuba, 18, 59, 98–100, 102, 143–44, 150, 182, 212
deteriorating infrastructure in, 273, 279, 283–84, 287–88, 292
and drugs, 151, 173–75, 228–29, 277
earthquakes in, 36–37, 43, 187
economy of, 18, 20, 22, 40, 59, 64, 66–67, 70, 94, 101, 123–24, 139, 141, 159–60, 163–66, 183–84, 207, 210–14, 215–18, 252, 264, 266, 267, 275, 279, 281–82, 287–88, 290–92
electrical grid in, 31, 180–81, 182–83, 208, 211, 222
emigrations from, 275, 289
Great Housing Mission, 282–83
Great National Moral and Illuminating Journey, 231–34, 236, 240, 250
history rewritten in, 187, 189–94
immigrants in, 187, 206
intelligence agencies, 38, 45, 128, 146, 171–72
internal discontent in, 47–48, 56–61, 70–71, 72–77, 82, 91, 93–96, 112, 218–19, 261–67

judicial tribunals of, 170
la lista Tascón, 101–4
land seizures in, 57
landslides, 43–46
list of registrants for housing, 282–83
literacy programs in, 231
los amos del valle in, 71, 74
Mi Casa Bien Equipada, 283
military forces in, 150–53
national strike (2003), 93–96, 108, 142
Venezuela *(cont.)*
national strike (2009), 214, 215, 218, 264
oil in, 2, 18, 20, 21, 40, 47, 53, 59, 63, 65–69, 71, 81, 88, 94, 96, 98, 102, 108, 112, 123, 141, 157–60, 163, 183, 212, 217, 264, 276, 280, 283–84, 289
opposition parties in, 18, 26, 38, 74, 76, 81, 91, 101, 108–9, 129, 153–54, 174, 275, 284–86, 290–91
opposition referendum (2003–4) in, 101–3, 108, 219, 283
population of, 42
provisional government (2002), 77–80, 94, 108, 112, 160
rain forest of, 117

rainy season, 42–46
social programs (missions) in, 102–3, 159, 163–64, 217–18, 219–20, 232, 274–75, 283, 292
superstitions in, 132
term limits in, 109, 111, 115–16, 154–55, 272–73
third faction in, 267–68
time change in, 136, 209
vice president of, 286–87
violent crime in, 232–36, 264, 267, 279, 284, 287
wars of independence, 20
Verdades de Miguel, Las (Miguel's Truths), 129, 198
Vicente Gómez, Juan, 135, 190
Vicente Rangel, José, 45

World Water Day, 136–37

Yare prison, 284
YouTube, 135

Zamora, Ezequiel, 11, 85, 88, 141
Zamora, Rhonny, 24
Zuloaga, Guillermo, 186

CHANNELLING GREAT CONTENT FOR YOU TO WATCH, LISTEN TO AND READ.